More praise for *Fat and Furious*

"Any woman who wants to permanently change the way she looks at herself and the world should read this book. Judi Hollis helps us break through the fear barrier—fear of success, fear of the good life, fear of joy—to care for ourselves and follow the adventure."

—Merlene Miller
Coauthor of *Reversing the Weight Gain Spiral*

"Powerful . . . When I began reading Judi Hollis's book, I was mad! When I finished, I howled like a wolf who was hungry for *life*, not food!"

—Kesho Scott
Author of *The Habit of Surviving*

"Hollis maps the journey of self-examination that women must take to heal food obsessions. . . . This book offers the true stories of women's journeys; it directs women to outside help; and it provides . . . writing exercises to promote self-awareness."

—*Kirkus Reviews*

FAT
and
FURIOUS

JUDI HOLLIS, Ph.D.

BALLANTINE BOOKS
New York

http://www.randomhouse.com

Library of Congress Catalog Card Number: 94-96741

ISBN: 0-345-39649-9

Manufactured in the United States of America

First Ballantine Books Trade Paperback Edition: May 1995

10 9 8 7 6 5 4 3

I have calmed and quieted my soul, like a child quieted at its mother's breast: like a child that is quieted is my soul.

—PSALM 131.3

Contents

Preface

"*History, despite its wrenching pain, cannot be unlived,
but if faced with courage, need not be lived again.*"
                                    —MAYA ANGELOU
                              "On the Pulse of Morning"

This is not an answer book. It is a question book. All the answers in the world don't mean a thing if you don't gain understanding and can't apply what you've learned to your own life. Real learning comes from asking the right questions—questions that rise up from within you. You've known them all your life. You were just afraid to ask. You had no model or mentor helping you learn to seek your own questions.

This is also not a beginner's book. It assumes you're already doing what it takes to modify your food consumption so that your body can become a resonant cavity in which you can hear your own questions bubble up. If you're still seeking a way to run from your own questions, to keep yourself sedated and silenced, then you haven't yet come far enough to take this on.

Other books can give you answers that stop your questioning. This book requires you to fill in the empty spaces. It knows that the only way out of addictive denial is to sit in your old wastes for a while and wait until you can begin to hear yourself. You may have to sit longer than you'd like. You may have to smell it, tell it, and shovel it out.

You and I know this path is necessary, for disordered eating and disordered bodies are the signals that let us know. The body doesn't lie. The head lies as long as it can. Bodies speak the truth. This connection between body and truth shows that those who are food-obsessed often have a keen sensitivity to truth. That's why we suppress it. We are as fat as we are dishonest. Our bodies show our distance from our true selves.

How far are we from our true selves? Well, it's impossible to pick up a woman's magazine today and not see an article that proclaims diets don't work. That's right! They don't work. Because disordered eating is not the result of failed willpower.

The current epidemic of eating disorders in America is something new in our society—it's a new measure of the distance between our lives and our true selves. Think about the three in ten Americans you see today who are obese, juxtaposed with one in ten who are anorexic. The irony is that, as a culture, we have yet to understand that obesity and anorexia are simply opposite poles of the same problem—disordered eating, disowned self, disowned power.

In twenty years of listening to the experiences of thousands of mothers and daughters who came to me for treatment, I began to see a strong connection between the mother's disowned power and the daughter's food abuse. I have learned that at the root of all disordered eating is an unhealed wound—the mother-daughter wound. In *Fat and Furious* I examine that wound in its many different forms, and offer a context for the probing questions that all of us as daughters must ask ourselves if we are ever to claim lasting healing.

Mothers, daughters, and food—it's an obvious connection. Where else but in motherhood, childbirth, and eating are beings so closely bound, so merged? How do these beings separate into their own individual selves? What's fascinating is the questions we don't ask about the mother-daughter relationship. In essence, it's a relationship that's all about giving and getting nurturing. And this sets the stage for disordered eating. So, why haven't we asked the right questions? What are we afraid to face?

In part, we're afraid to face the fact that daughters with eating disorders are carrying their mother's disowned pain and anger. Mothers have a powerful effect on their daughters' lives because girls watch their moms' every move. A mother's denied emotions are internalized by the daughter. No matter how mothers try to cover up their pain, they still serve as models for womanhood, and their daughters have a keen and vigilant eye. Too often the mother-daughter wound is based on unconscious enmeshment, a blending of boundaries, a failure to see where you begin and your mother ends. This failure creates self-destructive behavior that is played out on the plate.

Mothers suffer a great unhealed woundedness because the myths surrounding being a wife and mother promised them things that didn't come true. And then they've had to stand by and watch their hopes for their own daughters end in glaring disappointment. Yet, in spite of all they've learned, mothers still stubbornly struggle to make the old myths work. They haven't yet found the way to experience, and listen to, their own intuitive wisdom.

When daughters see that they can't heal their mothers' pain, they feel they've themselves failed, and they then stuff themselves. And since these things are rarely discussed openly, daughters resort to bingeing and purging. Until a daughter is able to consciously take a long, hard look at her mother's woundedness—at her unhappiness at being born female in a world that prefers males; at her inability to teach herself, or her daughter, how to make deep inner connections—the daughter is doomed to addiction and disordered eating to quiet her own inner cravings to be seen and heard.

Fat and Furious maps the journey women must take from unconsciousness to consciousness. It offers a frank, provocative, no-holds-barred look at issues that most women would prefer not to examine.

The process outlined here will help you learn to live with "rigorous honesty." It's about self-honesty. It's not about the lies we tell others so much as it is the lies we tell ourselves that make us ache, and then eat to sedate. And yet, it's exactly then, when we can't admit to ourselves that we're playing a game, that our Inner Self cries out for clarity and honesty.

To keep hearing that Inner Self, most days we'll choose to keep our food consumption moderate so we can come to trust our behavior, knowing we'll feel a deep unrest whenever we try to deny that we're living a lie. It's the denial that makes us overeat. *Denial* means: "DON'T EVEN NOTICE I AM LYING." It's when we're unaware that we're lying to ourselves that our spirit tugs at our coat sleeve to warn us. And that's when we have to fight off the urge to overeat to shut her up.

If you try to do this work alone, if you don't seek outside help and support, this book could drive you right back to the plate. In my experience it is imperative for women suffering from disordered eating to look at these issues, to ask the right questions, and then to find the support they need to weather the emotional storms that arise. You need mentors to help you stay out here, to help you stay conscious. All you have to do is ask for help. It's the first, and perhaps hardest, step of the journey. Living this way is difficult, but it's well worth doing.

—DR. JUDI HOLLIS
Palm Springs, California

Acknowledgments

Writing this book I cried big tears. None were wasted. I cried for my mother, myself, all women, all men. Birthing it caused almost as much pain and personal confrontation as birthing and raising a daughter.

My agent, Elaine Markson, helped us find a safe harbor to birth ourselves. She showed me how to weather disappointments and keep showing up for the next fray. It has been enlightening and encouraging to have such a quiet yet powerful woman in my corner. My editor at Ballantine, Cheryl D. Woodruff, has been a diligent and committed midwife, asking me to push and breathe so many times when I was tired and wanted to rest. Her faith in the wisdom of this project brought this book safely into the world.

My lifelong mentor and responsible guide, Dr. William Ofman, helped me to stay authentic and true to myself while facing much I preferred to avoid. Other professionals, like Roy Carlisle, Stephanie Covington, Sylvia Carey, Terry-Louise Fisher, Muriel Zink, Claudia Black, and Beverly Rubinstein, offered invaluable support. Dr. Lewis Yablonsky and Dr. Byron Lane advised and coached me. My dear friend, Gail Dubov, offered constant, loving support and wisdom, as well as a quiet retreat when I needed to run.

It was difficult to write such a serious book about such deep issues without lapsing into self-doubt. I have to thank a group of women therapists with whom I meet every month in New York City. These women are gifted professionals who celebrate the strength of our women's intuitive and perceptive powers, and we keep reminding each other to take ourselves seriously. They are Mary Ann Schottenfeld, Marta Elders, Susan Bogas, Barbara Kole Kiernan, Polly Howells, Laura Beecher, and Catherine Boyer.

I had much help from assistants like Jo Ann Fitzpatrick and Janet Hackney, who solved numerous computer and rewrite problems, and generally kept things running smoothly. Holding down the fort at my treatment centers was Robin Pinski, a dedicated professional who made certain our philosophies did not get compromised.

My brother, David Stockman, knew so well what I was trying to say. He loved me through all my confusions and was a keen and perceptive ally in the dance of separation. My father, Colonel Gilbert Stockman, was supportive throughout, constantly encouraging me to keep going, even instructing me from his hospital bed to get back to my writing. His energy is inspiring. My cousin, Carol Schaye, has picked up in mid-sentence each time we needed to encourage each other to walk tall and proud. Kristine Konold, a writer herself, has been a model for how an independent woman leads an exciting, responsible life.

Courage comes from the French word *coeur*, for heart. And in writing this book, I've become more courageous. My mother has also been courageous throughout this process, refusing to compromise who she is. I learned so much writing this book, and like the proverbial college student, was surprised at how much my mother learned as well. Together, we birthed a new relationship, a friendship, more separate yet more alive than ever before.

I am honored that so many courageous patients have shared their lives with me, and I am humbled by our human endeavors. Most of all, I deeply thank all the women and men in Twelve-Step meetings, known only by their first names, who gave profoundly of their "experience, strength, and hope." We paid exquisite attention as we stood together, channeling the light.

Introduction

Are you fat and furious? Does that sound a bit too harsh? Well, answer me this: What attracted you to this book in the first place? Did you want to hide the cover as you scanned the jacket copy? Maybe even that word "fat" is too much to bear. Maybe your body is thin, but your head thinks fat. Maybe your body is actually and noticeably fat, but you're such a sweetheart that no one can see your furious side—not even you. Well, just wait.

You *are* fat and furious, but it's not about food. It's about your life. You've been pushed here onto this Earth poorly prepared for the trials ahead. If anything, you've been trained to sublimate and distrust your one instinctive, wise, and knowledgeable ally—your Inner Self.

Now you find yourself addicted, depressed, and insatiable. But what you're really hungering for is to know your true self, to live an authentic life, to make your life count! The problem is, you don't know how to begin. That's why you're fat and furious. No one has taught you to journey inward on a voyage of self-discovery. No one has told you how to go about developing a loving relationship with your Inner Self. You've been out there dancing before you even learned the steps. That's what you're so mad about!

If you live in these United States, you'd be hard pressed not to be obsessed with your body image—and a tad pissed off. More than likely you've bought into Madison Avenue's dictates on how you should look, and you continually beat yourself up for not achieving its goals.

HIDING IN FAT

I was fat and furious all through my childhood, adolescence, and early adulthood. No one knew. I covered up my obesity and rage with extensive professional accomplishments. Despite my bulbous body, I had a charming personality. I was treating heroin addicts in New York City, then alcoholics in California. And while I was helping others, my alcoholic husband was beating me.

I was dedicated to mothering, to healing others. But I found my own nurturance in the plate. As my weight skyrocketed, I won accolades from treatment professionals who marveled at how "brilliantly" I understood the addictive personality. Actually, it wasn't brilliance at all. It was identification with my own illness. Like most overeaters, I could help others, but not myself. I dieted myself up to over two hundred pounds before I could admit that I hadn't a clue how to diet.

By 1974, I was so demoralized that I dragged myself to a self-help group. There I put aside all I knew and asked for help. As I curbed my eating, I began to hear a powerful internal voice—another being that I'd totally disowned. Here, I had the chance to befriend many other women, and I learned how to open up to a nurturance other than food. I discovered that I had spent incredible amounts of energy controlling my eating, dealing with the results of my eating, and explaining to myself *why* I was eating. I had three shoe boxes filled with "skinny" recipes and food plans I'd clipped from magazines.

I also had two shoe boxes filled with amphetamines I'd been stockpiling, just in case I needed them to prevent me from bingeing. How did I get them? They were the leftovers from my adventures with the medical approach to weight loss. I'd saunter into doctors' waiting rooms, endure weigh-ins from sylphlike young girls, and sit dumbly while a man who'd never suffered such ravages patronizingly explained the calorie count in four ounces of beef. I would feign enthusiasm as he passed a 1,200 calorie diet across a big mahogany desk. Then I'd promise not to disappoint *him*, and leave to do whatever the hell I chose. Despite the fortune I paid the doctors, at some point I'd usually stop taking their prescribed pills—and EAT instead.

Dead Ends

As I continued working with addicts for a decade—and watched them recover—I could see their joy. What light had turned on for them? I'd sit in staff meetings with my colleagues as we discharged yet another success story, my fat self crying inside. Wondering, "Why is there no help for people like me?"

The weight-loss industry takes in over $10 billion a year: Certainly they could help me! But I discovered they teach only failure—because most of their answers are presented as easy solutions. I'd never found it easy. All my battles with the bulge had left me powerless and confused about my life. I'd become a psychologist to try to figure out why I ate; but all my explanations kept me eating.

Then I turned to therapy. I studied my Jungian colleagues because their focus on feminine energy touched on what I knew was a key issue. But I couldn't seem to wade through the sea of gods and goddesses and other disembodied spirits. I just didn't relate to ancient archetypes and heavenly intrigues.

Next, I started reading feminist thinkers. In the 1970s, women gathered to help raise each other's consciousness about disowned power. But instead of going inward, to discover the muted voice of female wisdom, we turned outward and unleashed our rage and frustration at the men who'd helped shut us up. We didn't stop to consider a much closer stifling. We didn't see those generations of women stretching behind us, who had been trained to ignore their Inner Voices—and had taught their daughters to do the same.

In the 1980s, we grabbed onto what opportunities there were to gain economic and political power. We joined the men and became more acquisitive and outer-directed. But in reaching for what appeared to be equal opportunity, we strayed even farther from our deep feminine knowing.

Society pays lip service to women's equality, power, and success. But the deadly price of this success is giving up our powerful feminine self. Many women have grabbed for this brass ring, gone for the prize, and made it—according to other people's standards. But their reward has been to feel a gaping hole yawning inside them. That hole too often becomes filled with excess food.

We got a bit richer in some ways, but a lot poorer in terms of self-confidence and trust in our personal integrity. Our focus was on politics and economics, and on blaming men. But because we still didn't have a clue about who we were meant to be, we ate! We were so divorced from our heart's call that we became what Scott Peck called "People of the Lie."

Now, in the 1990s, we're stuffing and vomiting all those lies. Mothers and daughters are now bingeing and purging for their grandmothers and great-grandmothers and all those women's voices that can't be silenced anymore. These painful truths about the failure of modern society are showing up in treatment centers all over the country.

THE MOTHER–DAUGHTER WOUND

Finally, after treating thousands of families around the country, I discovered the hidden key to food obsession: the mother–daughter wound. Daughters are bingeing and purging their mother's disowned pain and anger.

Fat and Furious helps us explore the mother–daughter wound—being deaf to ourselves—an art taught by our mothers. It teaches us how to identify and come to grips with our mother's disowned pain, sadness, and rage in all of their various forms. It is the imprint of this unconscious and suppressed emotion—the rage that accompanies the inability to be heard—that fuels disordered eating. We learned to cut ourselves off from life and relationships by rigidly controlling our feelings and sedating ourselves with food, until we were left starving for real life.

Why do I place such emphasis on this relationship? Because national statistics declare that *after two years*, 97 percent of those in weight-loss programs have gained back all their weight, and even more. But I have witnessed 77 percent of my patients continuing their recoveries five, and even ten, years after initial treatment. Today I have found that true recovery from food obsession involves nothing less than:

Asking for help

Curbing eating—or starving

Rebirthing yourself into a brand-new way of life

No Blame

Unresolved issues in the mother–daughter relationship do not mean that your mother is bad, or that you are bad. It means that the innate dynamics of this relationship create profound tension around eating. The only way to address disordered eating is to fearlessly examine your relationship with your mother. Sons can take a look, too, though their books still need to be written. Men are invited on this journey, but the examples given here are mostly of women and their moms. Women suffer eating disorders in greater numbers than men; and women seem more sensitized to issues of penetration and vulnerability. These issues all revolve around Mom and food.

You'll find that moms often get a very mean rap in this culture. Much of the civilizing function is carried on by moms who themselves have received little or no training in celebrating life's joys and sorrows. The mother–daughter bond was supposed to accomplish this. It seemed especially close and promising. But moms found themselves forced into the false role of "civilizers."

Mothers taught us how to keep our external and internal hungers in check. This made it all doubly painful. Our mothers' inability to nurture and guide us, because they'd never been guided or taught to nurture themselves, caused us tremendous disappointment and resentment. WE had no models for ways to listen to ourselves because THEY had no models. So we dulled our hurts with food, running headlong toward our goal of living a pain-free life. Along the way, we lost ourselves.

Generations of women have never been taught to listen to their Inner Selves. When our voices are not invited or honored, we take them out to lunch. On some level, we all knew there were answers if only women could come together in a deeper way.

Remember, moms are daughters too. And although they've been blamed for the pains of their children, their moms never taught them how to listen to or honor their own voices, either. Our moms were concerned about survival, about protecting themselves and us, about living a safe life. It's what they learned from their own mothers, and grandmothers, and great-grandmothers.

Much of what moms do with eating-disordered daughters isn't conscious abuse or sabotage. It is the *unconscious* inheritance of generations of women before them, who'd been programmed to deny their true selves by a society built on keeping women in "their proper place."

For most of us, the tragedy of growing up is that, rather than befriending and celebrating their Inner Voices, mothers and daughters get into both *conscious and unconscious* power struggles and shouting matches—and both end up ignoring the signals from within. Those internal signals get hushed with excess food.

If this painful struggle is not healed, you will engage in a futile attempt to get nurturing by any means necessary. Too often you will turn to the plate for soothing. If you don't befriend your mother and her pain—and then learn to separate from it—you can't grow up to live your own life. You'll stay muffled and muzzled with food obsession.

I have learned from over twenty years of clinical work that healing the mother–daughter wound is the most crucial step in recovery from eating disorders. It alone provides the level of separation and individuation that can allow you to recognize and honor your OWN voice, instead of reacting to your mother's. That healing helps you move to a saner, less obsessed relationship with food—a position of healthy neutrality.

Even though you and your mother were born into a society that did not celebrate womanhood, your job is not to change your mom or the culture. Your job is to change yourself. Your compulsive eating is a clue that your own being has not been flexible enough to make that change.

Each of us is born with one true purpose—to live our own unique, authentic, and very real life. You've been eating to stop that life. In the process of awakening to your self, you'll discover that you hunger for some real guidance. You'll realize that you've always needed the example of a stronger, wiser woman who lives a life that works.

You can't do it alone. None of us can. Asking for help on your journey to reclaim your self is the strongest, bravest thing you can do. Your first instinct may be to ask your own mother for help. In this book you'll discover why you can't. And, in fact, you may ultimately pass the book on to her, or buy her one for Mother's Day—after all, she's a daughter too.

EATING OURSELVES TO SLEEP

Eating disorders have led us down a deadly path of emotional extremes—from passivity to aggressiveness; from unhealthy openness to rigid closing off. Did you drink to open and eat to close? Have you vomited to express and starved to suppress? Were you acting out a subtle death wish passed on from parent to child? It wasn't that you wanted to die. It's just that you wanted to sedate certain parts of yourself, you wanted them to get split off, you wanted to be less involved. You wanted a pain-free existence.

For your own protection, you tried to make life hurt less. You hoped to hang out on the sidelines, not to burn your own candle so intensely. You hoped to deaden your naive, hopeful, "happy puppy" self that is so easily disappointed, then despairing, and sometimes even devastated.

Yet, that innocent childlike self is where your spirit lives. When we were growing up, we needed to lose some of our spontaneity and vulnerability in order to become "civilized." We became so adaptive, so safe, that many of us had to become addicts to be able to pull it off. We used addictions to get back to that intuitive, vulnerable self.

Owning Our Anger

In order to recover from obsessions—whether food, booze, men, clothes, work, gambling, or sex—we must each turn inward to face the hollow of the empty, rejected self. For some that means separating for a while from anyone you've used as an authority figure. In some cases, that will be your mother. You'll find you need to choose a surrogate authority figure, one who can help you develop your own values—based on your experience, not hers. Then your anger can begin to subside.

In the process of recovery you'll begin to accept the parts of yourself and your mother that you have both kept hidden. You'll learn to tolerate feeling empty. Avoiding that empty place was your way of trying to feel a sense of security. But that "security" was not only unrealistic, it was ultimately deadly because it kept you locked up in raging anger.

By the end of this book, you'll be able to relax a bit and see your own mother more realistically because you'll be on speaking terms with your own real self. Your rage will dissipate in direct proportion to how well you're able to separate your own life from your mother's. At first, you'll turn up your anger and rage to burn away all those false notions of who you are that have been blocking your Inner Voice. Then you'll be able to sort out your own anger from your mother's.

Keep Your Ladies Quiet!

"But, but, but!" you exclaim. "I don't feel angry. I don't look angry. I've just got a few extra pounds to lose. Why do you keep saying I'm so angry!?"

I can only tell you that after a lifetime of treating food addictions—my own and other people's—and leading some of the foremost advances in the clinical field, I've never met an eating-disordered person—either bingeing or starving—who wasn't raging within. That was as true of the chronically depressed five-hundred-pounders as it was for the schizophrenics who appeared to know nothing about what was going on around them. It was as true for the moderate-weight vomiters who were so helpful and sweet to the treatment team, as it was for the waiflike anorexics who controlled their parents with an iron, though skinny, thumb. All of them needed to face and express their rage: Fearing such expression was what kept them controlling, alone, and unable to get help.

There is a strong impetus, even within the medical and psychiatric community, to keep that passionate anger in check. I have fought this in hospital settings. In one particular hospital, run by a nationally prominent corporation well known for treating famous male alcoholics, my treatment team was encouraging our patients to yell when they needed to in their therapy groups.

One day, the marketing director ushered a group of VIPs past a group room; he later protested that our racket was not attractive to visitors. I suggested that he rope off that corridor during group sessions, and take visitors elsewhere. Instead, the hospital administrator issued a directive: "No yelling in groups. Keep your ladies quiet!"

We moved our treatment unit to another hospital.

CHERISHING THE EMPTINESS

Most of us are angry at our lack of training for this inner work. But who knew? Parents of baby boomers scarred by the Great Depression were trying so hard to hold on against memories of loss that they couldn't teach their children how to let go. That "letting go" doesn't mean raging and pillaging whenever you like. It means developing a spiritual maturity. One in which you not only listen to yourself, but also learn to make wise choices about how to express yourself. Don't cast your pearls among swine.

Part of breaking the old generational patterns is facing how ill prepared we were to forge our own destinies. But first, we must mourn for those generations who have gone before. And then we have to grow up, realizing that we are psychological orphans, in many ways much more grown up than our parents.

Now we have to allow ourselves to surrender, to accept life on life's terms. In that surrender, we come face to face with our loneliness as well as our lack of preparation. And along the way, we grow up and find our unique, individual life. Growing up whole involves learning to be separate from, apart from. It involves welcoming emptiness.

Far from being a vacuum—a dreaded nothingness—spiritual emptiness seems a vacant place but is actually filled with strange, wild, and thrilling vibrations. Most of us have spent our lives trying to ignore that wild call because it was sending us pain signals. You and I used our substances or activities to muffle our soul's cry. We hoped that this would keep our personal rhythms in check, keep our desires at bay, and keep our focus on externals.

But what if that wild cry is the essence of who we really are? What if it is our Inner Voice calling? Most of us have had to be driven to the edge before we realized that our lives depended on listening to that wild cry.

As you become more and more comfortable with this emptiness, at last you'll begin to be able to hear. You'll learn to be accepting, to welcome in, to be penetrated by life. Our modern world is so eager to show us the fullness of life, so busy covering up personal and human fears and disappointments, that we haven't been able to acknowledge our vulnerable, disillusioned, disappointed side. That side had to eat. The time has come for us to fill that inner emptiness with the gift of consciousness.

SURRENDER

Those who truly recover from addictions become open, flexible, and teachable. They are able to let go of all their old ideas and grab hold of a totally new way of life. They seek out models for ways to let down without giving up, for reclaiming disowned power, for wielding it responsibly with personal integrity. Instead of bolstering up—something they needed to abuse their bodies to do—they're now free to fall down, to let go, to surrender to life. And in that surrender, they gain power—the very power they'd feared.

Whether you eat compulsively, starve, vomit, or do that and more, the same surrender is necessary. When you're able to surrender, when you're able to listen to your inner self, you will feel vastly more satisfaction than you ever got from any substance or activity. You will find yourself wanting to keep your eating in check so you can be quiet enough to hear that Inner Messenger.

One of the delicious surprises waiting for you is that you'll be filled with a vibrant, sensual sexuality that's even better than chocolate cake. Yet you'll be able to keep in touch with your boundaries so you're neither closed off and dead, nor melting to give it all away. You will be open to a relatedness that respects boundaries and offers choices. The goal is to be a semi-permeable organism, open to stimuli, but always true to its own self.

You'll gently hold yourself empty, and with respect. You'll cherish the excitement and preciousness of your life. Almost as a by-product, you'll achieve the proper body proportions that suit who you really are. For some, that will mean losing hundreds of pounds. For others, it will mean gaining fifteen or twenty. It's not about the weight. As you embrace your life, you will lose your old obsession with self-destruction. What you'll really be gaining is your own life in all its true dimensions—spiritual and physical.

To recover, you must die and get reborn. You must come back as a more powerful and gutsy lady. You must make friends with your Inner Self, your deep inner truth. That involves some interesting new relating with your birth mother, then a surrogate mother, and then all women—including your own daughters. It's a woman's thing, and a mother–daughter thing. Now, as we set out on that journey home to self, it involves facing how long we, our mothers, and all the other women in our lives have been lost.

FINDING THE PATH

It is crucial that you keep your food consumption moderate so that you can stay open and available for this life-changing work. You are now a long-distance runner preparing for a marathon. You don't just jump out of bed one morning and run ten miles. You take it slowly and gradually—each new day prepares you for the next.

Don't rush, and don't expect to know more than you know. This will be a grand adventure. It's all practice. It's all training for the next step. You will be laying your old self to rest and making room for the new self who will be born into a totally new way of life. You will move from a combative, closed-off stance to an accepting, opened-up stance.

The key to this rebirth lies in developing your spiritual consciousness. For a somewhat doubting New Yorker like myself this has been difficult. I don't really go for crystals and Birkenstocks. But I discovered that staying in touch with my inner spiritual wisdom helped me keep wearing the size 8 dresses I like so well. Eventually I came to appreciate the gift of surrender, the profound feeling of really letting go—embracing the emptiness!

At first, when you decide to follow that voice within that keeps telling you to "let go," you'll feel as though you're totally giving up your freedom as well as your responsibility to fashion your own life. It will feel like a cop-out. It will feel like death. But as you read this book, you may come to find, as I did, that it is actually our fighting and striving mentality, the fearful pusher and manager who is actually copping out. That persona has kept us Fat and Furious.

On the Rocks

AA members often instruct newcomers, "It's time to drop the rock." Don't worry—even if you let go, you'll probably pick up that rock a few thousand more times. But each time you'll let it fall a little sooner, and you won't hold onto it quite so tightly.

I got a letting-go message early in my journey. I had been able to lose so much weight by following this process that, without my even realizing it, I'd become a seeker on the spiritual path. I had begun to hear my Inner Voice. This inspired me to continue to curb my food intake, because I wanted to be available to those rumbling signals from my own deep wisdom.

I began to seek out forms of meditation and spiritual practices to help me quiet down so I could keep listening. Like many others, I had started out fat and furious, but as I met more and more mentors who were calmer and happier, I started wanting some of what they had. Their advice to me was, "If you want what we have, then DO what we do."

As you do the work in this book—removing the old waste that was clogging up your hollow space—you will experience a deep hunger no one has invited you to feel before. Once you start listening to that hunger, a miraculous transformation begins. You will have the strength to truly experience hunger pangs—even to use them as messengers to help you sort out what satisfies YOU, and what leaves you EMPTY. You will then trust your own instincts in the plate and in your life. You will hear yourself by listening to your body.

TAKING THE HEAT

This happened for me outside Santa Fe, New Mexico. I'd gone there for a sweat lodge ceremony with Grandmother "Little Moon." A sweat lodge is a tepee with a firepit dug into the center. Rocks heated white hot are placed in the firepit, and water is then poured over the hot rocks to create an extreme saunalike heat. A circle of people sits inside to pray, sweat, and spiritually purify themselves. It is like a rebirthing. Even though nothing is "expected" of those who are sharing the ceremony, all are participating in a ritual that is a living part of an ancient and sacred tradition. There are no rigid guidelines—the journey is between you and your spirit.

As the rocks heat up the space, the closeness of the people begins to feel unbearable. It takes tenacity and commitment to yourself simply to stay put. It feels as though the only way you can stand the discomfort is to leave your body and get the hell out of there. The experience is often quite rigorous; and you can leave if you must. The first time I tried it, I couldn't stand it—I left immediately. At later ceremonies I was able to stay. By then I'd faced enough of my own demons to be able to take the heat.

Juices and All

That turnabout came for me with a Lakota Wise Woman. My other sweat lodges had been led by white men who had been trained by Native Americans. I believe it was important at that point for me to be guided by a tribal woman. We were all nude women sweating together. Even though traditional sweat lodges excluded menstruating women, in this one we were encouraged to bleed onto the straw floor. We were invited to surrender ourselves, juices and all. We were earthbound animals transcending the body to contact the spirit.

Training in loving our female bodies and using them to go to God is something sorely missing in our Western tradition. Finding our Spiritual Selves involves falling back in love with ourselves as women. We have to melt down to feel our strength. In this book you will be asked to let go to get—to lose to win.

In that unbearably hot sweat lodge, I wondered, "What am I doing sweating here with all these naked fat ladies?" But then I answered myself. I realized it meant: DO THIS OR EAT.

As the lodge heated up, when I was ready to run from the agony, when it seemed that no breath or thought was possible, somehow I simply KNEW that this was a great place to be. You'll reach that place often as you work through this book. It will seem as though you're being asked to face unbearable and scorching truth. You'll feel caught between a hot rock and a hard place. You'll tell yourself, "I can't bear any more," and start to bolt. That's when you'll discover that it's in just those mo-

ments, when you "gotta get outta this place," that a keen awareness comes over you—that you are safe and secure, that there is
help all around you, visible and invisible. All you have to do is
ask!

We all need someone more experienced and wiser who can
help us learn to listen and trust our inner selves. A mentor who
can help us surrender to living the life we're really here for, to
dancing to the rhythm of our own tom-tom. Those of us who
keep walking this path know how hard it is. We won't hand you
platitudes about the joy and ease of this journey. We'll let you
know the pitfalls and the pains. But we'll also let you know what
makes the journey so worthwhile.

We have to keep asking ourselves why we so rigidly hold on
to the old life? Why do we keep resisting the new? Couldn't we
just give in a little? Grab onto a piece of the new way? As I baked
in that Santa Fe sweat lodge, gasping and fidgeting, it must have
been clear I was ready to run. That's when an elderly woman sitting next to me leaned over and whispered, "It's easier if you lie
down." I did. It was.

Lie Down, Listen, and Soar

For myself and for many of the addicts I've treated, to "lie
down" has become a rich and healing metaphor. Before accepting that I had to "give up to get," I'd been demanding that life's
pain and discomfort be soothed. Food, booze, clothes, and disengaged sex worked for a long time. I spent much of my early
life demanding that those needs be met. I'd practiced psychotherapy, taught assertiveness training, showed patients how to
get. Yet I didn't have a clue how satisfying it might feel to give
up some of my own demands. To simply walk away, saying, "How
important is it, after all?"

You're probably seeking very clear-cut answers, yet another
method that will fix you. You want a prescription, a formula, answers from me. But you know that in the past, those external answers got you lost. As you set out on your inward journey, giving
up to get, the path will seem rockier, and you'll be less sure-
footed. Each time you're faced with such a testing from the
spirit, you'll probably ask yourself, "Who needs this? Why am I

here? Why am I doing this? What proof do I have that any of this can work for me?"

It wasn't until I realized the greater value in listening to my Inner Voice that I was able to lie down and surrender into my own life. I kept watching others at Twelve-Step meetings speaking of the "letting-go" miracles. I scoffed and judged. But the pain of my obesity kept me listening. I was afraid of the hollow place inside where that clear, still voice lived. I kept listening to others, so that eventually I could listen to my own voice and begin to trust my own judgment.

I now welcome myself into that listening place, and I invite you to join me. In that quiet, empty place you will finally meet your true self—and other women. When you're able to lie down in more and more areas of your life, you will also be able to show up for more sensual and animal experiences. And to your delight, you will discover that they lead to more profound spiritual experiences as well. As the power of the body gets disciplined, the Spirit emerges.

Perhaps your first taste of surrender was buying this book. It was your response to an Inner Voice telling you, "You're ready." Reading it is a gift you're giving yourself, so you can finally get to know the real you. *Fat and Furious* is not a beginner's book. It's for those of us who are ready to lie down, listen, and then soar. If you are ready, no person, place, or thing can make you eat. Once you hear and trust—and ultimately embrace—your own voice, you will never be hungry again!

1

LIFE CALLS

IT'S NOT THE FOOD

If you picked up this book, right now you're probably more frustrated, upset, and angry than grateful. You may not know you're fat and furious, but trust me, you will! You're angry because you know on some inner level this is not the full life you were sent here to live. George Bernard Shaw said you can choose to live your life as a blowtorch or a candle. If you keep foraging for excess food, you know you're not living with all your burners turned up. You're only living a half-life—a style your mother taught to protect you. But ultimately, it stifled you.

You may say, "I want to relax more. I don't want such a full, hot life." Well, your struggles with food are a signal that you can ill afford such a luxury. If you're going to take in energy, the laws of physics compel you to give it back out—full blast.

It's Enough to Make You Eat

Are you irritated? Do you want to put down this book? If you've read this far, it's too late. You already know food doesn't work anymore. You may as well not eat but cry instead.

You may be like Brenda, a compulsive eater, who came to treatment while taking Prozac—but she was still crying *and* bingeing. She'd been prescribed the drug to alleviate her depression as well as to suppress her appetite. She'd expected it to work wonders, making her euphoric and thin. It helped for a while.

The problem was, her body chemistry had altered without any change in the way she was living her life. Her old life was still in session, and she knew there were changes she needed to make. She needed to take a cool, hard look at her marriage. Both she and her husband were being dishonest—"making nice" and pretending they still loved each other. She had to face her new "freedom" as the kids left the nest and she had no reason to stay in the situation.

The frightening possibilities opened up by that new "freedom" were too much to bear. Brenda was going to have to face her choices and be gentle with herself. She was going to have to accept herself. That was too difficult. She wanted to feel pushed against the wall, compelled by parental responsibilities. It was too difficult to actually say out loud, "I think I choose to stay." Instead she cried all the time.

Food had once worked gloriously to quell that crying. She could take one run to Baskin-Robbins, or down a medium-sized bag of Fritos, and those tears would dry right up. Now she hit Baskin-Robbins, 7-Eleven, Burger King, and the pharmacy, but the sobbing still continued. Food had formerly worked like plaster to plug up those holes, to make the world go away. Now she was like a giant sieve, bingeing, stuffing, running, crying. Brenda's life was in her face, full frontal and stark.

If only she could have been more gentle with herself, accepting her choices, finding and accepting support, giving herself a break. Instead, she was running scared, full of expectations and judgments of herself, insisting she should not feel what she felt. So she kept eating. But her best friend—food—had turned on her.

Perhaps, like Brenda, you're at that place where you can't eat and you can't not eat. In other words, you're between a rock and a hard place. There is both anger AND excess weight. There is profound confusion and lack of direction. You know you can't really eat the way you once did. It doesn't help anymore. It doesn't stop your crying. It doesn't keep your rage in check. It just doesn't work. It's over.

You picked up this book because your drug is no longer working. You're already too conscious for the sedative to work.

Your Inner Self is waking up. She wants to stop being stuffed. Your spirit wants to come out. It's a call to life. You may see this as a blessing or a curse. That's part of what you're so mad about.

ASK YOURSELF:

- *How did you eat today? Were you ravenous? Was "enough" never enough? Where did you eat?*
- *Did you leave your meal feeling energized and alive? Or did you feel leadened and deadened?*
- *Were you eating to wake up or shut up?*

The Starving Spirit

For two decades now, I've watched patients walk into hospitals seeking a medical solution to a spiritual problem. I have seen distraught parents of addicted children pacing hospital corridors, hoping for any diagnosis that could explain their behavior. Could their children be "hyperactive," "addicted," "dyslexic," "manic depressive," "borderline"? Any label was better than facing the fact that this might be the last throes of a human spirit trying to assert itself in a life that had kept it bound and gagged.

I got to see little ten-year-old fat girls, as I'd been, come into treatment with parents who were equally fat but worried more for their daughters than themselves. I got to see anorexics from thirteen to thirty-five who talked like little girls, declaring their abiding love for all the world, while for themselves they saw only weakness and incapacity.

There would also be the thirty-five-year-old obese women and men who could not grow up. They usually entered treatment excessively sweet and polite. But after four days without excess food, deep hostility surfaced. They objected loudly to all hospital procedures; but underneath they felt an even greater rage at themselves. They had no awareness of the disowned spirit. All of these people felt conflicted, wanting to find a fitting label. All felt unclear and ill-defined. They were ambivalent, unsure, out of touch with themselves. It was as though the body had to keep undulating, swelling or contracting, to show how conflicted the being inside really was.

The reason they were conflicted was because they'd been seeking power in excess fuel, all the while disowning their personal power—their inner spiritual compass that always points true north. There would never be enough food to compensate for that lost spiritual voice, and there would never be enough food to muffle it again. The use of food to disown spirit was over.

Labels Help Us Focus

Many tried to find a medical malady to explain their spiritual emptiness. My first book *Fat Is a Family Affair* and early treatment programs even helped in that effort. For these early patients and their loved ones it was important to identify the problem medically. This helped them get off their own backs, helped them see that the problem was identifiable and treatable.

We had found in treating alcoholics that their ability to come out and say "I'm an alcoholic" was often the most difficult stumbling block to recovery. Many preferred to call themselves a "problem drinker" or even a "no-account drunk." Anything was easier than addressing it medically. This is because, once it becomes a treatable problem, then the only issue is "Do I or don't I choose to take the treatment? Ask for help? Follow direction?" As long as we stay out there in that amorphous fog, unlabeled, we get to entertain the fantasy that "I can handle this myself . . . probably by Monday."

We found in the AA experience that the process of labeling only works when the individuals themselves found a label that worked. Each of us has a different tolerance for these issues. You will find your own voice. If your inner voice doesn't believe you belong in these categories, that's okay. You can still gain a lot of insight and lose a lot of weight. Just set aside what doesn't fit and keep on truckin'. Your answers will come at your own personal pace.

It Both Is and Isn't the Food

You know that your old relationship with food has changed and you can't go home to the plate anymore. You may as well follow this plan and open up a whole new spiritual and physical relationship with your true substance. In the beginning, there will be nothing more important than civilizing and disciplining your eating behavior. Your other medical or psychological maladies cannot be clearly addressed until this basic, physical, life-giving behavior becomes conscious. After all, eating is one of the basics—like breathing. We have to align these basics before we focus on other issues, no matter how important they may be. Until food is in order, you're not really available to work on codependency, shame, incest, rape, or anything else.

Empty or Full?

In order to become available to ourselves we first have to re-negotiate what we eat and how we utilize our basic energy supply—food. How we take in food determines the way life affects us. We'll learn to use our food intake as a metaphor for how we want to walk through this life. Will we gobble it up, keeping ourselves so stuffed that we feel nothing? Or will we stay a little empty, no more than half full, so that new things can penetrate and touch us? This issue of openness is very important, because food is one way we can allow entry without negotiating intimacy. We can only give up the satisfying, non-negotiable connection we get from eating if we find an acceptable substitute. This involves leaving home, mom's home, growing up, letting go. In some cases, it involves leaving mom behind.

Women's bodies are designed for penetration. Most of us never learned how to let the world in. Our work is to learn about separation and individuation, about independence and boundaries, about staying open, fluid, and resonating with energy. We then get the awakening and welcoming of our own Inner Spirit, what the Quakers call "the still, small voice within."

You can no longer eat the way you once did. Sorry. In *Fat Is a Family Affair* I explained the "tolerance change" addicts experience as their best friend turns on them. We cross an invisible line where we start needing greater and greater quantities to produce the same effects. We find that we get less out of the ac-

tivity and that the negative consequences—withdrawals, weight
gain, depressions—become greater.

The explanation of "physical" tolerance change also applies
to a spiritual and psychological tolerance change. Even though
Prozac is supposed to offer an appetite suppressant, that only
works for anorexics and vomiters. Overeaters eat right through
the Prozac. We are wonders to medical science. Our lives defy
prescriptions. You can no longer effect the same behaviors you
once did. You get more of the bad, less of the good.

We usually can't accept what is happening, so we just keep
looking for greater highs, hoping that each time our drug
doesn't work it just means we'd gotten a bad batch of something. With food, we always give it a second chance, scraping
mold off the cheese, or trying a richer pastry, or insisting they
must have changed the recipe at our last place.

We don't want to believe that WE changed, that the pastry is
still the same. If WE changed, that is a more serious dilemma. It
means solving the current problem and might even mean more
personal change. Most of my patients balk at this and tell me,
"I'd much rather change my food than myself."

Harold, a fifty-year-old accountant who had spent most of his
life in rowdy womanizing, smiled sheepishly as he told me, "I
don't seem to be able to bed a woman anymore without somehow falling in love with her." He didn't realize how much his attempts to keep up his former self-image—as a man who didn't
care about anyone but himself—were also keeping forty extra
pounds on his frame. We can no longer pretend to ourselves
that we're someone other than we really are. This hunger awakening within tells us that change is happening now. We don't
know yet what or how we want to change. All we know is, we
don't want to stay asleep any longer. And food can no longer
sublimate that knowledge. Life has changed what food can do
for us.

ASK YOURSELF:

- Is eating a reward or a punishment?
- What strong emotions or feelings have you tried to medicate with food?
- What event in the last twenty-four hours has caused you to reward or punish yourself with food?

A CALL TO LIFE

Louis Pasteur was the first modern scientist to realize that humans have something to do with the effects their substances have on them. He was the father of the germ theory. Before Pasteur, we in the West were so enamored of individual consciousness and integrity that we couldn't believe a lowly germ could subdue a human being. But once Pasteur convinced us that the germ caused the illness, we began to assume a passive part in our own health care.

This began the role of modern medicine as an authority figure and influenced how we regard our bodies. Pasteurization and other antiseptic medical practices were instituted. Belief in the power of microbes and the continual creation of drugs to subdue them created our dependence on chemical substances. As a result our streets are now overrun with addicts who bought too much of the package. Unfortunately, drugs *do* work, and foods *do* work. They medicate against pain and relieve symptoms. But they only work in the short haul. Life insists we experience it.

Now, after Pasteur, we're beginning to look past the germ, and past the substance. We're looking at how the individual *uses* the substance. Modern medicine is concerned with diseases of lifestyle, and how individuals use or choose health or illness. How they use or abuse themselves.

We've read Norman Cousins about the healing power of laughter. Cancer patients have followed directions from doctors like Carl Simonton and used guided imagery, and the power of mind and Spirit to fight cancer cells. Recently we've been reading best-sellers from doctors Bernie Siegel and Larry Dossey on how to mobilize our inner resources to choose health over illness.

Even Pasteur himself, in later life, began studying how the individual accepted or rejected the germ. Puzzled about why some people caught diseases and others didn't, he recommended that we think through and observe how the individual accepts and utilizes the germ. He saw that there was a reciprocal relationship between the germ and the host organism, the person.

Eating is a reciprocal, intimate experience too. We participate actively. As *we* change, so does the food.[1] Our attitude, and our intended use for the substance, are just as important as what the substance is. On his deathbed Pasteur proposed, "Forget the germ theory. The host is everything." We are the hosts for whatever players we bring into our lives.

It's a Death Wish

Now we're getting very close to the deeper meaning of compulsive eating. If we are active participants in the effects this overeating is having on our lives, then what are we after? Why can't we stop? What is it we're having such a hard time facing? We must face the fact that eating is not a search for nurturance, for life. It is just the opposite—a search for a way out, for death. We must ask ourselves why we're rushing head-long toward self-destruction. Is it because life keeps changing the rules on us and we don't feel at all prepared for weathering these changes? On some level would we rather run and hide in the place of no more changes—of death?

Compulsive overeating is a subtle and illusory death wish. Not knowing who or what we were killing we've used food to kill off our inner spirit, to hush up that insistent inner voice that tells us we're living off-track. Perhaps for you now, there just aren't enough peanut butter cups to turn down the volume. Your only hope is to develop your hearing so you can listen even better to the still, small—POWERFUL—voice within.

That voice is your greatest source of power. Listening atten-

[1]Dr. Hollis's conscious eating techniques are taught in the home video: "Dignity Dine," available through 1-800-8-ENOUGH.

tively to that voice will not make you suicidal. She will save your life by connecting you more deeply to your own life force. That voice wants to turn you on to a whole new way of being. She wants to talk to you, but she won't get into a shouting match with you. She will only speak softly and wait for your willingness to listen. Nevertheless, her soft tones have been incredibly insistent. But your compulsive eating has been escalating each time she tried to be heard.

How could you know? You were never trained to listen. But that Inner Voice did know—that's why you're reading this book. What this means is that, now, you can make a commitment to stop smothering her with food. And now, you can look for—and find—all the help and training you need to clean out your gut and your ears.

Sigmund Freud postulated that we all have an ambivalent commitment to both life and death. He pointed out that, like Hamlet, we're not actually sure whether we want to be here or not. This is the essential question for all addicts, codependents, and addicted families. It is the one most important question you must ask if you are pushing your *self* down with excess food. It is above all a woman's question. We are the birthers; our bodies are more grounded in the life force. We can't afford to be ambivalent. Bravely, we keep battling it out at a superficial level to avoid getting down to the deeper issues. Most of us have not been encouraged to listen to our internal debate.

Usually, parents had not allowed themselves to listen either, and they felt too guilty to let us question life. They wanted us to be "happy." The deeper dynamics for addicted families were dramatized by Eugene O'Neill in his powerful play, *Long Day's Journey Into Night*. The consumptive son, Edmund, tells his father about his own life and death struggle. He recalls the times when he was on the high seas, sailing and watching the gulls, and feeling totally at peace and in love with his life. At such times he was ready to accept whatever life or death had to offer. He felt detached from the human struggle and at one with the flow. He felt it was a mistake to have been born a man, that he'd have done better as a fish.

He describes his life struggle as: "Always a stranger, ever alone, always a little in love with death."

This speaks to a darker, more mysterious side of ourselves, a side our parents couldn't own. We kept it submerged. And now this disowned self EATS for us. Our parents made a decision to live a half-life, and trained us to follow them. Now you're facing a new decision—whether to answer that inner call to live a fuller, much more sensitized, more exciting life. Eating compulsively has really been a quest for resolution. Now you're yearning to re-own the parts of yourself you've tried to kill. These may be the same parts of themselves your parents tried to kill. You may be eating or purging your parents' disowned murder of themselves. Just think now of whichever parent you felt most involved with. It's probably Mom. Now, see what she avoided. Notice how easily you can tell her secrets. It may be easier for you to see HER avoidances than your own.

For example, Paulette, who was admitted for bulimia, saw her mother as raging, judgmental, and abusive. She swore she'd never be that way. She affected a charming demeanor, was a gracious hostess, always appeared interested in others. Her life worked well. The problem was that she was also obese. In treatment she affected the same personality toward staff and other patients. She was the Pearl Mesta of Hollis Institute.

During a psychodrama session we asked her to play her mother. At first she claimed she couldn't do it. She could describe her mother in caricature, ridiculing her mother's idiosyncracies. But she was quite uncomfortable actually "doing it." Our counselors insisted; so she staged an explosive reenactment of a childhood scene, with her mother raging. Her mother yelled while setting the table, throwing down silverware. Paulette, then ten, watched quietly, huddled in a corner.

Midway through that scene Paulette broke down into sobbing. In that instant she saw that her mother's rage masked deep sadness. She'd been trying to get some attention from her workaholic husband, Paulette's dad. He came home exhausted, demanding perfect meals and perfect grooming. Her mom always fell short and was met by his tongue clucking and critical glares. Paulette realized how sensitive and continually criticized her mother had been. She even saw how she had joined with her dad in judgments and meanness toward this woman. She felt deep sadness for her mother and herself.

Paulette cried softly for days after that session. She was advised to write about her sadness as if she were her mother. As Paulette wrote, the whole story unfolded. She saw her mother's pain. She saw how life had disappointed her mother, how she'd been left with very few options. Her mom's rage had to do with despair. She kept railing to avoid collapsing.

Once Paulette saw this clearly, she felt sadness for her mom's life. But she was able to get in touch with her own rage about the disappointments in her life. She too had married a critical man, and watched herself jumping through hoops to please him. Instead of raging like Mom, she had become compliant, hoping to keep his criticism at bay. While she was pleasing to others, she was very lonely in herself—disconnected from her own truth and that of other women.

Neither of these women could really help the situation they were born into. The healing gift of this process was that as Paulette got to see her mother's rage more clearly, she could then separate it out from her own. Now she was no longer afraid to show her own anger. She knew there were things in life she should be angry about. She didn't have to keep up the "goody two shoes" sweetheart image to avoid being like Mom. Her anger was important, and more than that—it was REAL.

As a result of letting herself get more angry, Paulette also became more three-dimensional. She was a bit less predictable, a bit more interesting. She was becoming an exciting person. Even more importantly, she was more interesting to herself. Instead of presenting herself as an "interviewer"—a foil for others' needs—she delighted in telling stories about herself. She was entertaining and excited about her own projects. She was truly alive.

ASK YOURSELF:

▫ *What parts of yourself have you tried to kill off with food?*

You may soon learn that you've chosen a destructive path to keep yourself from feeling too much. Despite its joys, life sometimes hurts. You may have minimized and weakened yourself as a survival mechanism, hoping to avoid hurt. It helped you adapt; but it has now outlasted its usefulness. It helped you grow up and live in Mom or Dad's house, but didn't prepare you for going inward to your own house.

As we take the journey of recovery into your own house, you'll find a way to re-own your disowned self; a self you've drowned with food. Parts of that being will feel safe; some will feel strange and disconnected. Some parts of that self will seem sinister and scary and a bit uncivilized. Thank God. This is the real being you started out with. You will come home to who you were always meant to be. In re-owning your disowned self, you will find parts that are like your mother; in fact, like most women. You must forgive both your mother and your self, so you can stop trying to be someone you're not.

If you don't do this difficult inner work you'll switch to other obsessions and continue to ride the merry-go-round. You'll regain lost weight, returning to vomiting, starving, drinking, or some other compulsion as your only way to feel powerful.

However, if you follow the actions proposed in this book, you will make this time the last time. You will regain your lost power. You will become centered in your own life. You will listen to the disowned self—she speaks through your body.

Ask Yourself:

- Describe your relationship with food. Do you have a love-hate relationship with food?

- When your body tells you it's ready to eat, what do you do?

- When your body tells you to stop eating, what do you do?

- Have you ever heard a message from your body? What did your body say? How did you answer?

It's Not Substance Abuse

I was one of the early pioneers in pointing out the similarities between alcoholism and overeating, comparing the woes of liquid sugar and solid sugar. Now I have had to eat my own

words. I've seen too many hospital admissions where people told
me they'd been sugar-free for years, but were bingeing on fat.
FAT IS WHAT MAKES YOU FAT.

These people had bought the addiction model I'd initially
proposed, but they had not focused enough on a moderate, bal-
anced food program. They had not understood that the purpose
of curtailing food abuse was to help them feel empty enough to
hear their Inner Voice. Although they had cut out sugar, they
continued to soothe themselves with excess fat. Fat not only
makes you fat, it also globs up your inner hearing and you get
the wrong messages. Since your soul knows that you're being
abusive to yourself, you feel guilty and are running scared, covering up, and being self-justifying. Your Inner Being knows.

Recently, eating disorder sufferers have been calling themselves "food addicts." Treatment programs teach this approach,
going right to the source of the obsession. But in some ways
they're not going far enough. While they're borrowing from our
experience with other addictions, they've only bought the substance, not the form. I have a special need to address this issue
since my first book, *Fat Is a Family Affair*, was one of the first to
teach the similarities between eating disorders and alcoholism.
But rather than trying to prove the similarities between sugar
and alcohol addiction, I wanted to show how the *treatment*
approach—a Twelve Step model—could be applied to both. I
wanted to show that the personality and lifestyle changes we
needed to make to help us recover were similar to those for
other addictions. Others have now overused that approach, focusing only on food, and ignoring important deeper issues.

Moderation in All Things

As I watched so many go only halfway, I became motivated to
produce this new book. Once your body is available to do the
deeper work, this book will help open your psyche. It can be
used by sponsors in Overeaters Anonymous to help them work
with others, and it can be used by mothers and daughters to
heal their mutual woundings. It could also be used in a study
group where you can help each other.

Whether you call yourself an addict or not, whether you go
to Twelve-Step programs or not, whether you follow my prescriptions or not, this book now welcomes you on the path to finding

your Inner Self. Every little bit helps. Even scientists are now touting more of this moderate course. Years ago we were told we'd gain no positive effects from exercise unless we did twenty minutes aerobically at least five times a week. Now we are told that a little dab could do ya—just get out there and do the best you can. I say, if you just lace up the shoes, that's a miracle.

I'd like to propose the moderate course with food. This includes seeking guidance from others farther on the path. You must realize that you are not alone. There are a lot of life lessons to share. It's not an addiction problem that we share. It's not sensitivity to a substance that we share, but a common way of *using* a substance to avoid living a too-sensitive life.

There have been endless battles within the professional community over whether food problems evolve from heredity or environment, nature versus nurture, calories versus emotions, behavior modification versus deep regressive therapy, energy intake versus energy output, et cetera. For our purposes, it's all of the above. This is not to avoid committing ourselves. It's just that there are no direct cause-and-effect links, no easy outs.

You probably picked up this book because you know how you have failed in the struggle to control food. That doesn't necessarily make you an addict. You don't have to call yourself an addict for this approach to work for you. You just have to consider taking the prescribed medicine even if your diagnosis is unclear. The medicine I prescribe will hurt nothing but your obsessive relationship with food.

It's Not the Poundage

It is not the food, and not the results of the food. This is not the time to worry about body image. The packaging will come into line when the psyche has grown into reality. Too much time has been spent on redecorating our cages instead of breaking free. Many manuals help us find more realistic body images. Research points out that most "normal" people see their bodies as heavier than they are, while severely obese see their bodies as thinner than they are. Both images are distorted. At my treatment centers and workshops, patients look at their bodies in mirrors with bags covering their heads. This is so they won't be distracted by a pretty face or an engaging personality. We just want a realistic view of WHAT IS.

Your honest recognition of body and food makes life more real. Your body will assume its proper form based on the life you need to live. Opera singers may need a large cavity for resonance of sound, swimmers may need fat and muscle, account executives may need a flattened bottom for conferences. When you live more in reality, your body will assume its natural shape. At this point it isn't important what YOU think of your body. Your shape is none of your business. You've probably used looking at your body as a way to beat up on yourself. Just consider that any approach at body image work right now is totally unrealistic. When your food plan becomes disciplined, you will have a chance to view your shape and your life from a realistic perspective. Right now whatever you see will be colored by a dense, opaque lens of self-abuse and feelings of inadequacy. Whether you're trying to lose a hundred or more pounds, or the same bothersome twenty or thirty, focusing on the poundage will not make your body perfect or your mind obsession-free. What I'm proposing here is deeper—it means changing yourself, not just your food. Often when nutritionists and medical experts talk about "lifestyle change," they're preaching switching restaurants, shopping better, building exercise and meditation into a daily schedule. That's not what we're up to here.

EVOLUTIONARY CHANGE

I'm talking about a deeper and more profound lifestyle change. I am suggesting trying on new behaviors in many important areas of your life, not just health and fitness. One's character is a given—changing how we operate in life, given who we are, is about working with our character as we evolve. I'm talking about an evolutionary change in your basic outlook. As you try on alternate ways of being, reorganizing how you approach your life, you will begin to generate and receive back different responses. Your life and your body will change. *You* will change. This involves giving up some values your mother taught you, and instead seeking what your own adult wisdom prescribes.

Right now this may sound pretty threatening. But you can surely see that the way you're living is not netting you the results you want. One value in seeking out others on this path is so you can come to know that you are not alone. You'll soon discover how many of us balked at the idea that *we'd* have to change. I don't know of anyone who easily and joyously volunteered for these changes. None of us marched right out, full of vim and vigor, to boil two eggs for breakfast and then change around our whole lives.

The Fruits of Change

All your previous attempts were probably of the "white knuckle" variety. You just "swore off." No one, not even you, knew the fruitlessness of such declarations. With that attitude, ego ruled supreme. Did you find yourself in a mad swing between gloating over successes, and then plunging down to the depths of despair when you felt defeated? That's why you're now going to learn how to find a mentor who's been there before you. This person will help you *see* yourself; help you change those behaviors that make you feel so bad about yourself; help you stay on the path when you feel impatient and want to slip away. You can't do it alone. None of us can. You also can't keep glorifying or minimizing the effort. Change your life instead of your cage.

Arnold was a successful lawyer who ate and smoked nonstop while he was in heated litigation trials. He slept little, worried a lot, and gained a great deal of weight. After each trial he resorted to obsessive dieting, and was able to slim down again. As he got older, the ravages of these bouts could not be fixed so easily. His "dieter" had broken down. Arnold came to treatment teaching our staff about the ways he'd always known had worked for him. When we suggested he adopt an attitude that included more "letting go" and taking care of self, he balked: "That crap isn't going to win me any cases!" We asked him to call another litigator who had followed our treatment recommendations and had become even more successful.

After the call, he relaxed a bit. He took a long look at his schedule and began setting new priorities. With our help, Arnold decided that part of his actual courtroom "preparation" would be:

- Getting a good night's sleep.
- Making sure his food plan was nutritious so he could trust his energy level as well as his mental responses.
- Talking sweetly to the secretary he usually barked at.

Why the sweet talk? Because we showed him that trying this new behavior would make him feel so good about himself that he'd have no need to punish himself with either excess food or losing a case.

As Arnold took on this new personal agenda, he found that creative moves he hadn't planned on often came to him in court. He developed an even faster knack of thinking on his feet. He also didn't react in anger and insult judges any longer. Arnold began to be fully present in his life, as well as in court. He was shocked and pleased, after a year, to report that his law practice had blossomed while his waistline had diminished.

Just as Arnold hadn't understood up front why sweet talking his secretary would help him reduce his weight, Evelyn, a film actress, couldn't see how a few kind words to her makeup artist could possibly help her stop reaching for the danish on the catering table. Evelyn hated getting made up, and she barked through each sitting. Understanding that the woman in makeup reminded her of a hateful aunt was fine, but she still had to change her response to the woman.

We convinced her that trying the opposite response to this woman would help curtail her bingeing. She forced herself to hold her tongue and smile sweetly. Her zipped lip carried her through the coffee break because she didn't have to binge to assuage her feelings of guilt over lashing out.

I'm not proposing here that we all become little Mary Sunshine. Some of us have to go the opposite route, and awaken our own passionate warrior.

Margaret served food in a high school cafeteria. She was withdrawn, shy, and a bit dowdy. For the most part, she was ignored by the students, who treated her merely as a robot, there to serve them. Some of the students actually abused and ridiculed her because she never answered back. She was hunch-shouldered and passive, available for whatever anyone handed out. After each luncheon service she vomited.

In treatment, we helped her straighten up, taught her to look people directly in the eye until *they* turned away, and we suggested that she hum songs to herself while she served. This gave others the impression that she was rather self-satisfied, content in her job, and occupied with her own concerns rather than waiting for "lip" from rude children.

She didn't understand at all how this would help her with

her bingeing and purging. But, as she followed these suggestions, she found that the students stopped picking on her. She
started feeling more confident and actually began to enjoy the
songs she hummed during lunch. She often felt so powerful afterward that she delayed having her own lunch until later in the
day. She was high and satisfied from observing her new SELF.

Ask Yourself:

□ *What event in the past twenty-four hours has caused
me to punish myself by not eating, or sedate myself by
eating? What feeling was I running from?*

---

*If you keep doing what you've always done, you're going to get the
results you always got.*
You probably need to consider taking a 180-degree turn
from your usual behavior. As a first step you'll renegotiate your
relationship with número uno—food. Then you'll begin to
change your attitude toward all the relationships in your life.
You'll stop being the person you were "trained" to be, and become the person you "choose" to be. You'll grow up. As you discover how difficult it is to change your own behavior, you'll ease
into a more live-and-let-live attitude toward everyone else. You
will forgive yourself, your mom, and life itself.

It's Not Easy

Facing that you're the one who has to do the changing is the
hardest thing you'll ever have to do. And doing it without excess
food is even more threatening. Learning how to be alive and
aware without excess food as a buffer—this is the difficult project every women's magazine advertises as "easy." In a world
where every cocktail party has weight losers boasting about their
recent success, don't we get the idea that any idiot should be
able to figure this thing out? Where do you go when you've tried
everything and still ended up fat?
There is no compassionate heart shown to those who don't

"get it together" both quickly and easily. Think about the other obsessive, compulsive disorders. They're all accepted, and oddly enough, respected. We don't see advertisements telling us how easy it will be to stop drinking, smoking, or gambling. The severity of the illness, the complexity of the involvement, the necessity for help is acknowledged and encouraged. But this is not the case if the problem is food.

The food problem is most stigmatized, most patronized, hardest to treat, and at the same time most minimized. Recovery from too much or too little requires even more significant and profound changes from the patient. It is much more life-encompassing; and it requires a greater commitment on a daily basis to make the change. It's hardest to face because it's usually the last! Whatever substance abuse you try to modify, it is always the last one that's most difficult. Why? *Because there's nowhere to run and nowhere to hide.* You're face to face with your life, and there are no alternatives and no escapes. Eating is a constant and insistent activity, and taking it away cuts closest to the bone.

Food is the toughest of the obsessive relationships to give up because you have to focus on it directly while not focusing on it at all. Compulsive eating is really a search for more power; but to get this you have to cut down on your food intake, your easiest source of power. You have to take time to regret the power you've disowned, while at the same time you're looking for new sources of power other than food. It's enough to make you eat!

No wonder you can't stay ecstatic about the prospect of getting your food plan aligned. You realize on some level that this struggle will be lifelong and chronic. Who needs it? Who cares? Why is life so unfair?

I can only tell you—if you follow my plans for an "empowerment diet," you will give birth to your own personal, real life. You will feel more satisfied, less hungry. Instead of lamenting the unfairness of your situation, you'll be grateful for your supersensitivity. You'll be giving yourself your best chance to connect with your real self.

ASK YOURSELF:

□ *Do you have a food plan? How do you feel about having to restrict your intake of fat, sugar, and salt?*

□ *How do you feel about hunger? How do you feel about having an empty stomach?*

□ *How do you feel about not having enough food? How do you feel about having too much food?*

DROPOUTS NEED NOT APPLY. Make this time be different for you. Don't expect insight alone to fill you up. You've already had a lot of that. Realize that you've picked up this book because you're hungry and thirsty for a richer, more satisfying life. Many patients come to treatment well versed in explaining childhood traumas. In a way it seemed that their explanations of the past were a way of showing off, acting in control, proving they knew what was going on.

However, as they were encouraged to stay abstinent and try on new behaviors, they found that some of the explanations they'd previously bought were not really helpful, and in some cases not even true. A cartoon I use in lectures says, "Some of the things that will live longest in my memory never really happened." Such patients sometimes found it more filling not to have so many answers.

Despite the tremendous help I and others have found in good therapy, there is a downside to it. In therapy, we spend a lot of time focused on problems—labeling and categorizing and figuring life out; but maybe we just have to live it. What if you faced one door marked "heaven" and another marked "seminar on heaven." Which would you choose? Is your life meant to be understood, suffered, endured, or celebrated? As we take this journey of celebration, your disowned self will become motivated to come out. And once you risk coming out, you'll never be the same.

Your inner self knows it's time to get going, but you don't have a clue how to start. You try bingeing, purging, or drinking. Now, these failed attempts to grow up and leave home have left you Fat and Furious.

Not Deprivation, but Invitation

We can take some comfort with the German philosopher Nietzsche, who said, "That which does not kill us makes us stronger." What if there may be great healing in opening up that hollow place inside you, that place where you always feel deprived? Instead of continuing to stuff it, why not empty it further? Why not really feel that hollow, vacant place? When you do, you'll discover a treasure trove of personal inner wisdom you've been choking off. Until you have truly allowed yourself to feel the emptiness, you can't really appreciate the satisfactions you get from minimal filling.

I know the idea of emptiness isn't an easy sell. Either you already know that's what you gotta do, or you want to be talked out of it. Isn't that what all the foraging for new food plans is about? Isn't it easier to keep talking about getting filled?

You'd be hard-pressed in this culture not to dwell on staying full, eating, and eliminating. It's almost un-American to be indifferent to food. At any table in the continental U.S. you will find people sitting down or standing up, eating and simultaneously commenting on what they are eating or not eating. Each person must take note and editorialize.

It's only a rare few who can take it or leave it. But when you too can view and think about food with a fairly blasé attitude, you will have arrived at a modicum of health. You will have entered "recovery." Such detached, nonobsessed people can show us what recovery from an eating disorder looks like.

In the next chapter we'll discuss what behaviors to focus on INSTEAD of food. You'll see what is prescribed in my treatment programs and what issues we face to recover.

2

FOOD KILLS

*I*F YOU BUY THAT FOOD HAS BEEN USED AS A PUNISHER INSTEAD OF A nurturer, if you see how it keeps you from hearing yourself, then you see how that turns everything upside down. Food use has been distorted. Instead of helping us grow, it's been killing us off. We can change that by changing how we live our lives. When we stop dying in the plate, we start living our fullest life. We get to die out of fear and anger to get reborn into a new way of life.

CHANGE WE MUST

The kind of life changes you need to make to truly effect and maintain a significant weight-loss concern nothing less than being born again. You need help to do that. I developed the first eating-disorders unit in a hospital in order to provide people with a birthing place to create new lives. And today I continue this effort.

I developed the procedures used at the Hollis Institute from my own personal experience—first as a chubby little girl, then as an obese wife of a battering alcoholic, who at the same time was a gifted professional in the drug addiction field. You'll benefit from seeing how this perspective has evolved and how it differs from some other approaches. Remember, although I was a professional therapist, I myself weighed over two hundred pounds!

While giving a lecture to the International Congress on Drug Addiction, I binged before my talk and belched at the podium. This was exactly what AA's *Big Book* calls "Painful and Incomprehensible Demoralization." I'd *paid* my dues. Despite my eloquent words, such actions kept me debased and self-loathing.

When I finally faced my own addictions I realized the truth in the Bible's dictum, "Faith without works is dead." I knew clearly that you would know a person by what they did, not necessarily by what they said. So, it was about action. My existential training at the University of Southern California said it as "We are what we do, not what we say." What I could actually DO without excess food fueling my fire was much simpler and less impressive than whatever my bingeing bravado accomplished. Reducing three moderate banquets to three moderate meals each day required a commitment and attention to detail I had never learned before.

As I learned about myself in action, I applied it to what I'd learned working with other addictive personalities. For many years I focused primarily on family issues and lectured internationally while supervising the work of many counselors.

Today, the Hollis Institutes in Los Angeles and New York have become training centers for counselors and therapists to help them do more authentic and longer-lasting work with addictive families. There, they are given experiences rather than lectures. The professional trainees are attended to as patients and assigned tasks similar to those of our addictive patients. They experience what it's like to walk the walk in addition to talking the talk. They feel the tremendous vulnerability and fear of being thrown into a new situation and having to ask strangers for help.

Most important of all, they gain a sense of what it feels like to have no answers, to be encouraged to go within to find their own. While they can never truly feel the desperation that our patients do, they experience a change in personal outlook and behavior. The method used to help them find their own voice is the method you'll travel through in this book. By the end of our journey, you'll be writing your own story.

Overeating Therapies

First, a word about the evolution of this treatment philosophy. My earliest work as a counselor was with New York City's Addiction Services Agency in the Phoenix House program. We developed residential centers where addicts could live and be given job assignments to help them focus on parts of themselves they'd denied. Accomplishing new tasks, new behaviors, forced them to own disowned parts of themselves. For example, a professional carpenter would not be put on the building crew, but might instead be assigned the job of arts and crafts director or flower arranger. We wanted each person to gain a little acquaintance with the side of themselves they might have been hiding. Whatever they had already mastered would not be an area of difficulty. We wanted them to feel what it was like to be confused and ask for help.

When I took all I'd learned to that point and opened the nation's first hospital-based Twelve-Step eating-disorders unit, that event triggered a number of debates in the professional field. Many are still unresolved. Interestingly, though, they've come full circle in the last two decades. First, there was the idea of addiction. Would people call themselves "food addicts"? If so, then how could you ever eat again? Was calling ourselves "compulsive overeaters" a sufficient label, or should we be "carboholics" to resemble our big brother "alcoholics"?

At my treatment centers we ultimately decided that "compulsive overeater" applied to all our patients whether bingeing or starving. But we also wanted to emphasize that it was not food or eating that was the problem. It was ourselves and the way we used food as medication that was the problem.

Early on I was challenged for including both overeaters and anorexics in the same treatment center. My response was that they all hungered for excess filling, and all used food in the same addictive manner to quiet an inner longing. Most anorexics start out as compulsive eaters, then find starvation a most effective way to control eating. Most overeaters also have long periods of starvation; some even qualify to be diagnosed as anorexics. They are the same disorders. Later I learned that each person, no matter which end of the spectrum they began from, had to make friends with their opposite side. Being in treatment with each other got them acquainted and less fearful.

ASK YOURSELF:

☐ *Have you ever gone on an eating binge and then seesawed your disordered eating from bingeing to fasting and/or starving?*

☐ *Did you ever criticize people who controlled food differently than you did?*

☐ *Did you ever say "I'm not that bad yet"?*

☐ *Did you recognize any of these behaviors as disordered eating?*

Another debate surfaced about the issue of whether treatment led to a cure or to the recognition of a chronic condition that required lifelong monitoring. Should we inspire patients to "overcome" their problems or teach them how to cope with chronic difficulties? Many colleagues were upset that I would encourage patients to go to meetings of Overeaters Anonymous and declare they were "compulsive overeaters." These clinicians said such a statement destroyed all hope and made the patient irresponsible.

All I knew was that my whole life experience had shown me that I repeatedly returned to food as solace. Despite long periods of firm resolve and what seemed like control of my eating, I could safely say that for me, it had been a lifelong tendency. I was a "compulsive overeater." But once I accepted that, I realized it gave me a new compassion for myself. It's my belief that, rather than making patients irresponsible, such an honest admission made them much more responsible. It helped them see that they fought an internal demon and needed help. They were then responsible to avail themselves of that help.

Entering the Treatment Center

Most of the people who call our center have read my materials, seen our former patients on television, or heard from friends, counselors, or relatives about the Institute. They know when they call that they're tapping into twenty years of experi-

ence in treating their illness. They know that they personally
have made countless attempts to control themselves and failed.
Therefore they hope to talk to staff who have a bit more experience than they do. Most prospective patients are wise and careful, and they check out the level of insight of our intake staff.
That's why we hire recovering people.

If you were a prospective patient, the intake staff would take
you through an extensive process of questioning to ascertain
how often, how ardently, and ultimately how unsuccessfully
you've tried to curb your obsession. This is not done to embar-
rass or humiliate you, but to help you face the severity of the
problem, the need for drastic measures, and the need to dyna-
mite your psyche into another dimension.

Some people find going to a treatment center far from
home an excellent and dramatic way to tell your innermost self
that you're taking big steps. You've decided to deal directly and
honestly with the biggest issue in your life. Your inner self knows
that if you don't get the food problem in order, you'll keep turning to food as a solace each time you need to face something
new. You may still do that from time to time, even after treatment, but you're not likely to stay out there as long.

Treating the Family As Well

During the intake process, our staff will ask your permission
to talk with family members, and possibly invite them to come to
treatment as well. This applies whether you still live with your
original family or are alone, but have an extended or absent
family. You, of course, have the right to refuse our request, but
our underlying purpose is not with just you in mind. We want
your mother and others to benefit as well.

In all my years of treating addicts, I've found that many others suffer their own traumas as they helplessly watch a loved one
in pain. They also need help when the addict goes into recovery.
In fact, the only patient I ever had who committed suicide was
not an addict, but a spouse. He shot himself three months after
his wife got sober. He was displaced and lost when his caretaker
role was taken away.

Family members need help in order not to feel totally responsible and a failure when a loved one comes to treatment.
This was especially true for mothers who admitted their daugh-

ters. They felt so ashamed that they had not been able to save their little girl, by somehow controlling her eating or starving. They themselves needed treatment.

As the programs evolved and changed, I saw more and more how important that mother–daughter connection was to the recovery process, and how both needed to find a way to gently renegotiate their relationship. I saw that those like myself—who kept significant weight off for decades—had renegotiated their relationship with food, and their mothers. Recovery involved mothers and daughters making friends as women and thus each befriending her own self, her own power, her own feminine wisdom.

Mother–daughter relationship struggles were so similar to the food struggle. If they were too enmeshed in each other, then there was smothering and not enough light or air or life. The merger weighed down both their lives, keeping them stuck and stuffed. If they were estranged, if they'd sworn off one another, that was a complete avoidance of the problem, like anorexia. And although the distancing seemed to bring relief, it actually kept the problem much more up front and center. Most anorexics secretly crave food all the time. Estrangement from Mom makes you just as hungry as enmeshment.

ASK YOURSELF:

- How is your relationship with food similar to your relationship with Mom?

- What food struggles—compulsive eating, bingeing, starving—did you observe on your mother's plate?

- How did your mother–daughter relationship struggle mirror your food struggle?

- What did your mom tell you about food?

- What did you observe about Mom's struggle to control herself and you?

All family members and sometimes friends and other relatives are invited to come and live-in with the patient for at least a week. They attend all educational seminars, eat the abstinent food plan, learn "Dignity Dine" eating techniques, and have their own personal counselor to help them investigate their own involvement with the eating disorder. The family members participate in multiple family groups. They too are given therapy and job assignments, just like the primary patients. But, in addition, the entire family is prescribed some task to accomplish together. We developed this program after realizing that although there was tremendous value in insight therapy—sitting and sharing feelings—families also wanted to fulfill a purpose, to do something together. With an action-oriented treatment plan, most family members flowered.

Sometimes we aren't able to get family members to come to treatment. We had found the same to be true in alcoholism treatment. At first, patients feel too guilty and don't want to ask their families to give up the time. Sometimes daughters didn't want to give up resentment and anger at Mom. Sometimes they didn't want their families to know too much, as things might change and then they'd have nowhere to run and hide if their eating disorder cropped up again.

Imagine how it might be if no one at home offers you a safe harbor when you get sick. That's very scary. Would you want such a family trained in "tough love," where they would let you know they couldn't help you and suggest that you go for help to strangers?

Sometimes families couldn't come for family week because it was too great a financial burden or logistics problem. We're hoping that our country's new health plans will make it easier for whole families to get treatment.

Since most of you won't be coming for treatment, and even if you do, your families may not, this book is designed to offer you important treatment concepts to help you experience a lifelong diminishing of the food obsession. As you read on, you will come to see how we've used food as a punishment. How it has taken us away from life rather than being the fuel we needed to enhance and energize our lives. Once that basic attitude is examined and adjusted, important changes begin to occur. You discover that you simply cannot keep ingesting excess food the same old way.

IT'S DEPRESSING. Most of my patients are admitted to the hospital with a diagnosis of depression. Of course! Who wouldn't be depressed by the hopeless cycle of gaining and losing hundreds of pounds. Many sense that they are depressed because they've lived so far from their true heart's message. They are so out of touch with spirit, so lost from their inner selves, that despite their sometimes superhuman functioning, they have become extremely depressed.

For many, that depression won't surface until their fourth or sixth day of treatment. That's when sugar withdrawals are the worst. Countless patients enter treatment full of smiles and gratitude, telling us how sweet the intake counselor was, how much they like the nursing staff, how they can't wait to get up early for exercise and meditation. But let's face it, most of them have been eating their "last supper" for at least a week before they come, so those smiles are really plastered on a walking glucose bottle. That draining bottle starts hitting bottom around the fourth day, and a raging, fuming, hostile combatant wakes up. Then she hates the nursing staff, feeling "they're all out to get me," and has a mile-long list of grievances at how inefficiently our unit is run. But as she weathers this storm of rage, it passes, and within a few days she is embarrassed and apologetic. No need for either. It's the nature of the beast.

Depression is anger turned inward, and without that coating of excess sugar and fat, it gushes to the surface. Curbing sugar and fat intake also creates a raw feeling. In that greaseless state, our brittle grief emerges. It's all part of that disowned self that couldn't be heard before. It's also about regret over wasted time, and fear about not making it. Who the hell wants to have this illness anyway? It starts dawning on people that recovery is about changing how we live, not how we pile our plates. It seems like such an enormous task—changing our whole lives. Can't we fix it with some kind of pill or something?

ASK YOURSELF:

▢ *Are you chronically angry or depressed?*

▢ *Was your mother chronically angry or depressed?*

The Prozac Problem

Many treatments today do turn us on to drugs as a cure. As one who has worked in hospitals for more than two decades, I can tell you that often those decisions about drugs are made by clerks at insurance companies who decide that a simple prescription is much less costly than helping you find who you were meant to be. Fewer people need these drugs than the amounts very randomly and indiscriminately prescribed.

The most blatant misuse of such drugs can be seen in response to the new miracle cure Prozac. It's being prescribed by nearly every general practitioner for today's daughters. Even though many report success with the drug's use, my concern is that it is too easily available and too ardently extolled as a panacea. I've seen that 85 percent of our admissions are women bingeing and crying while ON Prozac. Even though Prozac is supposed to offer an appetite suppressant, it only works for anorexics and vomiters.

I know that many of you may already be on Prozac. For example, when I lectured at the college town of Lawrence, Kansas, 90 percent of my audience said they were on it. If you are, please take no action, change no gears. Just realize that if you take a drug to soothe the pain, you are not learning how to FEEL the void. That void cradles your spirit. And the drug is preventing you from hearing the call from deep inside you. Avoiding the pain means avoiding your inner life.

Recovery Means Coming to Life

If you choose to leave your obsessive love affair with food behind, you will be setting out on the journey of recovery. Recovering what you initially threw away, you will reclaim and reinvent yourself. You will choose life over death. You will grow up emotionally and spiritually and leave your parents' home. You'll be free to make your own home in the world. You won't be able to go back to the dark side again. You will see your life clearly and take responsibility for the choices you make. Once and for all, you will have to become a psychological orphan and truly leave the nest—emotionally, and spiritually.

WHAT DOES RECOVERY LOOK LIKE? What do we mean when we say "recovery"? We all know we have to eat, that if we don't eat we'll be just as sick with anorexia as we ever were eating compulsively. So what does recovery from food obsessions look like? In Alcoholics Anonymous we plug the jug and go to meetings. In Gamblers Anonymous, we stay away from poker halls and don't bet on the Super Bowl. In Narcotics Anonymous, we are very cautious about even doctor-prescribed drugs.

So what happens in Overeaters Anonymous? It can't be that we stop eating! A binger who turns to fasting is then anorexic—the opposite side of the same coin. Total abstinence applies to other obsessions, but not this one. The alcoholic who quits drinking and abstains totally is not presenting a problem to his health, family, or society. However, total abstinence from food is deadly. Anorexia has the highest death rate of any psychiatric illness. Food disorders are much messier than other obsessions. There are no easy answers to this one.

FOOD IS NOT THE ENEMY

If food were the problem, we certainly would have mastered it by now. There is a $10 billion industry helping us do just that. The battle of the bulge is topped only by the arms race as America's number-one expenditure. Perhaps both battles have been fought on the wrong grounds.

You've probably been trained to approach this problem by labeling yourself sick, or by judging yourself weak and spineless. But what if you choose to see your food problem as a blessing rather than a curse? I'd like you to approach it as a symptom of deeper hungers. You are supersensitive, alive, and aware. You see and hear things so clearly and brilliantly that you try to turn down the volume with excess food. You are actually more gifted than cursed, but you've been running from the responsibility of that giftedness.

We all have a "response ability" to respond appropriately to the signals we pick up. Instead, our society has trained us to stifle our sensitivity and inner wisdom by hiding out in the plate, counting calories, focusing too much on the food. We've approached our problems too directly, focusing only on the symptoms—excess eating. Now is the time to shift our focus to the more oblique meanings—our obsessive need to fill up so we won't fall down.

ASK YOURSELF:

- □ *Are you supersensitive? Do you see, hear, and feel things in people's behavior or in the environment that other people deny? Are your perceptions later proved true?*

- □ *Have you acted out with food to keep your perceptions bottled up? How?*

Beyond Labels

Until very recently medical practice has been bent on naming things, but not on fixing them. Do you hang out in the self-help section of your book store seeking a new name for what ails ya? Would you like the book you're reading now to offer you checklists of symptoms that you could say yea or nay to? Wouldn't that make things a little easier? Wouldn't it be easier if we could just treat this disease called life?

Don't blame yourself for wanting your problem a bit more tightly wrapped and packaged for shipping. You came by it honestly. Most of us are running to labels to help us continue to deny that physically and spiritually we create our own lives. It seems too much to bear. Once you recognize this bottom-line, basic fact, you may sink into deep regret about wasted time. That can get very depressing.

Despite the comfort we may briefly feel from esoteric diagnoses, having a name for what's wrong with us is EXACTLY what is wrong with us. Our inner being knows there's much more to it than the medical label. She also knows that if we buy too much into the label mentality, we'll stop listening for her altogether. We might even work harder to shut her up. After all, most of our upbringing, our "civilizing," has been in the service of devaluing our inner yearnings.

Medicine has been part of that murder of the spirit by too readily naming legitimate human drives and needs as sickness. At the beginning of your journey to recovery you can use these labels to get help and support. Later you will be able to choose to throw the labels away, and find your own personalized healing.

Recovery means looking beneath the labels for who we really are. It means being more respectful to our elusive INNER SELVES. But our culture teaches the opposite. For example, I was working on preinterviews with the producer of a nationally syndicated talk show presenting "Women Who Hate Their Bodies." I'd been appearing on television for over a decade and was frankly quite nauseated at the gradual degeneration of media reporting and the tactics they used to increase their audiences. Although I was somewhat embarrassed at my continuing to appear, I was convinced that any way I could carry the message could be worthwhile for someone.

Our conversation got quite heated as the producer shouted that he needed four specific categories of guests: "I need an exercise freak, a vomiter, a plastic surgery makeover, and a starver. Maybe we could throw in a laxative abuser as well. Main thing is, they have to be average Middle America types. Not too serious, no one saying they have a 'disease.' We used that angle last month."

This producer didn't realize that he was actually bringing up a heady debate I'd seen brewing at professional conferences for two decades. Psychiatrists spend hours debating new diagnostic categories to decide if patients should be labeled anorexic or bulimic, or given the new label of "binge eating disorder" (BED). These fine line demarcations left me cold. The debate usually centered around consumption or elimination behaviors. "If she vomits only three times a day, we'll still call her anorexic, but if more often, she might qualify as bulimic."

Then there were those endless discussions of what purging meant. Could excessive exercise be purging? Was laxative abuse bulimic if done by a fat man? Recent studies had shown that even grotesquely obese women suffer from anorexia for long stretches at a time.

Considering all of these anomalies made categorization virtually impossible. Whose needs did these categories serve? How could medicine explain a three-hundred-pound woman who vomited six times a day?

I found diagnostic discussions not only boring, but a useless attempt to avoid deeper issues about treatment. Not knowing how to help these patients, doctors wasted everyone's time labeling. They were more concerned with accountability and making sure that THEY understood each other's nomenclature than with actual healing.

I tried to hold my judgments in check to see what I could learn from all this. I knew that no matter what the label, the same issues had to be faced in order to recover. I knew that many patients vacillated from one form of food abuse to another. I've treated many who spent their lives waffling back and forth along the continuum—one year weighing 85 pounds and the next 348. And what about those who are normally stabilized in weight, but who purge twenty times a day after spending four hours at the gym.

I've seen a 45-year-old, 400-pound man who vomited eight times a day. Which diagnostic category did he fit? Even more shocking is that these illnesses are still categorized as "diseases of childhood." The point is, patients have an unnatural love affair with the substance—it works to quiet a deeper longing.

How could I explain to the TV producer that these categories meant nothing to me. Everyone I'd ever treated was a whole human being, complete and subtle, and all of them fell into all of these categories from time to time. Such demarcations didn't work when talking about real people and real obsessive behavior. I couldn't for the life of me think of anyone I'd ever treated who fell into purely one limited diagnosis or the other.

Alcoholism professionals faced the same issues in their early days. They asked if a "periodic" was just as alcoholic as a daily drinker. We were thirty years behind the treatment programs for alcoholics where early patients came in full of denial, kicking and screaming, "I'm no alcoholic. I'm just a 'problem drinker.' "

What makes it a problem? It just depends on when in the progression of the illness you choose to take a cool, hard look and call a spade a spade. "When does a cucumber soaked in brine become a pickle?" When do you decide it's serious enough to label it? I guess the reason to delay is, once pickled, you can never go back to being a cucumber.

> ### ASK YOURSELF:
>
> ▢ *What labels have you given your disordered eating?*
> ▢ *What did the labels give you in return?*
> ▢ *What was your purpose in labeling?*
> ▢ *How did it help?*

USING THE LABELS—THREE DIAGNOSES

Let's look at some labels in order to USE them rather than be used by them. The labeling process is a tool you can use to see that you are not alone. It helps you realize that your efforts and disappointments are similar to those suffered by others. It helps you get off your own back. It helps you move out of the "self will" position of demanding that you and you alone should be able to take care of your problems. Labels help you stop "shoulding" on yourself. Try using them to help you become more compassionate with yourself; but be careful not to let them become your only means of identification. In other words, you are much more than your diagnosis.

Eating disorders are medically categorized as psychiatric illnesses—"diseases of childhood"—even though some are physical problems such as diabetes, heart disease, liver malfunction, gout, metabolic disorders, back pains, hypertension, and other medical and dental problems. These related disorders can be treated within the realm of physical medicine. And yet, when we help patients to hear and heal the psyche, many of these other problems clear up.

Compulsive Overeating

If your eating is out of control, you fall into the category of "compulsive overeater." Usually you will be moderately to excessively overweight. This label used to work well until some clinicians tried to prevent fat people from gaining access to psychiatric treatment. They felt fat people were simply a morality and "willpower" problem, but didn't need psychological help.

That is absolutely absurd, once you understand how many times the patient has tried to curb the obsession. When you look at how obsessive the love affair with food is, you know for sure that this is not a *physical* malady, it is most definitely a problem of the mind, the psyche, and the spirit.

Most of us continue to overeat in the face of all medical warnings. In March 1993, *Newsweek* magazine reported that Americans were very aware of all the harmful effects of excess fat in their diets. They still chose excess fatty "comfort" foods, giving as a reason that many of these people were out of work and fearful of the nation's future economic condition. When Los Angeles experienced the 1994 earthquake, bakeries and fast-food chains, as well as gourmet eateries, all reported increased sales and fattier choices. Facts didn't fight obsession or the need for comfort.

For a number of years, overeaters were separated out from those who overate and then purged. In 1992 at the International Eating Disorders Conference, a new diagnosis of Binge Eating Disorder (BED) was reintroduced to include fat people, making them again qualified to receive treatment. The label had again come full circle. You see, until you are labeled as ill, you have no chance to be offered help.

Bulimia

If you take in large quantities of food and then purge to avoid the results or consequences of your eating, then you will be categorized as bulimic. You are just as obsessed with food as a fat person, but there are different consequences. For a long time you can get away with secret eating with no one knowing.

This secretive aspect proves difficult to treat—we all like "getting away with" things. It's a false victory, but you still believe it. Many who stop vomiting then take up shoplifting or excessive lying, all attempts to keep "getting away with." So what is it you actually get away with? Your digestive system, your teeth and gums, your bloodshot eyes, and your swollen jowls give you away. But even more importantly, your soul knows and your body knows. As with other forms of addiction, your body grows accustomed to your behavior; but if you picked up this book, you're probably one of those people who has to keep increasing the frequency of purging behaviors. You may be obsessively increasing exercise, laxative abuse, or other purging activities. Often you will start gaining weight despite these drastic efforts.

Anorexia

If you think you can totally avoid this discussion, you fall into the category of anorexia. You may feel you have "no food problem." In fact, you probably aren't even reading this. More than likely your mother is. She's been reading lots of books, trying hard to find a way to help you. But you feel un-needy in every way. That's what the starving does for you. It helps you prove to yourself that you don't need anything from anyone. Even though anorexia was first labeled as "a loss of appetite," in reality most anorexics have large and obsessive appetites. They have resorted to NOT EATING as a way to cope with that excessive appetite.

Those are the three major eating disorders—and they're much more alike than they are different. No matter which eating disorder best describes you, the underlying psychological and spiritual hunger is similar for all—the hunger to re-own the disowned self.

No matter which eating disorder you suffer, the most important thing for you to keep in mind is: Your relationship with nurturance is unnatural. Whether you are obsessively drawn toward it, or repelled by it in fear and avoidance, it's got ya. You think about it more than other people, and oddly enough, you often don't enjoy it as much as they do. Early research, such as Hilde Bruch's on feeding patterns in obese infants, found that moms cut off feeding episodes early and weaned daughters sooner than sons. You weren't allowed to organically control your own nurturance. You were trained early to live in a little bit of deprivation, doing without. Food was a temptress and a punisher. You made it more than it is. But it's not love, God, sex, or rock and roll. It's just food. It has become a way to plug a gaping hole of loneliness and disappointment. When you don't have it you feel bad, and when you have it you don't feel good.

You can qualify yourself as eating-disordered if you see food discussions and weight loss or gain discussions dominating your life. Are you in a dress rehearsal for "When I get thin"? When the American Medical Association declared alcoholism a disease, their primary criterion for diagnosis was: "A person who has TRIED to quit." Obviously those who have willpower just QUIT. Notice how many times you have TRIED to quit unhealthy, abusive eating?

ASK YOURSELF:

☐ *Is my relationship with food natural or unnatural?*

☐ *What would a healthy relationship with food be like?*

☐ *How much of my time is spent controlling food or its effects?*

Life Is in Session

It is an attitude change more than anything else. You'll begin to do things that make you feel so good about yourself you won't need to abuse yourself so much! You'll become a person who stops "holding on" and instead you'll be able to "let go." You'll stop punishing yourself with food. As you develop a new personal philosophy, facing life and yourself on its own terms, you'll begin to like yourself a lot. These are the key attitude adjustments you'll be working through in this book:

- Action is the magic word
- Clean your own sidewalk
- Intentions count
- Crave the emptiness
- Forgive
- Surrender the ego

ACTION IS THE MAGIC WORD. There are so many good books about eating disorders and other addictions, and so many great philosophies of life. But they only work if you can truly live what they propose. You must take some action. It doesn't help to know the right thing if you don't learn how to DO the right thing. Most of the people who come to our treatment centers have already had extensive therapy; many are well read and educated. But what they knew did not help them lose weight. It's what they did that made the difference.

This is why in treatment we actually give assignments to help people face and walk through their greatest fears. Many come with the idea that they can talk about their fears, think about their fears, find comforting about their fears, and then somehow, as if by magic, they'll HAVE NO FEARS. Well, that hasn't been our experience. Our approach is to help people take action in spite of the fear. *Life Is Fearful.* We can't wait until we have no fear. We need to face the fear and do it anyway.

For example, if you tell us, "I can't lose weight because I'm afraid to be thin," then we'd say to you, "First get thin and then we'll talk about it." You won't really know how you'll feel until you're actually *in* the situation.

Jeanette told us that, in previous therapies, she'd discovered, "I've accumulated all this fat because I'm afraid of my sexuality. I don't want to attract men. I'm afraid they want to hurt me." Jeanette had deep-seated reasons for these feelings, and she understood why she felt as she did. She just didn't know what to do with her understanding.

I took her out with a group of patients on a FLIRT ASSIGNMENT. About ten of us, all women, piled into an old van and went to a car wash in Hollywood. There was our rickety old van waiting in line with many shiny new Mercedes driven by Hollywood types with car phones at their ears. Some of the guys who clean at the car wash are recently discharged from Federal prison—some even on weekend work furloughs. They're all friendly and flirtatious.

The assignment for all the women in my van was to FLIRT. As we piled out of the van, each woman, no matter what size or shape, was to quietly, unobtrusively, flirt with at least one man at the car wash. A fleeting glance was sufficient. The important thing was what each woman *did*, not what she thought. Afterward she was to register the response she got and report in group therapy on her adventure.

This exercise is wonderful for women who live in a dress rehearsal for life, the ones who protest, "I can't do this until I am thin and feel good about my body." Our attitude is, "Life is in session. Let's begin."

Jeanette LOVED the experience. She liked the power she felt after taking action. She kept smiling sweetly at one gentleman who kept returning her gaze all through the twenty-minute wait as our van was dried. Jeanette had originally come to treatment explaining to us her fears about what MEN would do. After the outing, she found instead that her fear was more about what SHE would do. As she felt the excitement of the blood rushing through her veins she realized, in action, that she both craved and feared the rush of power she felt. She loved the POWER! She turned around her theories from victim to actor— talking more about her concerns that, if thin, she might go raping and pillaging through the streets! As you take action, you find out who you really are.

CLEAN YOUR OWN SIDEWALK. You've probably spent a lot of your life focusing away from your own problems and toward someone else's. As a mother, you may have totally dedicated yourself to your children's needs and wants. It's often easier to focus on other people's problems rather than your own. If you are really good at it, you can become a therapist.

Do you know how many therapists it takes to change a light bulb? It only takes one, but the bulb really has to want to change. Well, as you will learn, the only bulb you can change is yourself. The closer you are to someone else's problems the more ineffective you'll probably be. This is a difficult message for mothers. If you're a mom, you will have to work doubly hard to keep your eyes on your own plate, and your mind on your own business. Many of our patients are sent to Alanon meetings for alcoholic families just to learn how to shift their focus off others and onto themselves. Some women become earth mothers in treatment, helping all the other patients while their own hearts are breaking. It is so difficult for them to move into the *receiving* role, to be nurtured and cared for by others.

Learning to Be Nurtured

Once you dedicate yourself to "doing the right thing" and working your own side of the street, you'll begin to feel deserving of help from others. For example, a very important issue comes up in treatment about who changes the toilet paper roll. "How does that relate to taking action and cleaning your own sidewalk?" you ask. Well, bear with me. It's just one of many treatment dilemmas. This issue doesn't come up in the hospital where we have janitorial staff who attend to facilities maintenance. However, in residential care, and during family week, we have many opportunities to experiment.

Since we always have many more women in treatment than men, we go through a lot of toilet paper. An entire evening's discussion group is devoted to the topic of who changes the roll.

When you come upon a roll near empty, what do you do? Do you leave an empty roll on the spindle for someone else to change, or do you place a new roll on it ready for use? What's your part? So many important treatment issues are dealt with as a result of how this is handled.

"How does this fall on my side of the street?" you ask. Well, it has to do with how you affect your world, how you find life, how you leave life. Who do you expect to take care of you? How much do you care for others? Is life fair? Should life be fair? Can you beat the system? Can you get away quietly without doing your part?

It all comes down to: Can you sneak a snack if no one's watching? This is what's involved in this simple action. How you act here has a tremendous effect on your eating problem. When you act in a way that makes you feel good about yourself, then you don't have to punish yourself with excess food. It may seem weird at first, but changing that roll can drastically change your role in life.

INTENTIONS COUNT. The world may not drastically change, whether you replace the roll or not. What is important is that YOU change as a result. By replacing what you use, leaving the world a little better than you found it, you're putting out your intentions to do as little harm as possible. The Buddhists say, "Enlightened action creates no wake."

An action as simple as this can have a powerful effect on your life. It's a matter of paying attention to your own intentions. You don't want to become a wimp. But a tremendous inner shift occurs when you focus on not creating too much hardship for others—while also not bragging about your good works. Doing the right thing, quietly and unobtrusively, creates a healing energy within your own organism. Your psyche knows and remembers these little nice things that you do.

The real payoff is in your food. With what seem like minuscule, inconsequential actions, you lose the self-punishing aspect of your food abuse. As you intend to put out kindness and gentleness in the world, you will expect to be treated the same way, although you may have to wait a little longer than you'd like. Here's where you learn one of the most difficult concepts in recovery: "patience and tolerance." Even if your rewards aren't speedily forthcoming, you know your intentions were honorable. You just need help to weather the wait.

CRAVE THE EMPTINESS. This brings us to the point of being able to be with and tolerate that interminable amount of time between wanting and getting. Many patients come to treatment totally unable to tolerate any sense of emptiness. They have suffered so many losses that their souls protest they can't take any more. They have to stuff themselves. Unfortunately, to succeed at this new life, they must find a way to appreciate and even seek after that feeling of emptiness.

I don't blame you for wanting to feel filled. The idea of eating whatever you crave is definitely attractive. There are even clinicians who advise you to listen to yourself to know best what and how much to eat. They advise you to eat whatever that voice tells you. But what if it's a hostile voice? We sometimes choose to abuse ourselves.

Advice to eat at will is not wise for newcomers. Until you have enough behaviors under your belt that make you feel "deserving," it's important that you listen warily to any "voice" that advises you what and how to eat. That voice may tell you that ice cream is fish. At first, you will usually choose excess and abuse. It's all you've known. It's comfortable and familiar.

Those who propose this approach warn that if we feel deprived of what we really want, we end up bingeing. Their solution is "To avoid feeling deprived, eat what you want." I have yet to meet anyone for whom this program has worked. I've treated many who came to me after it failed. They certainly wanted it to work and you can't blame them.

My proposal may seem difficult, even unreasonable, at first. But why not consider CHOOSING emptiness and a bit of deprivation? Why is "feeling deprived" such a terrible thing? I understand how you've been schooled to medicate discomfort, how life is hard enough without actually seeking out the difficult path. You'll have to make friends with the more difficult, seemingly "deprived" way to go.

Many of us think we're talking about a feeling of "food deprivation" but that's not it. Most suggested food plans allow us enough food to stoke the engine. What we're actually experiencing is an emotional, spiritual deprivation. We're not eating from a sense of food deprivation, but because we're unable to tolerate ANY feelings. We are running from our real selves.

The reason you and I have to surrender to a more difficult path is because we are hypersensitive. Others may get away with more abusive behaviors toward themselves or others, but when you and I live off course from our inner wisdom, we're harming ourselves at the core of our being. We simply can't get away with the things others do. If we coulda, we woulda. Twelve-Steppers call this feeling "losing conscious contact" with our spiritual selves. We're so sensitive that we actually feel that distance from our true selves as emptiness, pain, and loss.

FORGIVE. If we choose the path of recovery, we're actually choosing a more difficult life. There are many satisfactions from living such a life more fully and consciously, but you will still hurt more than others from time to time. You'll cry more, but you'll also laugh more joyously. It's like Garth Brooks sings: "Life is left to chance/I coulda missed the pain/but I woulda missed the dance."

As you grow to trust your own judgment, you'll develop a tremendous confidence in yourself. You'll gently and calmly begin to feel a loving compassion for yourself. And you'll come to realize that despite others' caring about you, and despite your acting inappropriately from time to time, no one has been hurt as much as you. You must apologize to yourself and then forgive yourself for all you've been through. At this point, you'll also be able to forgive others—especially your mom.

This is where the addiction model becomes so important. You're not a bad person trying to get good, you're a sick person trying to get well. That doesn't make you irresponsible. In fact, you're taking responsibility in seeking guidance, rather than continuing in your own solitary failures. You deserve compassion rather than judgment. You are now very responsibly trying to follow guidelines set down by those who have already walked out of addictions.

SURRENDER THE EGO. Once you start moving in this direction, you will feel no need for bragging or showing off. This is a gentle, continuous, lifelong struggle. When you tried to control your eating in the past, you probably came at it from a more ego-driven position, proclaiming firm resolve and willpower. How long did those promises last? Did you watch along with millions as Oprah wheeled out that wagon full of fat? Weren't we all hoping with her that the problem was finally, permanently solved? But with all that attention focused on her the fat returned!

Perhaps you need to take on this new approach more quietly and indirectly. Because this kind of recovery is hard to master, you need to sneak up on it sideways. You can't go at it full bore, because your inner being does not want to be controlled by your external ego's need for dominance. This is a battle you need to lose to win. But in the loss of ego gratification, you'll gain a much more permanent sense of satisfaction—your soul will sing. It will be difficult to explain to yourself, much less to others, that you're on the path, but not working at it. You've been schooled in all kinds of "firm resolve" talk and pushing and holding on and seeking power and CONTROL. This time you'll give up to get.

EGO means Edging God Out. Your "God" is your inner messenger. When you decide to overeat, you stop listening to her. In the past you may have tried to keep up with your ego's timetable; and then given up, blaming yourself for not moving fast enough. Hopefully, this time you're ready for things to be different. You're ready for YOU to be different. You've spent enough time, energy, and "willpower" on diets that ended in defeat, with top weights escalating or episodes of purging increasing.

You'll set off on this new journey with no fanfares from your ego. I'm suggesting a quiet, gentle, very, very dignified journey—a little less sure-footed, because there won't be any simple prescriptive guidelines or clichés. You won't necessarily feel good or look good all the time, but you'll be on the path. You won't feel the need to get into competition with others who seem to be racing past you with protein drinks, gym memberships, or some of your old tried-and-true failures. This approach may not promote ego gratification, but it will be more lasting.

ASK YOURSELF:

▫ *What one action am I willing to take today to change my behavior around food?*

▫ *What one action am I willing to take today to help myself instead of others?*

▫ *What feelings am I willing to tolerate today instead of reaching to food for an answer?*

▫ *What one thing am I willing to forgive Mom for today?*

▫ *What ego message (shaming and blaming) am I willing to trade in for a message from my Inner Voice?*

WHAT IS ABSTINENCE?

Since we all have to eat, there is no easy way to define abstinence from either compulsive eating or starving. It's not simply removing the substance. Alcoholics can plug the jug. We can't. My best definition is: "Abstinence is guilt-free eating." Finding that path will be ambiguous. You'll have to negotiate your way daily and personally. Your aim is to create a bit of a hollow place inside so there is room for your inner self to emerge.

In early recovery you will only feel sure, "not guilty," by talking with a surrogate parent, a sponsor in a Twelve-Step program each day about what and how you eat. The healing ingredient is letting someone else see into your plate. It starts with getting honest about what you're eating. That gradually expands into getting honest in other areas of your life.

Asking for Help: Why We Need the Sponsor

Now you will start to see how your eating battle has become your ticket of admission to a whole new way of life. All the help you need is waiting for you, all you have to do is ask. How can something so simple be so hard? Asking for help is your first big step on the path of recovery.

Once you have found a sponsor, you'll be face to face with the BIG QUESTION: what to eat or not eat. Although a nutritionist can help you here, this goes much deeper than what you put in your mouth. It involves issues of integrity and of honoring personal commitments to yourself. It's not just about knowing WHAT to eat—it's about DOING it. Your sponsor is the witness you will need to help you keep your promises to yourself. This person is not your judge or jury, just a witness. Your food choices are never clear cut, but they'll get easier once you begin to disclose your daily food consumption to someone else. TOGETHER two people can make daily decisions. It's hard for compulsive people to get rigorously honest. You will initially hate this experience. Decisions about food are extremely intimate, and can be very problematic. There are no definite right ways. It's difficult for us to tolerate such ambiguity. But when you find someone to share your food choices with, you'll be opening a channel to your inner self, and this intimate relationship will allow you to let yourself become more visible.

Footwork

If whatever you've been trying hasn't been working, I invite you now to try something new. This doesn't make whatever you were trying "wrong," but you may just need a change. It's just like your shampoo: Sometimes you just need to change brands. Don't you then marvel at how well the new shampoo works? Then in a few weeks, you'll get build-up from that one, and once again you'll need to try a different product. You need the same switch in approaching your food problems. After a while, this gets to be enjoyable.

We focus on food first so that later we can give up focusing on it. Having a disciplined food plan is what gets us to the starting gate, gets us feeling a little raw, so that our deeper inner signals can begin to be heard. In any event, please don't forget that the FOOD must always be attended to first. Think of your food plan as "footwork," or preparation.

For many years my Hollywood treatment center has seen many movie wannabees, and a few celebrities. Clichés in the movie business are "It's not WHAT you know, but WHO you know," or "You just gotta wait for that lucky break." Well, I've seen many who were given that "lucky break," but *they weren't ready* when opportunity knocked: They hadn't done their footwork! They got a chance at success, but because they hadn't done the necessary preparation, their "actor's instrument"—themselves—had not been developed enough to rise to the occasion. They were soon forgotten.

There were others who had devoted themselves to training and preparation and continuous study; when their lucky break came, they were ready to seize the opportunity. They had something deep, personal, and real to deliver. They had made themselves ready for success. Think of your food plan the same way, as a readiness for diving into your new life, seeing yourself in a whole new way, waiting for your "lucky break."

I saw this clearly with Jan, an early outpatient who came to group therapy every week, reported a perfectly abstinent food plan, watched many others share great emotion, sat quietly, and disclosed very little about herself. After six weeks, she hadn't lost a pound.

An easy answer would have been "life is unfair," or "Jan is lying about what she eats." The truth was, Jan was still lying to herself about who she was. Her food plan was just as she described it. The problem was that her feelings were still dishonest. Thank God she didn't drop out at this stage. Most treatment programs expect high dropout rates. Many gyms and behavior-modification programs overbook their classes, because they know many will leave after three weeks. If all showed up as registered, those locker rooms would be too full!

Jan was brave enough to keep showing up. And as she watched others begin to come out, her own inner self became awakened and encouraged to come out as well. One night, without warning, she came to group unable to stop crying. She'd been watching others, and finally her inner self felt safe enough to come out.

Jan told us that her weight had stayed on because she needed to hold down a lot of emotion. She was conflicted and blocked about the death of her only son in the Korean War. She had very heavy expectations of herself about what kind of a mother she wanted to be as well as what kind of a Christian; she wanted to model herself as decent and God-fearing and accepting of God's will. But when God seemed to have turned away from her, she found no way to cope except to eat. In our group she was encouraged not to eat, and ultimately to release her sadness. At the time of her son's death, she had taken care of everyone else, made all the funeral arrangements, never cried, and kept making big pots of spaghetti. She accepted it all quietly, subdued her rage with "It's God's will," and then ate nonstop for the next twenty years.

We all spent the evening encouraging her to come out. We re-enacted her son's funeral in a psychodrama session and helped her talk to him and say good-bye. The sobbing from all the group members was tremendous as we each remembered our own sadnesses and supported hers. The next week she had lost twelve pounds! Her body no longer needed to hold the sadness. Much of it got expressed that evening. More would flow out in years to come as she stayed abstinent.

This whole story may seem farfetched, and it would certainly be difficult to explain to a purely medical audience. It smacks a bit of California, "airy-fairy, fruits and nuts." I would be leading the pack of doubting Thomases here myself, if I hadn't seen this happen so often. Wilhelm Reich, inventor of the Orgone box and the earliest "body work" theorist, believed that we have emotions locked up in every cell of our being. According to Reich, each of our cells and muscles holds memories about our entire life experience. Reichian therapists will work with you to open up breathing and then do Reichian massage to ease and relax and move muscle mass. These techniques awaken and release long-dead feelings. Similar effects can happen with long-term food abstinence and a gentle invitation from others on the same path.

As with Jan, once the emotion is released, your organism no longer needs to stay blocked off, puffed up, filled and solidly packed. You become open, empty, and ready to be penetrated by new experiences.

Jan was doing the footwork, staying abstinent, getting ready for that evening. She was preparing for her lucky break. Once the sadness was ready to emerge, her body was ready to give up the weight. She wasn't sugar-coated or lard-locked any longer. When her psyche got cleared, her body was clear, and the gluing, blocking fat could melt away.

These things rarely happen according to our conscious timetable. I've now seen thousands who were able to follow these guidelines, seeking their inner souls instead of their outer shapes. Each time the body eventually caught up.

The First Step: Start Where You Are

You must now face how hard it's been. Despite the love affair, food hasn't really worked for you. Your inner self has been anxiously waiting for you to show up, anxiously waiting for you to slow down and listen. Food, and your struggles with food, have been keeping you two apart. You could almost say your real self has been in competition with food to get your attention. You're now going to make your relationship with food more conscious and then more disciplined—all in the service of meeting your innermost SELF.

Writing Down Your Life with Food

All through this book I'll be offering you questions to ask yourself, think about, feel about. As the answers drift into your consciousness and are spoken by your Inner Voice, you'll find that you want to remember what she has to say to you. A good way to do this is to start keeping a journal. Begin simply by jotting down the thoughts you have about your life as you work through the book. A journal is also a good place to record those intimate conversations you'll be having with your Inner Self. And it's the perfect place for the writing exercises I'll be asking you to do from time to time to get more deeply in touch with yourself.

Journaling is a time-honored method of contacting your Inner Voice. You may have kept a diary when you were young. It gave you a safe refuge—a place where you could call it as you saw it. A journal can do that for you now. You don't have to write in it every day. It's only for when you have something to say to yourself that you don't want to lose. It's a place to explore—and expand. A journal is a place to try on new ways of thinking and seeing and being. The journaling process doesn't care what your writing skills are, it has nothing to do with spelling or grammar. It has everything to do with communicating with your SELF!

Journals are very handy, you can carry them with you, or leave them by your bedside or at any special place you choose. They help you keep organized, because all your writings will be in one place. What your journal looks like is up to you. Some people like spiral-bound school notebooks in bright colors, others like to keep their writings in a three-ring binder with dividers so they have a specific place for dialogues, thoughts, written exercises, dreams. (This method is especially handy if you type or use a computer.) Other people prefer to have a beautiful cloth-bound blank book to write in. Some people use different colored inks for different kinds of subject matter. It's all up to you.

Once you begin your journal, it will serve another extremely useful function. Because you'll date each entry before you begin, and perhaps give a brief title to that entry as well, your journal will help you keep track of where you are in your own process. A journal isn't just for putting things in, it's also for re-reading and reconnecting with your own wisdom and self-discoveries.

Every few weeks, or when you have time, it's good to review what you've been writing: A journal gives you perspective—where you began, how you felt, what you thought. It helps you see where you're stuck; and helps you see who you're becoming, and where you want to go.

So grab your journal and your pen, or go to your favorite keyboard and start typing; you're going to sit down now and write about your primary, most important relationship: your relationship with food.

You need to approach your writing with an attitude of trust and excitement. It's best if you don't have a plan, if you don't know what will come out before you begin. There's a kind of magic that happens when pen hits paper, that gets lost if we linger too long in our heads. Right now, by writing freely, you can begin the process of "letting go," trusting that whatever you're meant to hear will be written down by your hand right now.

To begin, pick a quiet spot where you feel comfortable and private. No phones ringing, no one interrupting. Just sit quietly for a few minutes. Let your jaw relax; focus on your breathing. Feel your breath assume a natural pace, watch how your body takes in oxygen. Hold your pen lightly. Make a few circles on the page before you begin—let your whole arm move freely with the circles. Now, simply let the words flow, write down whatever floats into your mind. Don't worry about making sense, just let it all come out.

MY FOOD—RIGHT HERE, RIGHT NOW

Start where you are. Start with today. Focus on how you ate today. In Chapter 1 we asked you questions about your relationship with food. Here, you get to write down your answers.

Think about what you're doing when you eat. Think about breakfast, lunch, and dinner, and the snacks you had today.

1. How did you decide to eat? Was it your decision, or did the clock tell you, or did your stomach tell you, or did your work schedule, or social life tell you what, where, when, or how to eat?
2. How did the food come to you?
3. What was eating like?
4. How long did it take?
5. Did you enjoy the food? Did you love your food? Hate your food? Or love and hate your food?
6. Are there any similarities between your relationship with food and other relationships in your life?

MY FOOD—HOW IT'S BEEN IN THE PAST

When you've finished writing about your food for TO-DAY, begin to take stock of all your efforts to control it in the past. For your own clarity, it's important that you write a brief history of all your failed attempts at controlling this self-destructive behavior.

Pay special attention to the programs you began with firm resolve. And then—most importantly—ask yourself how you decided to give them up. Writing all this down will help you see that you've been trying your best. Your best efforts got you here. You will also begin to see clearly how you've often been your own worst enemy—that you've been giving up on yourself. And it will also show you that food just doesn't do it anymore.

1. Start by listing the various ways you've tried to control your eating: rigid dieting; Weight Watchers; bypass surgery; Jenny Craig; Nutri-System; Deal-a-Meal; health spas; gym memberships; inpatient hospitalizations; psychologist; psychiatrist; social worker; behavior modification classes; nutritional workshops. Add in your own.
2. Now, ask yourself how many times you gave up—it's IMPORTANT for you to see how you decided to abandon these efforts.
3. Ask yourself about the process that went on with each of those efforts: How did you feel when you started the project? Did you take on the control of food with firm resolve? What made you give up? What got in the way of your attempts at success? How did you feel about this?

You Did Your Best

We've all tried our best. As you review what you've written you can now begin to see how powerless you've been over controlling food. This is why I recommend that you go into a Twelve-Step program, such as Overeaters Anonymous. In this supportive environment you'll be able to find a strong, successful sponsor you can use as a mentor, as you begin opening up and listening to your Inner Self.

If you take this journaling effort to read to your mentor or to someone else you will be facing the first step in the Twelve-Step program. You'll be admitting your "powerlessness" over your lifelong attempts to control the substance. You'll also be getting ready to become more present, more visible.

As you review your efforts, can you honestly see the food game? Who won? Who lost? Questions about winning and losing bring us to the meat of the matter. In the next chapter we will look at why you failed so many times before. We'll also be asking: Can you stand the power of success?

Chapter

3

FEARING POWER

Bumper Sticker: "Whatever women do, they must do twice as well as men to be thought half as good. Luckily this is not difficult."

—CHARLOTTE CHILTON,
Former Mayor of Ottawa

WHY DO 97 PERCENT OF PEOPLE WHO TAKE ON WEIGHT LOSS ALL RE-gain the weight PLUS more? Why does the $10-billion-a-year diet industry keep winning new participants? Nearly every patient I've treated has reported some modicum of success in the weight-loss game, and could recall long or short periods when the demon was held at bay. How could they be so successful and then fail so miserably?

Perhaps it had something to do with discomfort with the success. Even after they'd reached their goals, their psyches were still wobbly. They'd felt more stable when they were fat. Why? Because they never had any training in how to feel powerful and live with it. For many, it had to do with growing up and leaving suffering loved ones. This meant truly emotionally leaving home. It was just too much to do alone. They had received help and attention while suffering, getting out of suffering, moving from fat to thin—then, nothing. There was no help or guidance for how to STAY in the good life, how to weather success, how to ENDURE our blessings.

We don't eat only over problems. We eat over the good times just as much. Success and celebrations make us eat. We don't know how to live the good life. There is a lot to weather in being successful. When you get there, you'll know. Your life is at stake. You may have been there quite a few times, had no comfort for your "problems of abundance," had no one to offer a few "there, there's" about how difficult it was. So you quickly regained the lost weight and gave up the journey. Even though we may be grateful for our success, we also need to face and acknowledge that we still have problems. We need to learn to "stick with the winners," those who support our efforts and struggles. We need mentors for success. We need help to feel deserving.

ASK YOURSELF:

- □ *Think about a major success you've achieved in your life.*
- □ *Did you feel deserving?*
- □ *Was success followed by compulsive eating—sporadic bouts of bingeing or starving?*
- □ *Did your success teach you to disown or celebrate your Self?*

In this chapter we'll look at some women who came into treatment when successful, because they realized that their inability to adjust to the problems of success was driving them back to the plate. They had to face how difficult it was to truly, psychologically grow up and leave home, while watching loved ones, particularly mothers, still suffering. They had to sever some emotional attachments. Avoiding this kept them feeling undeserving of their own achievement. The issues they had to face are things many others in our culture may never need to notice; but if you suffer from an eating disorder, you MUST take notice. Your inner self already has.

Most addiction programs were formulated by men emphasizing things that were important for men to face. Their treatment programs declare "alcoholism" to be a "serious illness," and food obsessions are merely girl stuff and insignificant. Because of this they never address one of the most crucial aspects of

recovery—healing the mother–daughter split. When food is cur-
tailed, that issue looms large on the table. The special needs for
separation and individuation that women face are rarely addressed.

Our work here is to learn about separation, independence,
and boundaries, while at the same time having the courage to
stay open (instead of shut off), fluid (instead of rigid), and resonating with energy (instead of drowning in stagnation).
Women face the issue of "powerlessness" differently than men.
Not so much because we are granted less power in the
culture—a cogent feminist argument—but rather because we've
never been taught how to wield the power we already have. We
don't recognize our power because we've been carefully taught
to disown it.

Didn't your mother try to help you enjoy being "a chick," "a
tomato," "a doll," or "a fox"? She was probably mercifully unaware that this objectification is violating. Perhaps the payoffs
she got made it more acceptable. She may have even liked some
of it. Maybe she didn't even notice the sellout. You probably noticed her pain more than she did.

In this objectification of women, Mom tried to protect herself and you by minimizing her pain, hoping it would go away.
This then delivered the message that feelings weren't worthy or
important. Women and women's sensitivities were trivialized.
What seemed like simple little avoidances at the time loom large
when we try to stop eating compulsively.

Recent drug addiction treatments have been encouraging us
to explore memories of incest and to confront the perpetrators.
But what about the millions of us who have suffered "lesser" violations than actual penetration, who still need to attend to the
constant violation of living in the modern world? Extreme cases
of rape and actual penetration are ghastly. But so are the minor
abuses from which we all look away. With no clues how to do it
differently, our moms did the best they could. And their daughters are bingeing and barfing to cope with the horror. All
women in this culture and many others have been brutalized
and trivialized. Your work now is to pay very close attention to
your own pain—be gentle with yourself and your mom. Reform-
ing the system happens as we re-create ourselves.

GROWING UP

Eating disorders are still classified as "diseases of childhood." They are more common to women than to men. Struggles between mothers and daughters surface as we see ourselves growing into our mothers, and we're forced to face their pains, their lies to themselves, their missed opportunities. Most little boys make a break from Mom very early in life. Girls are instead encouraged to model themselves after their moms. But what are they to do when they see how unhappy their moms are?

What did you do? Did you rebel and say, "I'll make my life happier than Mom's"? Did you strike out at Mom with "Why don't you make yourself happy?" Perhaps you conformed with, "I know Mom is really, really happy. I need to try hard to like what she likes."

If you bought into the idea that Mom was really happy, you more than likely also believe that Black slaves had it good in the Old South. I'm not saying there weren't some house slaves who slept and ate as well as their masters and had a good life. I also don't doubt that there weren't many desirable trade-offs in your mother's situation. However, just the way there was gross injustice in the entire institution of slavery, there are also painful violations in the lives of modern women. You are now living and eating that legacy.

Even though the condition of many women has improved—just like a number of slaves even inherited land from their former masters—we are still living with the ravages of institutions that reduce human beings to objects, to chattel. For some reason, eating-disorder sufferers are more sensitized to this violation than others. Perhaps that's because many of us were teased and taunted as "freaks" in the culture. We grew up viewing the culture from a different perspective, a bit outside and alongside. We weren't deluded or bought off by reaping so many of its benefits.

Powerlessness

We knew on some level that the game was about giving up our power. But the struggle to own or disown personal power is a struggle between life and death. Choosing food as your drug of choice is such a metaphor for your life's conflict. Food is the power source. The only way you access power is by ingesting food. We need to find other ways to feel more powerful. We need to discover food that will feed our spirit.

In my seminars, I show an ad from Eveready batteries that states: "If we can't offer you food, we'll offer you power." What a clear choice!

You were taught to disown power. You learned about the "terrible too's." You were TOO much. You were too strong. Too smart. Too outspoken. Too direct. Too, too, too. TOO MUCH! Too much for what? Too much to be mateable. If you fully expressed your energy, you might be too much for any man. Therefore your work was to minimize yourself. How degrading to both you and men!

You have spent a lifetime at war, battling between accepting your own strength and retreating to your plate. What you do with food directly parallels this struggle: all that bingeing and starving, dieting, exercising and restricting, vomiting and running, gorging and belching. It's all part of that battle. You have an ambivalent commitment to both life and death—the struggle to be here or go, stay or leave, live or die.

Think about all those times in your life when instead of being told to STAND UP AND BE COUNTED you were told to SIT DOWN AND STAY HIDDEN.

Write a few examples now. These instructions were well intentioned, and usually quite effective. For example, "Don't YOU be the one to tell them at work that Harry is fouling up the books. They like him there, and besides, you can't prove it."

Have you been instructed, "Try to sit and listen, dear. Men need their egos stroked, and no man is going to want to spend an evening with a woman who is too smart and has too much to say." When your best friend stole your boyfriend, you might have heard, "Don't be so upset. Women can't be trusted anyway. There just aren't enough men to go around. Why weren't you nicer to him?"

Treatment for Winners

When you become successful, you need more help, not less. But there's really nothing to do about it unless you're there. You must live it to know it. We'll discuss it now as both a warning and an invitation of what is to come later, and what to do when it happens.

The English have a saying, "Let us begin as we intend to continue." The Chinese encourage, "The journey of a thousand miles begins with the first step." Weight losers in Overeaters Anonymous quip about that last ten pounds, "Of a hundred-mile journey, ninety is halfway." Other Twelve-Steppers warn newcomers who want to slip away, "Don't quit before the miracle." They're all talking about difficulties coping with the good life, the accoutrements of success.

In Alanon we find people who were able to stay in abusive, alcoholic marriages during all the bad times. It was the good life of sobriety they couldn't stand. Marriages broke up in recovery. I know a woman who married seven alcoholics! As soon as they got sober, she divorced them.

INSIST ON THE GOOD LIFE. Going for that good life with gusto means feeling deserving. Addicts come into recovery expecting punishment. There is a common Alcoholics Anonymous joke about newcomers, "You spill coffee on them and they say, 'Excuse me.' " You deserve to be here, and you deserve to live the good life. You need not apologize for your existence. As you recover, you'll become more than pain-avoidant. You'll be pleasure-seeking. You won't just survive, you'll thrive!

Thriving may be difficult, but AA insists upon it. AA's program is "suggested only," except on this one issue. As we read along in the *Big Book*, eventually the sober person finds the one direction from AA that is no longer suggested, but emphatically required. "WE ABSOLUTELY INSIST ON ENJOYING LIFE." The literature insists we be "happy, joyous, and free." This becomes a most difficult task in recovery. To accomplish that task, you need to feel deserving. This involves laying to rest many demons. It means growing up and leaving home. It means making a full separation from your parents' sufferings.

Because there was never anyone to help you weather this separation before, you returned to suffering with food. But with a disciplined food commitment and consciousness in the plate, you'll be able to be open and available to your intended life, even when, as the good times begin to roll, your success may be difficult to take. You'll notice new gifts awakening within you. Unfortunately, despite all those fairy tales with handsome

princes and crowns bestowed on girls with little feet, in real life
to the victor go the spoils. As women we're stronger than we'd
like to be—stronger than our culture would like us to be—but
that's how we've survived. Life is a difficult battle, but when
we're conscious, we're well equipped to take it on.

Accepting this truth is bound to change relationships with
Mom, men, food, and life in general. Nothing will ever be the
same. If we're really strong, then everything changes. You may
still decide to play out the little-girl games, but you'll know it's
a game you're playing. You'll know the game is for effect, and
you'll take responsibility for choosing it. You won't be able to
fool yourself anymore.

Power and Powerlessness

Even though much of recovery will involve facing your powerlessness over your obsession with food, you still need to feel
empowered in ways other than eating. Our discussions of power
and powerlessness are different from men's. They were told to
become powerful, we were told to carefully avoid being too powerful. Not only are we afraid of our own tremendous power, we
were never taught how to wield it. Not attending to this dilemma
sentences thousands of women to further hospitalizations and
rounds of therapy—if they are that lucky. Some die and never return. Some admit to one aspect of their obsession, vomiting,
then declare they have that under control, but keep acting out
destructively in some another aspect, such as exercise.

Instead of trusting and exalting their resilient, fleshy,
bouncing-back woman's body, instead of owning its mysteries
and delighting in watching the ebb and flow, today's generation
of eating-disordered women think success and power lie in con-
stricting that body. They run to gyms, working out building muscle, reducing body fat, until they've lost their menses and
constricted all flow. Who emerges if they stop pedaling? Some
may never have to face any of this, as new sports medicine clinics
abound. They will continue to abuse their bodies, then get treatment for the results, and never even consider STOPPING the of-
fending behavior.

Women's great disowned power lies in our changeability and
flexibility. We have this fluid, undulating body. We're designed
to live our lives the same way, pulsating, vibrant, totally into the

ebb and flow of existence. What this means is that nothing ever stays the same. We can't hold on. Things must change. We must go with the flow. Whether we feel terrific or lousy, whether we're euphoric or depressed, "this too shall pass." As they say in Wisconsin, "If you don't like the weather, wait five minutes."

Instead of continuing to rage at men or our culture, why don't we begin with ourselves? After all, that is the only thing we can effectively change, and that all by itself is a very difficult project. In order to stop overeating or starving, we must examine all our compromises, all our decisions to give up on ourselves. How often did you give up on yourself because of the threat of success—the difficulties in truly going full bore into a new life? Of course you had good reasons for all the choices, but it still hurts to look at them.

■

EXERCISE 1

WOMEN AND POWER

Get your journal out. It's time to have a powwow with some powerful women. First we'll look at some women who weren't your mother so you can better understand the societal barriers that all women have had to struggle against for thousands of years.

1.   Read this entire list of remarkable women OUT LOUD! Harriet Tubman, Harriet Beecher Stowe, Carrie Nation, Eleanor Roosevelt, Mme. Helena Petrovna Blavatsky, Virginia Woolf, Indira Gandhi, Margaret Thatcher, Golda Meir, Justice Ruth Bader Ginsburg, Betty Friedan, Gloria Steinem, Helen Gurley Brown, Katharine Hepburn, Audrey Hepburn, Cher, Clare Booth Luce, Lucille Ball, Margaret Mead, Toni Morrison, Jacqueline Kennedy Onassis, Barbara Bush, Ntozake Shange, Alice Walker, Riane Eisler, Marilyn Monroe, Mary Tyler Moore, Carol Gilligan, Marija Gimbutas, Marie Curie, Lady Bird Johnson, Betty Ford, Sandra Day O'Connor, Judy Chicago, Louise Nevelson, Bella Abzug, Shirley Chisholm, Barbara Jordan, Carol Mosely Braun, Benazir Bhutto, Nadine Gordimer, Doris

Lessing, Donna Karan, Marian Wright Edelman, Phyllis Schlafly, Helen Hayes, Jessica Tandy, Barbra Streisand, Frieda Kahlo, Georgia O'Keeffe, Greta Garbo, Judith Jameson, Miriam Colón, Chita Rivera, Maxine Hong Kingston, Amy Tan, Nancy Reagan, Patricia Nixon, Ann Taylor, Edith Head, Martha Stewart, Julia Child, Fannie Flagg, Isabel Allende, Rosa Parks, Helen Keller, Mary Wollstonecraft Shelley, Terry McMillan, Madonna, Oprah Winfrey, Elizabeth Taylor, Diana Ross, Jean Houston, Claudia Black, Jane Fonda, Coretta Scott King, Hillary Rodham Clinton, Susan Sarandon, Michelle Pfeiffer, Bette Midler, Goldie Hawn.

2. Now, pick three of these women that you especially admire, and take this opportunity to write to them in your journal and tell them why you think they're so great! Can you be that great too?

EXERCISE 2

YOUR MOTHER AND POWER

This exercise will help you explore how your mother's attitude toward power deeply affected your own.

1. How did your mother feel about being a woman? Was she satisfied with women's role in society?
2. How did your mother relate to feminine body parts and biological functions?
3. Was your mother a powerful woman? Write the following statements in your journal:
My mother, _____, was a powerful woman. She owned her power when she_____
_____.
4. Now write:
My mother, _____, was afraid of her power. She disowned her power when she_____
_____.

(Please write as much about your mother as you wish. Consider discussing her intellectual power, her sexual power, her nurturing power. Explore your mother's unique gifts of power, and how she used them.)

Slim Pickin's

Obese people who lose weight usually expect an unrealistic major transformation. The media and press advertise dull, dowdy, fat people being immediately transformed into raving physical and intellectual beauties just because they lose weight. This false concept has led many to grave disappointment at the mediocrity of their lives after weight loss. Many regain weight rather than face this disappointment. If you're suffering with a food obsession, at least you have something realistic to pin your misery on. You surely don't have to cope with the difficulties of living successfully.

I, for one, lived most of my life thinking my only problem was my weight. Whenever I was rejected, I assumed it was because of my weight. Whenever I failed at any task, I also assumed it was because of my weight. If you didn't like me, I was sure it was my fat you were rejecting. It was devastating for me to lose all that weight and then discover that some people didn't like me anyway.

What if *you* won't like who you are when you're successful? What if you become the skinny bitch that you've always judged thin women to be? Perhaps you're really afraid of feeling too good and thus too deserving, and thus too demanding, and thus too cold and ungiving, self-involved, unavailable, and—God forbid—*in the competition.* What if the worst thing in the world was that you turned out to be a competitive, dog EAT dog, go-for-it gal?

If it had been easy to enjoy the good life we wouldn't be here right now. Happiness requires a deep and profound wrenching. We grew up watching our moms, our role models, suffering. As long as we suffered along with her, there was no threat of leaving home. If recovery REALLY involves eliminating unnecessary suffering, it also involves a threat few of us have ever faced—leaving Mom behind. It involves laying Mom to rest. Lovingly walking away. Lovingly leaving her in her own pain.

ASK YOURSELF:

Unclaimed power = anger or depression = suffering

☐ *How did your mother suffer? Did she acknowledge her suffering?*

☐ *What hurt your mother? How did those hurts hurt you? When your mother suffered what did you do?*

☐ *What compromises (loss of power) in your mother's life created her suffering?*

Beauty or Booty?

Can you stand to take home first prize if your mom didn't even place in the race? And which prizes do you want to take home? Can you forfeit that great prize of being "accepted, chosen, of service" and instead become more SELF-interested? Is that selfish? Does it make you feel less a woman? Does a woman have to do it all?

Can you appreciate success that doesn't devastate you? Can you be feminine and successful, or do you judge and diagnose your sensitivity? When do you bring your woman's power into the twentieth century? If you feel premenstrual tension, do you quickly label your sensitivity a disease process and find a physician who'll treat it as a Prozac deficiency?

Take a moment now and write a brief history of the times when you felt or were called "selfish." What were people really saying to you? Did "selfish" mean you were involved with your SELF? Was that seen as "bad"? Did the label "selfish" also go along with being "TOOOOOOOOO SENSITIVE"?

That supersensitivity has left you with many unresolved questions. But as you begin to feel more deserving, you'll find that you're asking totally new and important questions, questions your mom may never have been able to ask. This time you'll be asking them for both of you.

ASK YOURSELF:

- *What's in it for me?*

- *What am I going to get out of the experience?*

- *Why am I doing this?*

- *Why am I always giving all of myself away—always trying to help others?*

- *Am I always in a flurry of activity so I can avoid looking at my own empty cup? Isn't that using others? Are they distractions from Self?*

- *Who will be threatened by my success? Am I a threat to game players who want to push for power?*

As you ask these questions, let yourself become quiet and relaxed. Allow yourself to become consciously aware of what your Inner Self is answering—not your head.

A gentle, recovering person is not a wimp. On the contrary, the fact that you're beginning to own your own power is quite threatening. You have a responsibility to be fully and completely ALIVE. As you follow this path, you may become a threat to *some* of the people in your life. When you're tempted to return to the old compulsions, ask yourself to seriously consider the options first: Are you going to make yourself invisible again, to make others comfortable? Are you going to let your Self down? Or, are you going to keep on walking your own true path—even if that means being alone?

As you get to see how well your Inner Spirit serves you, you won't want to abandon her so easily. You'll be too strong for many people. You'll see what conflicts this causes as employers balk and spouses walk. You'll find yourself catapulted into new relationships because you're seeking friendship and support from those who foster your growth and success. You will have no guidelines or rules on how to proceed and will just have to show up for life. It's a leap of faith.

YOU HAVE CHANGED

Many encounter relapses at two and five years into recovery. These are important demarcations in your journey into the good life. By then you KNOW on a deep level that you can't go home again. YOU have changed. You've left the world of your childhood, with no guarantees about the new one. It can be exciting and inviting, but also terrifying. Proving yourself in a world Mom didn't create, you will experience life in ways your mother never dreamed. Where are the models? You are! You have to become a model for Mom.

Now you have to face your SELF. *YOU* HAVE CHANGED. It's difficult enough to accept that people and circumstances change on you, but to accept that YOU have changed feels like you've abandoned who you are. Let's face it. You had to change or die. What else was there?

This is when you need a mentor and a structure like the Twelve-Step program to become comfortable with enjoying the good life. But this time you won't need to share the pain. You'll be looking for models of how formerly suffering people have learned to live joyously and guilt-free. You grow in a direction totally different from your previous programming. You will take on aspects of yourself formerly disowned. Sometimes you won't really trust who you are, you'll think you've become a phoney-baloney. Speaking to this dramatic change later in life, Carl Jung said, "What is true in the morning of life can be a lie in the afternoon."

You may not be able to personally pinpoint how you have changed, but I can guarantee, if you have been following a more abstinent, slightly restrictive food plan, not acting out eating whatever you want, then you have created some change in your own consciousness. You have been signaling to your inner sensor that you want to listen and be aware. As such abstinence continues, you will start feeling more deserving.

Running the Race—Playing the Game

Life is in session and you must be present to win. Be careful that you're not living your life in a little room filled with plants telling someone about your painful childhood. That's not REAL

LIFE. That's therapy. And therapy is only a tool to help you EN-HANCE your life. If it starts feeling more real than real life—take a breather.

As you make abstinence from compulsive eating or starving the new litmus test of your progress, then self-examination is only necessary if it helps you not act out. If it promotes bingeing or starving, STOP!

A former patient, Mel called to tell me he was looking into his "family of origin issues." He had also gained back twenty pounds. I cautioned, "STOP! If you have to overeat to face these things, then you're not ready yet. Let your food plan be your guide. Only examine what furthers your abstinence." I caution you all, investigate what furthers your current goals. Set aside what gets in your way. There will be plenty of time to deal with those issues later.

Sometimes difficulties in your present life will throw you off balance, and you'll find yourself seeking excess food. Then you HAVE to look at what's going on. But you also have to remember that it is emerging from your present reality, not your old stuffed self. And you're dealing with this issue from your present vantage point of success. Your new life is working. Staying in the present will take us to whatever home we need to go.

The idea that healing lies in keeping our focus on the present—in doing what's put in front of us—is quite controversial in treatment circles. Actually, you will find few psychotherapists who promote such an idea. Some behaviorists, yes. But most therapy is oriented toward what happened in the past, as opposed to what's going on in our lives right this minute. This is why I so strongly support and recommend the Twelve-Step programs. Most of the meetings are devoted to current concerns and future behaviors. The idea is that we can heal by picking up the stones in front of us, rather than trying to pick up all the boulders littered behind us. If a boulder looms up in the present and blocks our way, then yes, we will attend to it.

Take the case of Marlene, who successfully lost a great deal of weight, but then found that her sensitivity and insight still kept her a bit outside the norm. Problems in her successful present were forcing her to examine her current and past life. She was having new problems with food, getting a little sloppy, caring less, seeking sedation more. Food was her litmus test about what did and didn't work in her life.

Marlene had seen me in private practice initially to face her depression caused by obesity. Notice that I didn't express this the other way around. Her depression did not cause her obesity. She was depressed because she was obese. As we focused on her abstinence first, her increased self-esteem and ability to see life clearly (rather than sugar-coated or lard-laden) lifted her depression. Marlene didn't necessarily need to examine all her childhood trauma then. She had enough to do simply walking through current life changes. I was certain that when her food got in order, much of her depression would clear up. If for no other reason than she wouldn't be constantly responding to sugar withdrawals and the mood swings generated by the fasting and purging syndrome.

Little did I know then that years later I would be leading a wave of clinicians trying to explain to the medical community and insurance companies that we could only help patients like Marlene by clearing up the food obsession FIRST, and then seeing how much legitimate, long-term, or chemical depression was really there.

Marlene grabbed hold quickly. She began going to OA in conjunction with my therapy and classes, and ultimately lost over fifty pounds.

That's when her troubles began.

She began to experience problems both at work and socially. These went hand in glove with her newly enhanced self-esteem and self-acceptance. In recovery, we warn, "Be careful what you pray for. You just may get it." With all her weight-loss success, Marlene was on a roll. Then she realized that some things were getting worse. Marlene could have brought these adjustment struggles to our sessions for the next thirty years. Seeing that these were not "characterological" issues, but adjustment reactions, I had to help us both discontinue therapy at that point. These current life issues needed guidance from a sponsor, not a therapist.

This is an important decision for a therapist, and I regret that some of us keep patients in treatment far too long. But because I so adamantly support the Twelve-Step approach, I want patients to learn about living life in anonymous groups rather than solely in my office. (A word of caution here, though. Some people begin to live their lives at AA clubhouses and don't make the break to real life there either.)

Make sure that whatever you do enhances your current life and helps your abstinence. Those who retreat into therapy, and pretend real life isn't ready for living, start believing therapy is reality and the real world doesn't exist. If you think about it, why wouldn't we opt for that? In therapy you're nearly always right and supported. You get to talk about what THEY are doing, and you have a whole block of time devoted to you and your concerns. You're master of the universe and totally in control. But that's not true at Twelve-Step meetings, where neither you nor anyone else is "in charge," where you hear others having the same concerns you do, and where there is no "cross talk," so you are left to trust your higher self for guidance. When you find that others have struggled with the same issues, you begin to see the broad picture of the human condition, that you need to follow disciplined direction, and listen to your inner guidance. You see that life is hard to face but learn to accept that "this too shall pass." With this recognition comes some measure of comfort.

As gently as any mother sparrow nudging her chick from the nest, I told Marlene that she needed to consult her sponsor on how to deal with current situations, and that our work was essentially ended.

"But what about my past?" she asked, startled. "Don't I have to work through all my childhood issues?"

"Why would you want to bring up all your past, Marlene?" I said. "That would really be asking for a lot of pain."

"But, I thought I had to face it so I can get over it."

Like the rest of us, Marlene had been taught to distrust the ever-open pregnant present. Like most Americans of her generation, she distrusted the present and blamed everything that went wrong in her life on the past. *It was as though she—and we— wanted to ascribe reality to events long ago and far away, which can't be changed.* That was safer than facing the current moment— brand new, all options open—with full accountability to herself on how she'd handle it. Could it be true that no matter what her parents, and our parents, had done, no matter what we'd been through, or all the "good reasons" we had for failure, we could still create a rose garden from here on out?

My job was to cast Marlene out of my office and into that rose garden of life, showing her my confidence in her ability to trust her instincts, seek guidance often from her OA sponsor, and proceed on her path. As Sartre said, "Freedom is what we do with what was done to us." It's so scary to believe we're not sick. That is often the most traumatic bad news I bring to patients: "You no longer need my services." That has nothing to do with wanting, however. If someone wants therapy as an aid in the growth process, that can be accommodated. But I believe people must be clear about the differences between NEED and WANT.

As for Marlene, I felt she needed to place abstinence as her number-one priority above psychological awareness. If bringing up the past would get in her way, cause her pain, and send her back to the refrigerator, how could it be helpful at this point in her life? So she'd "work through" her pain and "get over it"? Are your feelings and experience something to move aside?

That's what Marlene was asking for as we debated stopping therapy for a while. I explained to Marlene that some things in life we never get over. They're our battle scars, our badges of courage. All our life experience has culminated in the package we now have to work with. I told her, "By facing life squarely NOW, you'll find out which personality traits you've taken on work for you and which ones are nuisances and need to be discarded. That way you'll begin to see the exquisite value of all you've been through. You won't learn that by going back, only by going forward. In the past you were too weak and scared to appreciate the lessons you were getting. Now is the time to live."

I assured Marlene we would meet for six-month and yearly checkups, but that her sponsors—her models for her new life—were the right people to go to for suggestions on what to do today.

Over time Marlene did uncover a lot about her past, but she only took a look when it was a need generated by unfolding awareness in the present. As we cross the threshold into our new life, we panic at the prospect of leaving the old one behind. Nothing brings up past pain more quickly than current successes.

Handling the Competition

As with many overeaters, one of Marlene's most difficult life conflicts involved competition and jealousy, especially with other women. When she was fat and depressed, she'd never had to face this issue. She threatened no one, and no one bothered her. She never had to look for underlying causes for disappointments or failures. She explained it all away with "It's because I'm fat."

I have listened to countless formerly fat women talk about their feelings of loneliness and alienation around other women. Their expectations of "sisterhood" are so great, their hopes for mutual understanding and support are so vast, that when the reality of competition sets in it's devastating.

Marlene first shared her feelings about that pain at our first yearly checkup. Actually, she called me in great distress asking that we schedule an appointment a few weeks earlier: "I'm crying and shaking here over something that happened at work. I really feel I need to figure out why this is so painful. I've been pacing around my house, holding myself with folded arms and rocking as I sob. I feel like I'm falling apart. This is exactly what my mother used to do."

We met within the hour. She arrived in a sweatsuit, hair disheveled, bleary-eyed, and sniffling. This was a far cry from the impeccable outfits and fashionable makeup she'd been sporting since she'd lost weight. She jumped right in: "We have this really gamey broad at work. Everyone is sick up to here with Adele's coyness and slimyness. She gives indirect digs, doesn't do her job, and then faults others. And if she's confronted she strikes out by 'psychoanalyzing' anyone who catches on to her games. She makes it THEIR problem and always gets off the hook.

"Oh, coincidentally, Adele also happens to be dating one of the senior VP's. We've all been told that should make no difference, and that we need to expect the same standard performance from her as from anyone else. Unfortunately, no one seems to have told *her* about these expectations. Well, I was put in charge of supervising this little prima donna. I'm valued there for being a straight shooter and honest person who doesn't play games. Damn it, recovery programs made me like this—I used to love to hide and back off from responsibility and pretend I didn't see and didn't know. Now I have to show up and be alive. Well, I feel like I'm gonna die trying.

"We had a staff meeting on Friday," Marlene continued. "In consultation with my supervisor and some of her fellow workers, it was decided Adele should be held accountable as a team player. She was going to have to cooperate with everyone else and hand in customary reports about what she was doing. We planned to get this all straight with the whole team present so Adele couldn't resort to the excuse that had worked so well in the past: 'Oh, I didn't know I was supposed to do that.'

"Well, Jude, I really thought the staff meant what they said. I believed they wanted the situation to change, and that they wanted me to change it. So, I gently but firmly, as a matter of course in the meeting, told Adele that she would have to hand in a weekly report like everyone else. And we especially needed a report on why one of her accounts was not paying off. These were standard requests asked of any employee. Not to Adele, they weren't."

Marlene was barely holding back her tears. Shakily, she continued, "Well, that night I got a call at home from the district manager, raking me over the coals. Hadn't I understood the delicacy of this situation? Didn't I realize how fragile Adele was? Didn't I know that such directness would destroy her? She'd gone home that night and dramatically cut off her hair. Then she'd called her VP lover and sobbed, 'I'm so worthless I want to die.'

"The district manager then lambasted me for being 'too strong.' He said I shouldn't have been so direct, that the situation had needed more tact. I should have 'played the game' a little more. Jude, I don't know how to 'play the game.' And I wasn't being abusive—just real."

She broke into soft sobs. I let her cry it out while she kept murmuring, "I was just being real. I was just being real!"

The Weak and Helpless Types

Like so many women in business today, Marlene had not been trained in such gamesmanship. She hadn't realized that the last thing being called for here was reality. There are many situations where honesty is discouraged, and subterfuge prized. Many people report that they feel safest at a Twelve-Step meeting because it appears to be the only place where honesty is encouraged and allowed. However, I also suspected that the painful level of Marlene's response to all this indicated that there might be many deep underlying issues. I asked, "What's hurting you so about this?"

"It's that 'gameyness' that WINS!" Marlene replied angrily.

"That convoluted, slimy behavior gets the gold, but straight people get shit. I'm in trouble now for calling a spade a spade, even though everyone wanted it done. Adele's high drama with the haircut gets SYMPATHY! I happen to know she was planning to get a haircut next week anyway. But if I confront her with that, I'll look even more stupid and overly invested. Apparently, you're not supposed to say what you see. What do I get for my efforts?"

"I guess virtue is its own reward," I began feebly. But then I suggested that perhaps Marlene's deep tears were for the alienation and loneliness she was feeling. Here she'd gone out on a limb, taking a risk for her coworkers, only to have her support system fail her in the face of wily manipulations. Her supervisor could not support her because of pressure from higher up, and Marlene was left to face the music alone because she'd tried to deal with a situation everyone else knew but no one was willing to challenge.

She continued sobbing, "It's like when I was in college and my fiancé left me for another girl. I remember him telling me that I was strong and could handle myself. But the other girl was a frail thing who would probably kill herself if he left her. And here it is all over again. It's those weak and helpless types who rule the world. Why can't I play that one out? It really works!"

"Why can't you?"

"Because it's not real."

"It's not real for YOU."

"You mean their stuff is real? They really believe their own bullshit and don't see through their own games?"

"That's right. Who else in your life is like Adele?"

"My mom. She's exactly my mom. Playing weak and helpless. Ruling the whole household from her drug-addicted bed, shouting orders and criticisms. All the time playing too weak to be confronted or asked to be accountable."

"Right. Some choose to do it one way, and some another. Adele's way and Mom's way are going to win them certain prizes. Your way will win you yours. It's just a choice when all is said and done."

Her sobbing stopped and she stared at me quite a while. Then a sweet, proud smile spread over her face. "I guess I'd rather do it this way. I'm willing to pay the price."

She was beginning to see that we all choose certain behaviors because they work—for us! And when we think about it, we're usually willing to pay the price. Of course, we need to realize that "our way" might not work in situations where the majority of people have made different choices. In certain races, we simply need to let them win, and be content with the fruits of our decisions.

The same issue arose in Marlene's third year of recovery. She'd been working with an older woman, Inez. They enjoyed each other, saw many things the same way, and were able to communicate well. Marlene felt very good with Inez alone; but as soon as a man showed up, her friend changed. When men appeared, her dear friend disappeared. Inez became someone else. In describing it, Marlene said, "It was like she was magnetized by a male crotch. My clear-headed friend was cockeyed."

Marlene told me that she'd developed a crush on one of their fellow workers. The man was in Marlene's age group. She'd felt daughterly, sharing confidentially with Inez her fantasies about him. A slow, casual dating ensued, with Marlene keeping Inez informed of the details. Marlene cherished their friendship, relished telling Inez intimate feelings she couldn't yet share with the young man.

But then she began noticing a subtle ill feeling whenever the three of them got together. It seemed as if Inez went out of her way to make sure the young man knew she was up on ALL that was going on in the relationship. Marlene felt clearly violated, but excused the behavior as "Inez just wants to fit in and belong."

That intrusive intimacy was soon followed by jokes with sexual innuendos, and Inez showing how cool she was. A few times Marlene got a clear flash, "This woman is flirting with my man." Again, dismissing reality, she explained to herself, "That's impossible. She's older than my own mother!"

With an abstinent food plan the body doesn't lie—there's nothing to sedate its clear responses. If you have a faint sick feeling in the pit of your stomach, more than likely something really is amiss. Again, Marlene's overall feeling was of violation and abandonment, but it all seemed so unreasonable. How could a woman thirty years older—and a good friend—be interested in her younger man? Well, why not? Of course the woman might be attracted. But it was what Inez was doing that was so painful. Marlene fell back on her old response. She decided again to dismiss her concerns with "Well, I've been fat all my life, I really don't understand the dating and flirting world. Just because she flirts doesn't mean she'd act out on it."

I interrupted. "It's not her future intentions that hurt you," I said. "It's what Inez is doing NOW. It's the fact that she's not in your corner, supporting your interests, as you would do for her. She's presenting herself in a competitive, adversarial role, and you feel abandoned and disappointed."

"Yes, but I really think I'm wrong here. I must be making it up. There is no way this woman would want to take this man. He's not even her type."

"The issue, my dear, is that he's YOUR type. She doesn't want him or his type. She just wants to win him from you."

"Oh, come on," Marlene protested. "I can't believe that."

As it turned out, the young man was transferred, and Marlene's interest waned. There wouldn't be any reality-testing for a while. Marlene had first come into recovery pretending to be tougher than she was. Then, seeing manipulative "helpless" players winning in the game of life, she had subdued her more direct, confrontational style and started holding back. We often see people in early recovery operating on a pendulum swing from one emotional extreme to another. Marlene found that most of the time now she chose to back off from confrontation, and silently withdrew from people who hurt her. Her friendship with Inez faded with neither mentioning it.

THE LOWDOWN. Two years later at our regular yearly checkup, Marlene came in exuberant because of a recent revelation. She'd met a woman who had known Inez years ago when Inez was still married and raising kids, and hadn't yet entered the business world. The woman reported, "Boy, that Inez was a hot one. She was always having outrageous fights with her daughters."

"Yeah, what about?" Marlene asked.

"Oh, she was always trying to steal her daughters' boyfriends."

Marlene squealed when she told me. "Can you believe that? See, I wasn't making it up. She was actually on the make. Why, if she'd do it to her own daughters, she'd do it to anyone."

"I never doubted what you saw," I told her. "But I also realized that, quite understandably, you wanted to. The truth of this competition and grabbiness is really hard to take."

Marlene stared at me quizzically. She cocked her head and said, "You're right, Jude. It's really hard to take."

"What's hard?"

"Well, it's not about the man. It's that the woman isn't there for you. It's like you're sisters—up to a point—but then they have to turn on you. It feels so tragic, like she can't help herself. She must prove herself by moving in on me. If I have what she doesn't, she can't let it be. Most of all, I feel so stupid and hurt at my naiveté—believing it would be different."

"Marlene, you're not naive, it's just that you need to move up to a better class of people. You'll need to surround yourself with friends who have nothing to prove, people you can depend on. The road gets narrower."

She lamented to me that it still seemed so unfair that things would have to be this way. At first she wanted to blame herself. "It must be something I did. I probably didn't let her know I was really interested in this guy. Maybe I acted too casual, so she thought I was a swinger type and wouldn't mind. Maybe . . ."

"Enough, Sweetheart. You had every right to expect to be understood and acknowledged. The woman knew the situation. She just wanted to win over you! Accept it."

Marlene gave a heartbroken cry. "Isn't there something I can do to make it different?"

"Well, if you want to invest in the relationship, you could tell her what you feel and see if it changes anything. You could try to talk about her competitiveness." Marlene decided to let it lie.

There is no need to worry about confronting or not confronting. It's always an issue of timing. The important lessons of our lives will keep returning and we'll be given ample opportunity to check them out, commit the same mistakes, or learn from them and change our responses.

Marlene sobbed, "Geez, this recovery is a lonely road. Can't I just put up with the bullshit I see and never mention it? Can't I pretend?"

"Why, sure you can if you want to go out and eat a side of beef. Your other choice is to accept that some relationships simply don't work out. Don't find yourself wrong or them wrong. Don't HANG ON tenaciously. Move aside. It just didn't work.

Don't try to fix it or fix yourself. Let it be. You've got to be yourself. Your job is to keep taking care of yourself and being alive. Those who mind won't matter, and those who matter won't mind."

ASK YOURSELF:

▫ *What areas of your present life are causing you pain or suffering? How does your suffering correspond to your mother's suffering?*

▫ *How do you feel about competition—and winning? How did your mother feel about competition?*

▫ *How do you feel about competition with men? With women?*

INTIMATE RIVALS

Most women, and even mothers and daughters, are rivals. Not for Dad, as so many Freudian analysts would have us believe, nor for men's toys or gifts. It's actually worse than that. Daughters need to compete with their mothers to prove that Mom was wrong. They don't seem able to share the spoils and gifts of success. It's another aspect of the self-hate we learn at Mom's knee. Other women have to be beaten. They deserve it because they are so much like me! It's a variation on Groucho Marx's line, "I wouldn't be a member of any club that would have me as a member."

This competition has to be acknowledged. Pretending it isn't there is deadly, dishonest, and keeps us addicted. Marlene's story was painful because her friend could not admit she was competing with her. If Inez could have been honest about herself, there wouldn't have been any conflict. Too few of us can tell ourselves honestly how powerful and competitive we really are. Accepting this outright, acknowledging that it's always been there, seeing ourselves rev up for games we never thought we played, is a way to accept *unconditionally* that that's just how it is.

Why can't that be okay? Boys get a chance to revel in their competitive games, but girls are supposed to deny theirs? Boys admit they seek to do better than their fathers. If you can't acknowledge a longing to be the victor, you can never claim the spoils. Boys learned a great deal more about being competitive and weathering defeat. But girls don't learn how to come back well after defeats, and they certainly don't learn how to handle the stress of success.

OBJECTING TO OBJECTIFICATION. In eating-disorders treatment, we have to help all women—mothers and daughters—discover and unite in their feminine wisdom. They haven't been trained to celebrate their successes, or to listen carefully to the messages from their wise, resilient bodies. The way it's done is that each person, mother or daughter, first needs to develop an awareness of herself, and to see herself as a woman raised in a culture that devalues women and sees them merely as objects, as merchandise. How is one supposed to act?

Your mother is probably much less aware than you that anything is missing. She may have felt a vague unrest, but could never really consciously express it. But you, that perceptive, intuitive baby, picked up on her sadness. She didn't know how to address this pain, or change the system, so you as her closest friend took it on. You are now bingeing and purging your mother's disowned pain and anger. As these violations become more and more clear to both you and your mother, you'll be able to hug each other and cry together.

Birthing Yourself

To truly own your power, you will take on a mentor or sponsor to act as midwife and get yourself reborn within this very lifetime. You will have to accept some parts of your earliest programming, your cultural conditioning, which you can't simply shake loose; it keeps being reinforced all around you. Your response will require a form of surrender as you realize how inescapable much of this has been.

For example, as much as Reneé fashioned herself a career woman who wanted to change government policies in Africa, she was a workaholic—until she fell in love. Each time she became attracted to a new man, her career was put on a back burner. She gave it all up for that "love thang." Joan Crawford had a great line in an old 1940s movie: "A woman can do absolutely anything she wants to do! . . . unless she falls in love."

Well, for Reneé nothing much had changed since the Forties. But this was not something for her to reject about herself. She didn't have to label herself a "love addict." She didn't have to swear off dating or give up a career.

What Reneé needed to do was to find a way to moderate both those sides of herself. It wasn't as simple as integrating the career with the "mommy track." She had to accept that no matter what her "head" told her she wanted, her basic programming was to give her life over to a man. She'd learned this at Mom's knee. And though she'd rebelled against it because she saw what it had done to her mom, eventually she had to accept that it was a large part of herself as well. She had to grow up WITH her programming, not in spite of it.

Chooser or Chosen

Your eating disorder is an attempt to resolve this conflict for both you and your mother. This is sometimes a personal, clear message that you refuse to enter the dating race. It is a race in which you are the CHOSEN rather than chooser. You are packaged and put on display waiting for the chooser. This dilemma will only be healed when GETTING CHOSEN is not your major agenda.

There are many women who will argue with me about how "modern" and unaffected they are by such pursuits. They insist that they're content and satisfied as career women. I can only report that in recovery meetings, and in treatment centers, most women's primary concern is still with relationships with men. It's still about being attractive and marketable.

Much of what you hear in the popular media and in feminist literature would have you believe that women are no longer primed for plucking, no longer encouraged to get married, that, in fact, they're being prepared for contented careers whether they're chosen or not. I must tell you that 99 percent of the patients we see in treatment are still singing the hit title of Sandra Bernhard's Off-Broadway comedy revue: "Without You I'm Nothing." The image of a strong, manless woman may be cutting edge in some circles. But that is not the case in Kansas City,

Syracuse, Birmingham, or Austin—nor in my treatment centers in New York or L.A. My patients have bought into the marriage myth. Despite achieving successes in other areas, they still feel that "getting chosen" by a man is their most important achievement. If they are not chosen, they believe that there is something drastically wrong with them. Their reaction is to find out what they can fix about themselves. This attitude isn't given up easily—if at all. We were programmed to be mated, not sated.

Ask yourself about your own programming. Were you packaged as an object or prepared for being a person? Were you trained to use your power or to minimize your strengths? Were you primed to take action or to wait to be picked? Do these battles show up in your plate?

IT'S YOUR ASS OR HERS. On some level, for you to truly claim your power will mean killing off your mother's. This may sound too harsh to bear, but your mom is cheering for you to do it. She wants you to make the break out of the programming you both suffered. She may be too embedded in the system to make the break herself. But there's always a chance that you might be able to come back for her, if you make a clean enough break first. To save your own life, you have to both accept and forsake your mother's. If you are addicted to any self-destructive activity, you can't afford to play nice, little-obedient-daughter games any longer.

All the dieting in the world won't gain you permanent results, if you don't come to terms with your own power struggles with Mom. You need to recognize which battles are hers, and which are yours. You need to pick up your own flag while laying hers to rest. I've seen eating-disordered people working feverishly at everything but this—their relationship with Mom. Many focus on anger at Dad, reenacting incest events over and over. Although this may be necessary work, it can't be done as a way of avoiding the mother work. Many women try behavior modification classes to learn assertive techniques. Although they may begin to act stronger, for the most part they feel like charlatans. This is because they haven't resolved what their being successful will mean to their mothers' lives.

Lifelong recovery from food obsessions requires two things: developing a new relationship with food, and also developing a new relationship with your mother. That's the only way you'll be

able to effectively wield the power intended for you. If you remain in conflict about this power, it will show up on your body.
Dieters who resort to excessive control become anorexic, running scared. Those who stop vomiting run to gyms, exercising to
excess. Achieving moderation in the food/body obsession game
means celebrating yourself as a woman. It also means owning
the parts of you that are like your mom.

The reason Marlene was so finely attuned to competitive
women is because she observed it and suffered from it while she
was growing up. She watched her mother's personality change
when Dad was around. She saw her play dumb and incompetent
to get her way. She saw her ignore her child to focus on her
man. She saw it all in Mom. And once she was abstinent, her inner self picked it up immediately in her adult women friends.

And yet, it doesn't really help to know all that. Knowing you
learned it observing Mom doesn't take away the pain you feel in
the present. It even compounds things, because now you feel
your mom's pain as well as your own. This is NOT a childhood
problem. Please don't dismiss it, when you see it in the present,
by calling it childish. It feels bad to be abandoned by the woman
closest to you. Your greatest abandonment occurred when you
were taught to disown your power—and above all when you were
taught to doubt your perceptions by the most powerful woman
closest to you. It was no one's fault—not even Mom's. It's cultural and it's unconscious in us all.

So Long, Mom

Yes, "boys will be boys," but what will little girls be? At the
same time you're experiencing betrayals and abandonment from
other women, you're also feeling poorly schooled at playing success games with men. You may have to redefine yourself and learn
new rules. One big rule to break is about what it means to be a
woman. Laden with excess food, you thought your job was to bolster men, feed mentors' egos, enhance the well-being of others.

If recovery is your agenda, all that changes. You must live up
to YOUR potential, not theirs. But when you go for it, it's a slap
in Mom's face. As you face success, you fear for you both. If you
fail, you fear for yourself; if you succeed, you fear for HER. All
the great books on imposter syndrome and fear of success don't

help us say good-bye to Mom and actually watch ourselves walk away and leave her.

In recovery, you will seek out new mentors and role models in successful women. You'll watch what they've faced. You'll look at the seduction of the workplace, and how pleasant it is to actually categorize and tally your successes. You'll need to watch the prices you pay for success. Just like men, you'll need to be warned of some of its trappings. You'll face what it really means to give up all your symptoms and be problem-free. You'll have to ask yourself, What if there's nowhere to go? You'll have to remember Peggy Lee's song: "Is That All There Is?"

You will need to learn to balance the marketplace demands with your inner vitality and energy level. Make sure you aren't sacrificing too much. It is in the strength of your vulnerability that you can stay successful. As a woman, you will learn to be taken care of—the way men were before you. *You* may have the secretary, the maid, the supportive spouse. In my seminars I show a cartoon where a queen tells a friend, "I hired someone to rock the cradle, so that I could rule the world." Maybe we all need a wife.

Crotch Watch

You'll find it's time to look at some power games women never learned from their moms. Men know how to dance around each other's gonads so that no one gets too threatened. Women, however, are not aware of the power they wield. This means they're ever in danger of threatening male parts they didn't even realize were in the game. They're called "castrating," although they have no idea what prize they've supposedly won.

Theresa spent three weeks calling before she ever got in to see me. She wanted to talk hurriedly and get quick telephone answers. She'd make appointments for our initial "no fee, get-to-know-each-other, eyeball-to-eyeball quickie" evaluation session. She liked that I invited prospective clients to briefly interview me before committing to an ongoing investment of money and time. Theresa was a successful lawyer, and getting her fair share was terribly important to her. Each time, at the last minute, she'd have to cancel because business called. She was happy to be important and "needed" by clients and colleagues. I finally told her that I would schedule one more freebie for her and if she canceled that, we'd be through. She showed up early and ready.

The aggressive energy of young corporate women on the rise walked in three paces ahead of her. I felt the piercing eyes, the firm handshake, the excess of poise and confidence. It's a trick they've all mastered. You can see it best somewhere around the edge of the mouth. But that's also where it crumbles first. I was a little surprised at her diminutive stature. The red suit gave her a bit more impressive bulk, but I was not at all surprised by the bow tie, the briefcase, and the squiggly Picasso pin.

Even though she seemed rather tough, I stared warmly into her cold, darting brown eyes. Her eyes stopped moving after a few evaluative runs around the room. Theresa finally settled into my gaze and stared straight at me without blinking. Then giant tears melted out of the centers of her eye sockets, down exquisitely made-up Lancôme cheeks, and onto the lapels of that red wool suit.

"I vomit every night," she said. "I hate my life. I'm making it very well in my career. I'm satisfied with all that. It's just the vomiting I want to curtail some."

I said nothing.

"It's not the weight gain I dread. It's the loss of the relief. I need the relief of this outlet. Do you understand?"

I nodded and a tear started for me as well.

"It's just not working. I'm falling apart. I'm a barracuda. I've ripped and torn men and women in my path. Mostly men. Poor guys. I wonder how they felt later going home to their families. I couldn't help it. I had to. I had to win."

I nodded. Theresa cried.

A few silent but full moments passed and then I commented, "You've spent your life swimming through shark-infested waters and now the sharks are inside you."

Her eyes began to dart around the room again, as if that last statement had penetrated too deeply, as if it made her too visible, too vulnerable. There had been such an immediate connection with her pain, I felt invited to come in too soon and too fast.

Theresa was so aware of herself and so available, it was very likely that many others had also penetrated too quickly as she let down her facades and asked for closeness. I would learn in subsequent weeks that she had no time for anyone who noticed her pain who couldn't handle it gently. She was a very smart woman and extremely sensitive to being treated as an object. She had warned me immediately that she wanted no part of being a psychotherapy experiment. She'd seen me take patients on some national television shows, and told me she felt I had no business exposing those people's lives to the media.

I agreed with her and explained about refusing some current TV projects. I also assured her that no one was ever forced to appear with me, and that I spent a good deal of time before, during, and after such events working through whatever we all learned in the process.

Theresa's major area of current pain was about competition and jealousy. She'd worked so hard to get where she was, and she felt secure and nonfearful in most areas of her life. However, she'd found that women friends, male mentors, and especially her own mother were excessively critical, gossipy, and worst of all, excluding of her. On the way up, while women friends chattered incessantly about boyfriends, corporate gossip, and lifestyles of the rich and famous, she'd hung around, bored but participating. But now she just wasn't interested in "girl stuff." During visits to her mom, she had very little to say.

While she was moving up the ladder, Theresa had incorporated the values and styles taught by male mentors who knew the ropes. She also kept pace with them at the health spa as she worked out with the boys, talking shop and sweating bullets. She even tried to get her body fat percentage down closer to theirs! Her periods then stopped. She was losing her body, her menses, her blood and guts, her self, and her soul. Her career had begun to consume her life, and there was no more room in her life for gossip about friends' new boyfriends or Mom's concerns. She'd become obsessed with work, the arena where she learned sharp new skills, where she felt vibrant and alive, always facing new challenges.

Her mother was the most abandoned of all her old acquaintances. Theresa's father had left for ports outside the home—probably the office. But her mother had been abandoned even earlier by her own mother, who had been a career woman long before it was fashionable. She'd been raised by a governess before day care and "sitters" were the rule. Now her daughter was leaving too. With such intergenerational abandonment and pain, her mother railed, "You're just like your dumb father.

You'll give all your life to a corporation like he did, lose the love and respect of your family, and end up depressed and withdrawn. Is that what you want?"

Theresa never answered when these diatribes started, but she vomited one extra time when she got home. As part of her treatment with me, she would read Hilde Bruch's *Eating Disorders* and learn about fathers of eating-disordered daughters who were demeaned in the home. Despite whatever was accomplished out in the world, when they crossed that threshold, their wives berated them with "What does that job do for me? What have you done for US lately? Why aren't you ever home?"

These fathers were actually codependents on the "runaway from home" circuit. They saw their wives' pain, but not knowing how to fix it, they ran. They were trying to find approval in the workplace because they felt inadequate on the home front, and their wives didn't know how to show them the way to intimacy. But why should anyone want intimacy anyway? Intimacy was so messy and unpredictable. Not like work.

Eating-disordered women like Theresa grow up to assume the same corporate seat as their dads, all the while criticized by themselves and the culture for leaving home and hearth. Often these judgments are expressed outright by mothers seeing the same, repetitive loss of family to the workplace. The daughters had stored so much data from watching their parents fight that they not only took up their father's role but the guilt that went with it. Consequently, they were in a continuous state of disequilibrium, going for the prizes their male professors and mentors extolled, yet feeling guilty and a bit unsettled at leaving Mom and something of themselves behind. In recovery, they would have to find that disowned momlike part without rejecting all the positive successes they'd earned in their present lives.

These women now face the same struggle little boys were primed for early on. But, unlike the boys, they were to be socialized and trained by a same-sex parent, Mom, their primary love object. Little boys would be schooled early in how to grow up separate from Mom, so they could win battles foreign to hers. Today, girls like Theresa are being asked to learn men's rules, to be more like Dad. But how are they to find a place for the part of them that's still like Mom? These daughters vacillate between being career women and emotional bag ladies. How can they find a place for the mom side of themselves, the part that longs for intimacy and connection? Many, like Theresa, find this part of themselves in toilet bowls late at night.

They are fighting someone else's battles, the old war between Mom and Dad. But the war they witnessed all their lives is now being waged in their own intimate battlefield of body and soul. Most don't complain, or even know they're in this conflict. They hear the newscasters' alarming reports about the epidemic of bulimia, but they think that applies to the younger girls with excessive behavior, the ones who keep "getting caught" and vomiting in school lavatories. As long as their lifestyle keeps working for them, they have no reason to seek help.

Theresa's first calls to me were not so much to stop the vomiting as to stave off a suicidal depression brought on by an office coup, where a "lesser qualified" colleague was made partner and she was passed over. She knew she'd have to leave the firm, but had no idea how or where to go. She was living what her mom had predicted for her dad. She'd sold it all to the company store, lost sight of anything meaningful to herself other than work, and had become a workaholic to maintain her self-worth. At least work was dependable and wouldn't fail her. She could invest herself and get reasonable returns. Relationships—her mom's world—were just too unpredictable and volatile.

Oddly enough, Theresa was discovering that the business world was equally unpredictable. As much as she'd been groomed for success and power, she now found that she was being eliminated because she'd never learned how to wield it. A certain realization began to dawn: She was not "one of them." The more she spoke up, the more she was shot down. She jumped in at meetings—where she was the only woman— confronting and speaking directly about what she saw going on. They simply couldn't hear it from her. She was perplexed. Reading up on feminist authors, she examined the power shifts within the company, trying to attack some lack of opportunity for women. But it wasn't really that. Women were afforded opportunities, they just hadn't been taught how to walk on eggshells well enough. They hadn't learned the "crotch watch." Since Theresa had passed her female colleagues long ago, she had no one with whom to discuss this dilemma.

She'd certainly learned all the female airs and graces that worked in intimate relationships; but she thought that in business playing with the boys meant playing straight. In actuality, the boys had a way they'd learned to talk with each other that got things done and said, without anybody actually doing or saying anything. She would sit in meetings and watch them dance around each other's egos. They'd say nothing, but all of them understood what was going on. It was an elaborate dance men had perfected from their common experiences.

They seemed to know the limits of what each man could tolerate. After all, they all had the same genitalia to worry about. They all had the same "male ego" her mother had tried to warn her about. And while she was home watching Mom and Dad fight, they were learning combative etiquette in backyards and sandlots. Girls learn to negotiate, to take turns, to share rather than take power. They don't learn how to take pleasure in the fruits of their victories. Boys learn to compete—win or lose—and then play a new day.

Theresa, unschooled in wielding power, came on like gangbusters—too direct, too assured. Even though men can be strong when they need to, they also know how to dance around one another's gonads with finesse. She'd become a threat without even realizing it. Word around the company was "She's a real ballbuster." Theresa came to me despairing and pleading, "But I never wanted their balls. Who does?"

I answered her as gently as I could, "THEY do."

In recovery, you may learn that you are actually much more powerful than you ever imagined, and such power is a threat to both men and women. For Theresa, the tragedy was that she had incorporated so much of her father's values, and rejected her mother's. When the corporation turned on her, it was as though all the meaning in her life had disappeared. In recovery, she would have to re-own her feminine side. In doing that, she would come to accept that she was actually much more powerful than many men but had to learn new tools for wielding that power.

Keep Your Legs Together and Your Mouth Shut

Girls have to be ever mindful of boys' gonads, while also covering up our own. The prohibition has always been to put down women who are too powerful! We've been conditioned to disown power. To deny our lively energy. To squelch our invaluable life force. We picked up our culture's message about how powerful our genitals actually are. In early childhood and into adolescence we got warnings about how powerful that crotch shot could be. You were to keep your legs closed and your panties hidden.

Sharon Stone showed it all in the movie *Basic Instinct.* But most little girls learned very early to keep their legs together. In my extensive collection of Marilyn Monroe memorabilia, I found a photo of her with no panties and everything bared. The instinct was basic long before Marilyn or Sharon. She just put it out there. What would it mean if women honestly and forthrightly made use of their sexual power? Marilyn played dumb enough to get away with it. Most "proper girls" learned to hide out. We had to be ever mindful of who looked at us and how. We were taught to be packaged and marketed correctly, not taking action, but waiting for the action. Men act, women react. Men look at women and women are ever mindful of themselves being looked at. This determines not only most relations between men and women, but also a woman's relationship with herself.

Pocketed Power

Too often women choose sickness as a cop-out on life. Pauline's mother was sick and frail and necessarily focused on her own survival. Focusing on what she COULD do, Pauline scrubbed floors, attended to the sickbed, and tried to help. Her mom neither resented nor appreciated her. Illness was their mutual cross to bear. There was never any reason to question their lots. They both suffered in silence. Pauline knew Mom had some vague sort of lung problem, that she had great difficulties breathing from time to time. She asked if it was asthma. "Well, not exactly," her mom replied. It was a vague, all-encompassing malady, and its lack of definition assured it would never be cured.

It was also quite assured that Pauline, as the only girl in the family, would stay home as long as she could and take care of Mom. Dad and the boys showed periodic anger and irritation. It was almost as if they were mad at Mom for being sick. They seemed to think she could manage differently than she did.

Pauline was always Mom's champion, explaining her illness and keeping the mean men at bay. She learned from Mom's

complaints that women were compassionate comforters and
men were unfeeling bullies to be understood, but not counted
on. They also got angry, which women never did. Women took
to their beds instead. Pauline vowed never to cower like her
mother. She argued with her father and criticized him on her
mother's behalf. She was fighting someone else's war. And Mom
kept feeding her ammunition by complaining of the traumas
and degradations of marriage. She promoted a feeling of camaraderie between women around the sickbed. It was no accident
her daughter became a nurse.

Pauline never questioned why she chose to be a nurse instead of a doctor. She had the smarts for it, but the power was
more than she wanted to consider. While in training, she studied
the books of Carl and Virginia Simonton, who worked with cancer patients, teaching them to use creative visualization to create
a healing relationship with their own illness. This approach
sometimes led to remissions and even cures. Pauline brought
some of this new learning home to her mother and asked her to
give it a try. Her mother rose up on one arm, enraged that Pauline would even suggest such nonsense.

"Don't you think I've tried every single alternative known to
man or beast as a way out of this dilemma?"

It was a weird, rhetorical question, but it stopped Pauline
cold in her tracks. The answer of course was "No." With light-
ning clarity, Pauline's mind sped quickly through all of her
childhood experiences, remembering numerous instances when
Mom could certainly have tried harder. But she had chosen to
wimp out and give up. Pauline also remembered the rage she'd
seen on her dad's face. At that time, she'd thought he had no
legitimate cause to complain.

Then it hit like a thunderclap: Her mother had essentially
ruled herself, her daughter, a husband and two sons through the
power of her illness and never-ending recuperation. Whether
the illness was psychosomatic or not was not the issue. The real
issue was power. Mom's use of power had been indirect and manipulative. No one ever got a straight answer from her. She expressed many critical judgments through innuendo, and thus
escaped any retribution from those she'd wounded. Over the
years, Pauline had felt vague rumblings of rage. But she'd managed to save them for toilet bowls where she vomited weekly,
then nightly, then *seventeen* times a day. When she entered treat-

ment for bulimia, her vomiting was almost uncontrollable. Despite her half-hearted attempts to keep smiling, she telegraphed rage. Her volcano was erupting, anyway.

Had her mom been wielding power in ways that brought her what she wanted, we'd have no cause for discussion, no patient to treat. Mom had a tremendous amount of power, but she'd been unwilling to own and declare it. Why bother? She already had Pauline to fight her battles for her, and three men who buzzed around her. Quite common with purgers and compulsive overeaters is a secret pact between mother and daughter to keep the lid on things while orchestrating others' lives. Such women can never show outright and directly how truly powerful and managerial they are.

Pauline confessed early in recovery that she'd made a vow to herself that, no matter what, she wouldn't turn out like Mom. Unfortunately, her opinions of other women who exercised direct power was that they were unfeeling and too forceful—like men. She faced a daily dilemma trying to be a decisive nurse while having to cajole and manipulate doctors. In effect, she ended up just like Mom, turning her rage into sickness. Mom used the bed, she used the toilet bowl.

DAUGHTERS WANT TO HELP

How often have we seen women suffer? Daughters watching their mothers suffer learn to become long-suffering themselves and miss out on living their own lives.

We saw this clearly when ten-year-old Angela was brought into treatment despite her mother's objections that "she really hadn't been affected by eating disorders." Angela suffered as she watched her mom's pain, watched her mother's weight spiral upward despite all attempts to control herself.

In our approach of treating mothers and daughters together, we ask each of them to write a history of their attempts to control the other's eating. Here is what Angela, who was not overweight herself, wrote while watching her mother's fights with food.

Sometimes I felt that I had to remind my Mom to start dieting. When I would remind her to diet, sometimes she'd get mad at me and say go away or leave me alone and [I] felt so angry that I would ignore her for a little while. I didn't really check on her, but I would ask her about her diet. If she stayed on it, I would be happy and do my chores, but if she broke it I would be so upset I would pick fights with her. I would eat junk food and hide it under my bed so she wouldn't find it and eat it. If she didn't find it I would be glad but if she did I would be so mad that I felt like screaming at her or asking her why she did, but I didn't because I was afraid. Sometimes I ate diet foods with my mother mostly because I liked to, but I also wanted her to diet. I didn't need to diet at all. When mom was dieting she would give me money to go buy groceries and I would buy healthy foods or diet foods for her then I would be glad knowing that she was eating the right foods. I would always feel a little embarrassed when my mother would go to my school because she was so overwait [sic]. So I asked my father to go instead.

Let's look more closely at what Angela wrote. You may notice that when expressing strong emotion, especially anger, she leaves out "I." She meant to say "I felt so angry." Often children of addicts have difficulty writing "I" when it is coupled with strong emotion. Angela's first comment is about the reaction she gets after pointing out Mom's destructive eating. Mom gets angry at her daughter's intervention.

Later, Angela responds to the counselor's question about checking on diets by saying that she doesn't, but she admits that she asks her mother about her diet. Couldn't we call that "checking"? It's hard for her to see herself and how much she's been affected. Many would say we shouldn't even bother her with this. We have to. Many would say, "Well, she's only ten." But at age ten, daughters begin to notice that they will soon be growing into their mothers.

Angela goes on to show how arguments with Mom are generated by how Mom is doing with her food plan. Also, notice Angela's responsive, reactive behaviors, helping with housework if Mom is on her diet, going to her room angry if Mom has broken it. Notice how she hides food. Then, she wants to confront Mom, but is afraid of Mom yelling back. This is classic in troubled families, where we see this blurring of generations, and children are conflicted about who is the parent and who is the child.

In training seminars, I show therapists Angela's actual letter so they can see how the last sentences are misspelled and printed backwards. Up until this point the penmanship and spelling have been perfect. But the last sentences are so hard to write that they are fraught with misspellings and dyslexic character juxtapositions. Her statements appear to be rather innocuous and understandable: "I would always feel a little embarrassed when my mother would go to my school because she was overwait [sic]. So I asked my father to go instead." As understandable as the embarrassment might be, it was actually gut wrenching for this little girl to say it out loud and write it in print. She needed to cry in groups of other daughters, who also shared the same pain watching their mothers' struggle.

Eventually she told this to her mother in a family group and they both cried together. Saying it out loud to Mom in a supportive atmosphere healed her sense of excessive responsibility, and also helped her mom acknowledge her own feelings of helplessness and struggle. Mom shared how hard it had been for her, and how much better she felt now that she was asking for help with the problem. They were able to cry together and then each work their own side of the street.

Without this early intervention into her life, Angela would have grown up feeling like a failure since she couldn't heal her mother. She might have gone on to marry an addict or become one herself, trying to mend Mom's woundings. With this early start, we were able to relieve her of her mistaken sense of responsibility.

For daughters like Pauline and Angela, recovery involves grabbing onto power, becoming direct, and feeling your guts again. Vomiting is giving up your guts. Recovering women are gutsy. They walk with power. They know they have the potential to take care of their own side of the street. When I give seminars in the deep South and speak of this power, women stare at me blankly, as if I'm suggesting something outlandish and unnecessary. In my slide presentation, I show a dinosaur above the caption, "History is full of giants who couldn't adapt." Many women respond like Scarlett O'Hara; they play out that Southern Belle rhetoric in a world passing them by.

EXERCISE 3

WHO'S WHO—MY MOTHER, MY SELF

Here's a chance to interview your mother—and your self—to discover your opinions on a wide range of topics. Remember to keep good notes in your journal. Be sure to complete your interview with each subject from your mom's point of view first. Then go back and do your own.

	MOM'S OPINIONS	MY OPINIONS
On Power:	_____	_____
On Success:	_____	_____
On Men:	_____	_____
On Sex:	_____	_____
On Body Image:	_____	_____
On Motherhood:	_____	_____
On Pain & Suffering:	_____	_____
On Food:	_____	_____
On Diets:	_____	_____
On Love:	_____	_____

Your eating disorder is a signal that the old rules are no longer working. In the next chapter we'll see how some of your failure with food was an attempt to salve the wounds of Mom's disappointments. Was she disappointed in marriage? She dated and mated—but was she left unsated?

4

STAYING HOME

AT THE END OF THE POPULAR WOODY ALLEN MOVIE *ANNIE HALL*, there is mention of a brother who thinks he's a chicken. When asked why he wasn't taken to treatment, his family replied, "We need the eggs."

Is there some reason that you need to stay in your food obsession? What purpose does it serve? What are your good reasons for continuing to hurt?

Your disordered eating has been an effort to stay at home, to avoid growing up and emotionally cutting the cord, to avoid leaving the nest and living your own life. Let's see what made you stay—so you can now be free to leave.

We are now going to look at how some of your continuing failure in the food obsession game has been "needed" by your family. It's been a way to maintain the status quo. Failure to grab hold of the brass ring of abstinence means being emotionally arrested, unable to grow up and leave home. For many with eating disorders, that has to do with a deep, loving connection to Mother and an inability to separate from her to live your own life. Often, fear of separation comes from a deep attachment to the pain she has lived through. Although Mom may appreciate the comfort you want to give, on a spiritual level, she really wants you to go. She wants you to claim your freedom. At the same time, she's also going to feel abandoned and possibly alone. That's just how it is. You will both need help in weathering this monumental change. For both of you, this separation may prove the most difficult of any breakup you suffer.

SPITTING UP MOM'S PAIN

You are very finely attuned and sensitized to Mom. It may be just this sensitivity that makes life between you so difficult. According to a 1993 Gallup poll of 1,239 adults, 43 percent said that boys were easier to raise than girls. We say girls are more difficult, because of our fears and protectiveness toward them. That's one easy explanation; but from what I've seen in treatment, I'd say it is also because girls demand more honesty from their mothers. Daughters confront their mothers.

As a loving daughter, you moved in to fill Mom's need. You became the message carrier for the family, the one who would declare to the world that there was a problem. You served as a beacon of light signaling the way for relief boats to come in and help. Unfortunately the beacon burned too brightly and you got your wings singed a bit. Recovery will involve letting Mom find her own voice, shine her own light, as you get out of the way.

Your visibility and open presentation of problems gave voice to Mom's concerns. It's like Mom's inner spirit wanted her to be honest, so she birthed a daughter as ally. When Mom lives honest to herself, no one else has to act it out. Right now, neither of you can help it.

———

EXERCISE 1

TELLING YOUR MOTHER'S STORY

Watching your mother's life hurt you. She couldn't hide her pain from you. You wanted to make it up to her, but couldn't get in. You hurt yourself instead. The only way out of this interwoven expression of pain is for you to make conscious what you have been doing unconsciously.

It is amazing how finely attuned daughters are to their

mothers. They are able to give many specific details of their mothers' lives, able to *feel* Mom's emotions readily.

Write now about your mother's life—through her voice! Take out your journal, sit quietly for a time, following your breath. Feel your mother's presence. When you're ready, make a few circles on the page, and begin. You will be amazed at how easily this material comes to you.

Use any or all of the following questions to access your mother's story. This is a stream-of-consciousness exercise. You don't get graded on it! Its purpose is to focus your inner and outer awareness on your mother's life. Even if you are a mother, forget your daughters now. Just be with yourself as a daughter watching your own mother. You are tracing back to your own origins. You will now enter into your mother's head as she is pregnant with you, contemplating your birth. This isn't about judgment—it's about understanding.

If you know nothing about the circumstances of your birth, try interviewing your mother. Or if your mother can't remember, ask your grandmother or your older siblings or relatives what was going on in your mom's life then.

Start by introducing yourself, as your mother, using her name. For example, if your mother's name is Sylvia, begin with: "Hello, my name is Sylvia. I was born in Warsaw, Poland, in 19— . . ."

Mom's Story—Part I: Pregnancy and Birth

1. First, identify yourself by name (using your mother's name).
2. Where were you born? When? What is your age now? Where do you live now?
3. Who were your parents? What were they like? Did you have brothers and sisters? Were you the youngest, oldest, middle, or only child? How did that feel?
4. Where did you spend your teenage years? What was happening in your life then? How did you feel about it?
5. Did you get married? Whom did you marry? Why did you marry? How did you feel after the vows were sealed? What were your options?
6. If you didn't marry, why didn't you?

7. How long were you married before you got pregnant? What is this pregnancy like? What is the world like now? What is the news of the day?

8. What does your mother think of your pregnancy? What advice does she offer?

9. What does it mean to you to be pregnant with the little girl who is now writing this exercise?

10. Tell us about your pregnancy.

11. What is the quality of your life like during this period? What happiness, joy, worries, pain, or disappointment are you carrying?

Mom's Story—Part II: Daughter's Childhood

1. Again, identify yourself by name (your mother's name).

2. How did your life change when your daughter was born?

3. Tell us about being a mother to your daughter when she was five years old. How old are you now? Give us some of the important details of your life in this period.

4. What is your relationship with your daughter like? Are you close? Do you enjoy her company?

5. Do you have other children?

6. What is your relationship with your husband like?

7. Are you working as well as caring for your family? What is this like?

8. What is your life like now?

9. What was the texture of your life during this period? What worries, sadness, pain, and disappointment did you carry then? Still carry?

Mom's Story—Part III: Daughter's Adolescence and Adulthood

1. Again, identify yourself by name (your mother's name).

2. Tell us about being a mother to your daughter when she was fourteen. What was it like to raise a teenager in 19—? What was the texture of your life during this period?

3. Describe your relationship with your daughter when she turned twenty-one. What was your life like then?

4. Tell us about your relationship with your daughter now.

5. What is the quality of your life today? What worries, sadness, pain, and disappointment are you carrying?

In treatment or weekend seminars, we would now ask you to speak to the group "as if" you were your own mother. I never cease to be amazed at how easily this exercise is carried off. There is rarely balking, difficulty, confusion, or resistance. It is an automatic and well-known exercise you've been practicing all your life. You give great "mother."

There is often a key phrase that mother and daughter hook into easily. For example: "Mel really didn't want this second baby," or "I was going to leave him, but my mother said the baby would make him settle down," or "All my girlfriends were getting pregnant, so I just knew I'd want to also. I didn't question it much." Even if these key phrases seem very offhanded or contrived, the underlying expectation is that the mother is going to somehow "get out" of her situation. Moms are always expecting things to get better.

Here's what Judith wrote as Esther, her mother:

It looks like the war is going to end soon. I pray each day that Herb will come home safely. It's hell living here with my dad. I thought marriage would get me out of this house, but instead here I am bloated, lost my size 9, and scared to death of this delivery. I feel sick all the time too. I'm not so sure we should have gotten pregnant like this.

Herb was running around quite a bit even before he went overseas. I feel like I don't even know this guy. He's a city type, with a great gift for gab. And he's so strong willed. I sure hope with the baby he'll take care of me better. But, why does he leave? I hope this baby is a boy so he'll be happy. Maybe he'll stay home more, teach the boy about baseball and stuff. If it's a girl, I don't know what I'll do. My mother was sickly. I never learned what girls like. I don't even know what I like. What can I teach a girl?

I'm not even sure I want to have kids. But with Herb it seems like his whole ego is tied up in this thing. I'll do it for him. Maybe it'll make him happier to be married. But how do I talk to a child? No one ever taught me. Those maids we had were busy with the housework all the time. They didn't have much to say to me. I read a lot. I guess I can read to the kid.

I hope Herb gets home before the baby's born. I wonder why I say that. He's never really been a help to me anyway. He criticizes me all the time. He'd probably even have a better suggestion on how I should deliver the baby. Well, maybe all that controlling stuff of his will change once the baby's here. We can both focus on our project of raising the child and we won't get into so many personality squabbles with each other.

In actuality, Herb did not get home for the delivery, and Esther was abused further by her father after she got home from the hospital. It was six months before Herb got home from the war, and he immediately began to criticize the feeding schedule she had for the baby. It never stopped. Scared about parenting anyway, Esther had birthed a little girl, who became the constant source of more criticism from her husband as well as a growing sense of inadequacy within herself. When the little girl grew into adolescence, she began criticizing Esther too. It's what girls did. Judith did it automatically. Her father was the "powerful adult" in the family. She became what Jungians call "a father's daughter," as she joined him in judging females.

The conflict of being a "father's daughter" critical of her same-sex parent became Judith's lifelong struggle. Because she'd been trained to hate women, she hated herself. She grew up to choose abusive, critical men like her father and grandfather, and ultimately puked her rage late into the night. In treatment, Judith would have to own her more feminine side—the side that could "receive" caring. She would have to learn how to receive from both men and women.

Whether your mom is alive or not, you need to mourn for the sadness of her life. More than likely, you felt all of Mom's pain and wanted to soothe and comfort her. But she couldn't fathom such a role reversal, and so she pushed at you and hit out, needy, trying so hard to cover up, never escaping your knowing glance.

You knew most of this already. You knew everything about your mother's disappointments. As a baby, you made her the object of careful scrutiny and attention. Those less empowered have to understand those with more power. Just as domestics understand their employers, dogs scout out moods of their owners, and women psychologize their men, daughters keep a vigilant watch on their mothers. Since Mom was supposedly the more powerful, you watched and picked up most of her worries. Your mom, however, may not have liked such close scrutiny, and remained defensive and fearful of your vision.

ASK YOURSELF:

□ *Which of Mom's secrets did I always know?*

□ *What disappointments of Mom's did I see?*

□ *What pain or sadness of Mom's did I try to fix?*

Who Benefits?

Addiction treatment has to take a pragmatic approach. We can't afford to be swayed by the latest fads and casual cocktail conversation. We're dealing with life and death struggles and must take a hard look at what works, what doesn't, and why. We must ask, "What purpose does a daughter's illness or failure serve in the family system?" This has nothing to do with causality. Careful of guilt! We don't want to blame parents who are doing the best they can and making the accommodations they have to make. They're operating in a survival mode. We're just seeing what works and why. And we're asking if we need this behavior anymore, and if not, how we replace it.

We see clearly that Daughter's "problem" has become the family problem. It gets everyone's attention, and takes everyone's mind off any other problems in the home. In fact, there will often be another sister who is a perfect, model child. If one sister gets into recovery, the other develops an illness. If the family system needs the illness, someone will take it on. I have treated addictions for more than two decades. Most of my work is in southern California, where three out of four marriages end in divorce. In the heartland of such painful statistics, I have never treated a pure anorexic who came from a broken home. The parents' marriage remains intact while Daughter dies.

When we see this so often, we've got to question, "What purpose do problem daughters serve in a family?" The answer is twofold: DISTRACTION and EXPRESSION. The daughter's primary if unwitting purpose is to keep Mom distracted from her own personal problems, especially problems with Dad. You may have seen the Sally Jessy Raphael show where a mother served as a counselor in her daughter's "fat camp" rather than confront her obese husband.

Often the daughter's life-threatening illness serves to unite Mom and Dad in a common bond—fear of losing their daughter. The sicker the daughter, the closer the couple. These couples need extensive counseling. Their conflicts are so deep-seated and hidden that it takes months before they acknowledge any difficulties. They protest ardently that they have an idyllic marriage, that they'd like to retire together to a romantic island alone. They plan to do that as soon as the children are raised.

However, children resorting to obsession and addiction are not getting raised. They're not being helped to grow up and move into their own lives. They stay at home to rot. How odd that the maturing daughter, ready to leave the nest, suddenly comes down with major life-threatening problems that keep her parents from living out their "dream." The problem child is protecting the parents from watching their house of cards crumble. The daughter's sickness is protecting her mother from disappointment and severe disillusionment.

If you are an eating-disordered daughter, you are helping to save your parents' marriage. You are providing a diversion from Mom's pain, a distraction from her deeper marital problems. Illness preserves the family system.

ASK YOURSELF:

▢ *What were the most striking features of your family system (family problem)?*

▢ *How is the energy of your family system (family problem) alive and well in your life today?*

Unholy Alliances

In treatment, we sometimes see parents appearing as a loving couple, upwardly mobile, middle-class, psychologically aware, with "very little wrong" in THEIR relationship. In fact, they usually report that their lives would be perfect were it not for this poor dear daughter who is starving herself and throwing up. The sickness is keeping the parents together.

The mothers are often immaculate, well groomed, fashionably thin. Despite their gracious smiles, they often speak in a controlled deliberate manner that sometimes sounds like ice cubes clicking in the veins. The daughters affect the same kind of pose. But later, in group therapy, they describe with almost sexual abandon what a powerful release it is to vomit.

We also see *not* so slim and fastidious mothers, in less than idyllic relationships, who expend great energy trying to help their daughters, but also bingeing with them. Obese mothers and daughters are both caught in self-abuse rather than personal expression. These daughters unite with Mom in complaints about how "rotten" men are, whether in the home or out. The bottom line is, they expect little of their men, and seek most of the intimacy and contact in their lives with each other, or with other women. Selling the guys short usually means they've given up wanting men for anything other than physical contact. Although they can never admit it directly, their behavior resembles the more male perspective of only "looking for one thing."

It really doesn't matter which extreme the daughter's weight reflects. The bottom line is that Daughter has not witnessed Mom being truly vulnerable to and then nurtured by a man. In the "perfect couple" scenario, Daughter's wise, intuitive side picked up that everything wasn't as sweet as its image told her it was "supposed" to be. In the more estranged families, the daughter watches a mother whose needs are clearly not getting met. She gets no training in vulnerability, intimacy, or honesty in watching her parents. She goes for a sublime merger with excesses of food, or swears off completely, opting for starvation.

In both cases, the daughter is declaring that she needs no one. In actuality, she just doesn't know how to need anyone. The overeater says, "Thanks anyway, but I'll take care of all my needs

myself. Watch me guzzle." The anorexic says, "I don't need anybody. I don't even need food. Watch me live on air."

All of this pain has been carried unconsciously, but acted out
with food. In order to stop the acting out, you must now investigate further to make your unconscious motivations more conscious. You need to become more aware of falling into what
used to be automatic behavior patterns. This is not to put blame
on anyone. We aren't trying to determine what caused your
problems. This is about your developing clarity about what your
motivations and intentions have been, so that you can make a
choice now about continuing your behavior, or changing course.

ASK YOURSELF:

◻ *How did your mother feel about your father?*

◻ *Did you ever witness your mother being truly vulnerable
to and then nurtured by a man? How did that make
you feel?*

TRIANGULATION

A basic tenet in family therapy is that "The acting-out child is
acting out the unresolved conflict of the parents." In our case,
eating or starving is the acting out. If you've been lucky and wise
you may have had the sense to get out of this system. But if you
suffer an eating disorder, you were probably very deep in this
doo doo before you began to have a clue about what was really
going on.

You have to ask yourself if you want to remain the message
bearer—Mom's speaker of the house. Or, can Mom do her own
work, find her own voice? Did you have major flare-ups with
food obsessions when you were negotiating important life pas-
sages and trying to move away from Mom's pain and live your
own life?

You've been in a lifelong struggle to separate from Mom and
get born again. You became the "pointman" in the family

drama. Your pain became the repository for all the family's pain. This is called "triangulation."

———

EXERCISE 2

A TRIANGULAR AFFAIR

Bring out your journal now and take some time to think about the triangles in your own family relationships. This time, instead of writing, make these interconnections graphic and visible by drawing and labeling the triangular relationships in your family.

1. Draw a triangle that represents the power dynamics in your relationship with your mother and father. Where does the power reside? What is the problem? Label the people at points of the triangle.
2. Draw arrows pointing to the directions in which power *moves*. Which two people are unified in their attitude toward the third? How do they lock power to keep the other out?
3. How does this loosely structured balance of power serve the good of the whole?
4. Draw triangles that represent various ages in your life—as a child, as a teenager, in your twenties, today. Do the patterns of relationships shift over time? How?
5. Draw triangles that represent other relationships in your family. How do they affect the whole? How do they affect you?

Remember, disordered eating is about confusion. It's about ambivalence toward power. As soon as you draw a triangle and write in the names of family members at the points, an "AHA!" will start to bubble up for you. You'll find that you already know what I'm about to explain. You KNEW. You always knew. You just couldn't look before.

You are now looking closely and you're seeing the coalitions of power you experienced throughout your upbringing. Look at these family power coalitions to see how two people collude to lock a third person out. In anorexia, it is usually Mom and Dad locking the daughter out. However, if the daughter's obese, it's usually Mom and Daughter locking Dad out. Mom and Dad can move to lock Daughter out, as you'll see later in Jenny's story. At the same time, Jenny's story later exemplifies mother and daughter locking out Dad. We saw that with Pauline, attending to Mom's sickbed while the men stayed out. It may have been father and daughter locking Mom out, as in Judith's case.

All of our families have some aspects of all the triangles. To get a handle on what was the most clear power coalition in your family, watch where energy travels in your triangle. All family members participate equally in triangulation—the lockers and the locked. Two people are close along the base of the triangle, focusing attention and energy toward the tip. This third point gets a lot of attention, but it's shut out. Whoever holds that point is perceived as an object, treated with scorn and contempt, or even "concern," another form of objectification. The two people stay focused on a third to keep from getting angry with each other. It keeps them from seeing how absolutely NECESSARY that object person is.

Sometimes we mask anger with excessive worry and concern. For example, parents may show grave concern by vigilantly monitoring a daughter's eating. Parents may be consumed with worry, and use this as an excuse not to get involved with anyone else in the family, namely each other. Maybe mother and daughter are united worrying and raging over alcoholic Dad. The problem person serves to unify the other two. The family system needs the family problem. We need the eggs.

As we investigate triangulation, we can see how Mom's pain and anger was shunted into the daughter, who stuffs it down with food and later pukes it into toilet bowls or garbage bags. Most of the time, family therapy shifts to "couple therapy." Mom's getting her own mating life in order, whether staying or leaving, will help daughters separate and grow up. Daughters taking on their mother's sorrow are secretly enraged, because they're fighting someone else's war. Their souls know they're in the wrong arena, and they must decide whose war is really theirs to fight. Addicted daughters serve as substitutes and salves for Mom's loneliness, making it up to Mom "for all she's been through."

Let's see how focus on the pain of others has sifted down through three generations of women.

Shirley had been overweight most of her adult life. Both her parents had eating disorders, although they'd never admit it. Her mother used her "food allergies" as an excuse to maintain her birdlike eating patterns. All the women in her father's family had been huge. Fearing their plight, all his life he'd struggled successfully to keep his weight in check. But there were those occasional binges when he'd scarf down everything in sight.

When Shirley began drawing the triangles that represented her family's relationships, she realized how these patterns had been repeated in her own life. She began with a triangle that represented her parents' relationship before she was born. They'd married to focus on illness.

When Shirley's parents married, her father was very ill and wasn't expected to live very long. But good nursing and no more cigarettes and TLC and wifely monitoring kept him around for another thirty years. Their bond from the beginning was about fighting his illness.

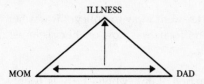

ILLNESS

MOM   DAD

When Shirley was born, the pattern of parental bonding shifted. They made Shirley, a chronically ill child, the focus of their attention and concern. Shirley moved in to fill the illness vacuum. Once again, it was a bond between Shirley's mother and father against illness. But now the illness was Shirley's.

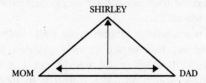

SHIRLEY

MOM   DAD

Shirley's sister was born when Shirley was eight. She was two months premature, and so entered the family triangles as another illness. Shirley was now declared well to become her mother's helper.

In Shirley's teen years, her mother's focus was almost entirely on controlling every aspect of Shirley's life—her food, her clothing, her dating life, all her activities. They formed the base-

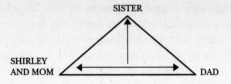

line, and squeezed out her father and sister. Illness had been replaced by puberty, which her mother seemed to consider an acute illness of its own.

However, as family ombudsperson, Shirley, plus her sister Mary, formed a separate triangle against their very controlling parents.

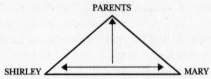

When Shirley went away to college, it was her turn to be out in the cold. The focus was now on her sister, who was entering puberty herself.

Shirley married Ralph when she was twenty-five. He was a man who binged and starved—two aspects of both her parents in one. Although he was slim and athletic, his hobby was eating as a gourmand. Food was the focus of his life, and he made certain it was Shirley's as well. Whenever Ralph had been on a bingeing spree, he'd starve himself back into shape for several weeks afterward. Shirley wasn't so lucky. She slowly ballooned from 135 pounds to 210.

But there was another problem as well: Ralph had severe emotional problems, that kept everyone on edge. He raged constantly. No one knew when he would act out next. Shirley needed a lot of support, and she found it in her friends. The alignment was Shirley and her friends versus Ralph.

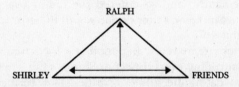

When Shirley's daughter Gina was born, a new triangle was formed. Shirley and Gina bonded into a new baseline. Gina became Shirley's support system, with Ralph's problems still the focus of their attention.

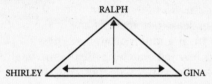

Shirley and Ralph were divorced when Gina was ten, and Shirley became a single working mother. Interestingly enough, the baseline didn't change from who occupied the point of the triangle. It was still Shirley and Gina bonded together, but now it was "You and me against the world, kid."

Gina, as Mom's ally, put on weight herself, even though Shirley was now on a health food kick.

They came to treatment when Gina was twelve, just experiencing her first menstrual period. Her mother was constantly dieting as well as grooming for the manhunt. "Gotta stay in the race," she'd gibe as she warned Gina that no man would have her fat.

Gina heard daily about the pressures of single motherhood and how Shirley's burden could be significantly lightened if she had a man. At the same time, Shirley lamented her previous marriage, often telling Gina about "your rotten father." She both needed and resented men. Gina picked up this ambivalence and hostility, and set about eating in earnest to remove herself from the race. She'd seen her mother act as caretaker to her dad; but she never saw her mother receive from a man. Mom said she wanted something, but she kept choosing men who wouldn't give her what she wanted. An excellent picture of this dilemma is drawn by Mona Simpson in her novel, *Anywhere But Here*. Daughter watches her mother on the desperate manhunt, then lapsing into ice cream binges and shucking the whole act.

Shirley gave Gina many conflicted messages about seeking men, seeking self, having power, letting go. She'd dress up, go out and flirt, date a few times, stop seeing a man, and then complain to Gina, "Men are no damned good. Who needs them!" It was like "Mom doth protest too much." Shirley didn't know how to talk with her daughter about what was really missing in her life. As she developed an abstinent food plan in treatment, neither dieting obsessively nor indulging any food fetish, a rawness oozed out of her, which made her feel more vulnerability than she'd ever known. She felt an emptiness she knew even a man couldn't fill, at least not men as she'd known them. Shirley's marriage had been a union around sickness—a pattern she and her mate had learned watching their own families suffer. She knew now that there was a deeper issue to deal with. She expressed it well in her own separate group long before she was ready to discuss it with Gina.

"I really don't have a clue how to be with a man in a cooperative relationship—where we are both there FOR each other. I can help a man if he's sick. I can unite with him in helping others who are sick. But I don't know how to focus on growing together. How can we invest in health? I'm really bogged down in generations of pain and sadness. When I was hurt by my husband's sadness, I ran away. I used my daughter to commiserate with, making her my best friend. She's learned that illness gets attention. Now I'm starving, she's fat, and neither of us knows how to receive nurturance or how to get enough. We're never enough and we never get enough."

Shirley was asking the right questions. While bingeing or starving, these questions never even came up. Her daughter Gina knew they were there, but she ate them away. Since Shirley was facing her life honestly, admitting her confusion and lack of direction, she was open and soft and in a good position to talk with her daughter. She decided she'd like to explore her ambivalence out loud with Gina. If you have adolescent daughters, you may be fearful that your daughter will reject what you say, or worry that admitting your confusion will encourage her to rebel against you or hurt you more. Our experience in treatment is that if you feel resolved and calm about being "enough," you can talk with your daughter about anything. You will speak as a fellow traveler rather than an authority. From that perspective, answers will come to you. You don't share this for her, but for you. Guess what? She knows anyway.

Shirley began the next family group talking with Gina as an ally, first acknowledging the difficulty of breaking such patterns:

"Gina, you and I come from a long line of caretaker, helper, self-hating, man-hating women. I showed my hatred for men by letting your father get away with temper tantrums and raging. He had no right to treat us that way, but I somehow 'understood' his abusiveness. I didn't respect him enough to fight squarely to make him cut that shit out. I was a nursemaid instead of a partner. It felt safer than truly being alive with a man, being of value to him, feeling of value myself. I see this so clearly now as I date men who appreciate me and it makes me cry. I am really afraid of being loved. I want so hard to protect you from growing up as closed off as I am. To do that, I'd like us to right now separate a bit. I need to find women my own age to help me. I won't be complaining to you about my single life. When I placed my confidences in you, that was no way to treat a daughter. I gave you too much authority before you were ready. I don't want to lay my prejudices on you. You might not even think of wanting a man. Why do I have to make them so important? It's a way to avoid myself.

"Now I see that I am even more confused about settling in to my single life, maybe not even wanting to mate again. That could be a choice for you too. I want to stop pushing so much for the marriage thing. What's the big deal? I think we both need some time to feel out what it's like to just be a woman. I really don't have a clue yet. We need to find teachers. Maybe that sweat lodge thing could be a start."

Gina picked up on "just be a woman." The rest had been heard, but she didn't know how to respond. She had a response to the "woman" stuff because she was so fascinated with menstruation. Her response was not directly to her mother's concerns, but obliquely said it all. It was in the form of a question: "Ma, do men like sex when you have your period?"

Shirley got it. She offered her daughter a wise woman answer in the form of another question: "More important, honey . . . DO YOU?"

SURVIVAL DECISIONS. As you look at these coalitions, try not to move too quickly toward blaming someone. While these are the factors involved in your problems with food, they *didn't cause them.* You may want to find the culprit so you can pin the rap on someone and get yourself off the hook. But it just doesn't work that way. It's not that easy. Our job is to get conscious. Others are not as lucky or as courageous. They will stay unconscious. So try to keep an open, compassionate heart. View this sadly, seeing how everyone is simply trying their best to survive. Once you begin to see how certain ways of functioning are organized as SURVIVAL decisions, you'll have more respect for how tenaciously we've all managed to hold on. You'll see more clearly *why* you couldn't easily give up your pointman role in the family—even after you became an adult, even after moving away. There are a lot of lives at stake, and a lot to give up. This is all much more complicated than simple "cause and effect." These things defy direct investigation. Your deepest psyche will only answer the call if you approach obliquely, from the edges of your awareness. All of the factors involved will be slowly revealed over time, but they usually take at least one lifetime to figure out.

ASK YOURSELF:

▫ *What was your mom depressed about?*

▫ *What was she angry about?*

▫ *When your mom was sad or mad, what did you do with food?*

Daughters Save the Marriage

Jenny's story is so classic that a video was made of important demarcations in her family's recovery. Jenny's eating disorder came on at a very critical developmental stage—when it was time for her to grow up and leave home. Jenny came to us for treatment right after her seventeenth birthday. She was vomiting twelve times a day, starved herself most mornings, collapsed into compulsive bingeing after she got home from school, and finished off her stashes in midnight raids which ended with a solemn oath to "fast" for the next day. She was thirty pounds underweight and ashen. You'll later see why treatment for her vomiting was such a necessary rite of passage for her eventual maturation and separation from her family. Jenny's mother, Aggie, said, "I thought she was feeding the neighborhood." Aggie found herself rummaging through kitchen cabinets, counting bread slices, measuring jam jars, and doubting her own experiences of shopping and stocking shelves. Aggie's major diversions from her own life were watching Jenny's food consumption and spying on Jenny's chaotic relationship with a drug addict boyfriend who held wild, raucous parties on weekends. She just knew if she could get her daughter away from "that boy" she'd get some control back.

There was also another woman involved, the boyfriend's mom. Often, when trying to break away from a tightly held mother–daughter bond, the daughter will seek an ally in another woman outside the family. This is someone who she feels really "understands" her. Such relationships have less engulfing attachments or expectations. Jenny liked this "other woman" who stayed drunk most of the time. She wouldn't have to feel any of the guilt and recrimination she felt when she was around her "proper and straight" real mom. This woman gave her support for her disordered eating.

Quite by accident, I eventually met this "other woman" seven years after Jenny left treatment. Watching Jenny's recovery had motivated her to get to OA, and I met her at a meeting where she was maintaining a 130-pound weight loss!

During initial consultations with Jenny and her family, we sketched a brief outline of her history and our possible directions as a treatment team. Her parents, Aggie and Rod, had separated and divorced when Jenny was five. Whenever Jenny asked about the divorce, she was told it happened because Mom's work moved to a new location, an hour away, and the commute hurt the relationship.

Jenny would later tell us in group therapy that she thought this was the weirdest reason she'd ever heard for a family to break up. But her parents were so upright and straight that Jenny was sure this had to be the reason, and she must be evil for even questioning it. For Jenny, like many others, initial doubts unexplored led to compulsive behavior as a way to avoid further questioning.

Such failure to pursue one's initial rumblings of confusion and doubt provides a fertile ground for eating disorders. Instead of trusting their instincts, children see Mom and Dad as perfect and themselves as evil. They choose to punish themselves instead of questioning further.

Upon receiving our evaluation that Jenny DID qualify for treatment, both parents sighed with relief. They expressed gratitude that at least she wasn't "an addict or something." Even though they'd been divorced for twelve years, the Barrows continued to function as a family unit. It was as if the couple had never really acknowledged the reality of their divorce. They couldn't face their pain. We'd later learn even more about that. Dad visited every weekend, "to see Jenny," often staying over "as a friend," and the three of them went on outings together and operated as a commuting triad. When they learned we'd want both parents in family groups three nights a week, Rod admitted it would be a hardship, but he wanted to do all he could to "support Jenny."

Family nights lasted for three hours, during which time each family member attended separate groups where they could share any secrets, practice any new approaches, and generally let their hair down without loved ones present. Aggie would be in a moms' group, Rod with other dads, and Jenny in groups with recently discharged patients who had returned for aftercare. After a short break, the families would reorganize and come together in multiple family groups to learn new ways to talk with each other.

Counselors and fellow patients from the first groups would also be in these later groups to help advise families on which issues needed confronting and which were best left for individuals to handle separately. These decisions are extremely important with addictive disorders because it's so difficult for sufferers to establish boundaries and determine which is their private territory and which is the family's domain.

An early aspect of treatment is learning the concept "We're as sick as our secrets." During the initial psychosocial evaluations, patients are asked to tell the counselors any secrets they harbor that they feel may get in the way of their recovery. They are assured of confidentiality, and that we will not pressure them to divulge what might harm them. We let them know, however, that we are required by law to report to authorities our knowledge of child abuse or incest, past or current, and also bound to warn prospective possible victims of any threatened injuries.

We do caution them that since we are family therapists, we will want to protect some individual secrets as necessary, but our "patient" is the entire family system and we will want to proceed in a manner best for the health of all. We can't keep secrets within the family system. We will encourage eventual, careful disclosure. It might be enough just to say, "I've got a secret." You won't necessarily have to say what it is, but if you pretend you don't when you do, that makes others around you feel crazy. They *know*.

Your Secrets Make You Sick

Jenny's major secret was about her own victimization when she was twelve. She'd stayed late at a schoolyard with girlfriends, playfully taunting some older boys, and was raped. Aggie feared that if Rod knew, he'd declare her an unfit mother and take Jenny away. Instead of helping Jenny heal her own wounds and remorse, Aggie quickly enlisted her as co-conspirator against poor Dad's supposed inability to understand or handle the situation. Mom's primary concern was making sure Rod would not find out. She couldn't focus on her daughter's pain. So it was sent underground. The two women colluded in believing women were strong enough to handle things men couldn't.

A common theme in eating-disorder treatment is women disrespecting and distrusting the strength of their men. Even if his work brings him great accolades in the world, he is often berated at home for being emotionally unavailable or unable to handle "feelings." It's like a well-worn tune learned in childhood. It may not apply to today's situation, but the melody is oh, so familiar. Despite all the fantasies played out with macho men and doll's house marriages, in reality addicted women don't expect much of men or have much faith that they'll be there when the going gets tough. Aggie and Jenny effectively froze Dad out. In treatment, Jenny wanted to clear up that bit of subterfuge.

Sometimes we find patients in early recovery wanting to deal with past trauma as a diversion from CURRENT work. They make an unwitting deal with themselves and a therapist to work on the wrong issue. Some eat right through such explorations—though their souls know it's the wrong war.

We had to make sure this was the work Jenny needed to do at this time, and that Jenny would work on her own true dilemmas—not Mom's, or ours. We decided to focus first on getting Jenny painfully aware of what she was currently doing with food. We'd help her develop a support system at Overeaters Anonymous and wait until she'd had a few months of abstinence from vomiting. We knew she'd probably gain weight in recovery and wanted to help her through that PRESENT trauma rather than focusing on the past. There are many therapists who would give equal importance to this rape.

However, in addiction counseling, *we go first for the current destructive behavior* and cope with the difficulties of stopping self-destruction.

This is always a judgment call. And it's difficult to make. One clinician alone may have too many of her own personal biases and avoidances operating to make it. At Hollis Institute, we practice a team approach, where such decisions are made with the entire clinical staff present in weekly "staffing sessions." There we make decisions based on patient needs, checking to see if anyone on staff is avoiding, or pressing for or away from certain work. Patients and their families benefit from the best thinking of a group of experts.

Also, we professionals monitor each other in any areas of our own avoidance or denial. In staff meetings we might ask each other, "Is someone on staff overly anxious to work on the rape, or is someone particularly hesitant to open up that issue?" In this case, the team unanimously voted to focus on here-and-now issues with Jenny, to deal only with what came up in the present as a result of her abstinence. We knew that once people become abstinent, unresolved pain will eventually surface. We then invited Jenny into the staffing to explain our "treatment plan." We keep no secrets from the patient.

There was certainly enough to work on. Jenny and Aggie had many discussions about jealousy and competition with other women. Aggie sensed rightfully how much her daughter resented her, but nothing was ever said directly. Both these women were committed to "making nice," talking sweetly, and complying in any way they could. Jenny's compliance led to vomiting.

Jenny was confronted on her "syrupy sweetness" and asked why she felt unable to be direct. We found it particularly healthy and significant when she got into a minor skirmish with another resident while marketing and argued over which brand of yogurt to buy. The facade was starting to break down. As her own sweetness was confronted and unmasked for the avoidance it was, she made it clear that she wanted to pull off Mom's lace collars and find who Mom really was.

In response, Mom's facade got tighter and tighter. She sensed the growing air of openness entering their family life. We soon learned that Mom had the most to hide. As Jenny dressed more casually, was able to leave her work assignments imperfectly completed, and even told sexy jokes with other residents, Aggie's collars got starchier, her eyes darted ever more fearfully, and she tried to get Jenny into conversations alone between groups to form a pact about what could and couldn't be discussed.

Rod showed up semi-regularly to groups. He came across as so many men in eating-disordered families do, like an unnecessary appendage or, at best, a foil for the women—generally ineffectual in the feeling realm. He had a rather cold, "scientific" demeanor, and seemed not to be in any way needy or even aware of sadness or other feelings.

Some evenings Rod called, absenting himself from groups because he'd had to work late, and the hour drive in L.A. rush hour wouldn't get him there on time. Months later we'd get to see how well timed and less than "coincidental" those absences were. Most of the work Jenny needed to do in group centered around the mother–daughter–boyfriend–future mother-in-law dyads, so that's where we focused.

Jenny's recovery began to stabilize. She got a sponsor in OA, an older woman to present yet another competitive surrogate for Mom. She was eventually discharged from treatment with a fair prognosis if she could just learn to be a little less perfect. Aggie had mellowed out some and was going to Alanon. She was learning how to keep her eyes off Jenny. As she started attending more to her own life, she didn't even know or care what was in the cupboard. Eventually she even started dating and going away on business trips.

Six months later all hell broke loose. Jenny broke up with her boyfriend, attempted an overdose, started continuous bingeing and vomiting, and came back to treatment thoroughly depressed. She'd had a smattering of feeling good, knew what recovery felt like, and trusted us enough to come back when the going got rough.

She was readmitted as a relapse patient, and the treatment team moved to make decisions about what was missing or not working in her recovery plan. We looked at what paths we'd taken in the past that might possibly be changed for the present course of treatment. We asked Jenny, as we do with all relapse patients, to make the same evaluation.

After initial consultations with Jenny, we decided it was now the right time to discuss the rape. We also wanted assurances of "perfect" attendance from Rod so that he could assume his rightful place in his daughter's life. Even though Jenny was more into dating and moving away from the family, she didn't know how to negotiate spending more time with a dad she really liked. They needed to talk. (After a few weeks in this second course of treatment, Jenny shared that during the past family groups, just as she was mustering up courage to talk to her dad about their relationship, that would be "just the night" the freeways seemed too crowded for Dad to get to group. Some of the "coincidences" we learn about in family therapy are so bizarre that we hear strains of the "Twilight Zone" theme echoing in the background. There is so much more communication going on than our little pea brains dream of.)

Investigating her relapse, Jenny decided the guilt of not telling Dad about the rape was weighing heavily on her conscience. Notice it was not the rape itself, but the secrecy. She didn't need his counsel at this point, she just didn't like keeping secrets. When it had happened she was too young to fathom all the choices she had in the matter. Now with later maturity, she realized she had bought into her mother's fear and effectively colluded to lock her father out.

Recovery involves a lot of forgiveness—of yourself and of others. Jenny felt she wanted her father's forgiveness. She decided to tell him about her lies. These issues are not easily decided. They need the guidance of sponsors, counselors, and others outside the family because family members might advise you to hold secrets and spare loved ones. Or, conversely, family members will advise confrontation and attack as a way to stir muddy waters and get you to do THEIR work. When you run these options by a therapist or spiritual mentor, sharing secrets will be viewed with a focus toward trying not to hurt anyone, including yourself. It takes some work to make sure whether sharing or hiding is the more painful route. For Jenny, it was time to come clean.

Work began on preparing her for telling Rod the truth. She wrote out scripts in the form of dialogues, emphasizing what she wanted Dad to know, and how she'd help him understand it wasn't his fault it happened or that she chose to hide it from him. She practiced in psychodrama sessions with her peer groups, setting the proper stage and experiencing all her fear and trepidation. By the night of this "come clean" family group, Jenny was super-confident and prepared.

As many patients have found, if you do enough homework and preparation, nothing you'll experience in real life will be half as difficult as you've imagined. An important value in treatment programs is the opportunity to practice and get feedback from uninvolved, caring others. All fellow patients and staff were primed for the family group, and everyone was prepared to help Jenny and Rod weather the truth. No one was prepared for what happened instead.

It was Aggie who threw a giant monkey wrench into these well-laid plans. Before Jenny got her throat cleared, Aggie jumped in with "I've got something to share." This was not offered as a request; there was none of her usual hesitation or pause. She raced on with "I know Jenny has been curious for years about our divorce and I think it's about time I cleared up any confusion." Aggie had never mentioned this as a dilemma in any of her groups with other moms. As far as we knew, it was a minor inquiry on Jenny's part. We had no idea it was a strong issue for Aggie.

Counselors stared, dumbfounded. I must admit I felt somewhat usurped as I'd, in all my glorious awareness, led my treatment team toward mending the father/daughter split. Didn't this woman know we were on a timetable? We'd been rehearsing Jenny all week. Too bad. Aggie continued on her juggernaut without waiting for any sign from the counselors. "Jenny, I think you should know, your dad and I divorced because I was having an affair with another man!" She then burst into hysterical sobs.

Why now? Why had Aggie chosen this moment to spill the beans about long-past, unrelated events? Unconscious and unknown to her, she was operating from deep codependency. Sensing her daughter had major pain to share, Aggie threw in the gauntlet and decided to divert attention and any strong emotion toward herself, so her daughter could be spared the pain.

Notice this as a form of triangulation. From my early drug counseling days, we called such behaviors "throwing a bone." Aggie thought she could throw out some interesting material for the group to chew on. If she could get us interested in this past topic, perhaps Jenny would give up on talking with Dad about the rape. On some level, Aggie sensed that her daughter was going to come clean. She tried to distract attention onto herself. It worked for a while.

Jenny exploded with anger. "You mean YOU—lily-white, perfect, Miss Virgin Queen, always impressing me about being a 'good' girl—you had an affair? And here I was trying to live out some kind of bullshit morality that had nothing to do with reality. Why couldn't you tell me the truth of who you are?" Jenny raged on for a full five minutes, and then fell in a heap, sobbing. Her mother's composure was certainly bent as she sniffled quietly, staring holes into the carpet. Finally she offered, "I'd like you to forgive me. I hope you can. I'm sorry I misled you. These are things I tried to deny even to myself. I hope someday you'll understand."

Jenny wasn't ready in that moment to engage with Mom. Their healing would wait for a later session. Perhaps Jenny's strong motivation and direction toward health would not let her be deterred by this unconscious tactic of her mom's. She turned instead toward Rod. "This side of the family has been dishonest too." With that, the tears flowed freely and Jenny sobbed about being raped and how badly she felt that she'd hidden it all these years. She hugged him, gulping, "You've always been there for me, and I didn't come to you. I'm so sorry I closed you out."

Rod's immediate reaction was to question Mom, as he asked Aggie, "Why didn't you let me know?" Before she could respond, Jenny answered for her, "We were scared and we were afraid, and we're sorry." Jenny, in answering for her mom, didn't yet see that she was unable to separate her own feelings from her mother's. She'd been operating from MOM'S fear, not her own.

Rod glared at his ex as he hugged Jenny to him. His own pain finally welled up as he thanked her for being able to trust him now. And he reassured her with "We'll work it out. I love you." Jenny then broke down into bigger sobs, and said, "I love you too." Mom sat quietly on the other side of the room, huddled and alone. This time she was locked out.

Healing progressed gradually over the next few weeks. In private sessions, the parents began to talk with each other about how inadequately they'd handled their divorce and how they still felt so much genuine caring and commitment to each other, but hadn't known how to talk. With all the family secrets out in the open now, there was a lot of talking. The dam for all three family members couldn't be plugged. They got to see what they'd been avoiding. The parents didn't want to face the pain of their divorce. Jenny saw how she stayed Mommy and Daddy's sweet little girl so they'd have ample excuses for seeing each other. Dad began visiting every weekend, and they had family outings as if no one had ever been divorced.

This couple loved each other, but they'd had no ability to weather the crisis that had entered their relationship. As long as Jenny stayed "their little girl," they never had to confront their pain. If Jenny were to grow up and leave, they'd be left alone with each other. Jenny had dutifully developed an eating disorder to keep herself from growing up, to bring attention to all this unresolved pain. Working on Jenny's eating disorder had brought that pain back into the spotlight. As a natural rite of passage, it was now time for Jenny to grow up and leave the family nest.

How could Rod and Aggie continue to spend weekends together without her as the ostensible excuse? They'd have to face past hurts to become ready for future joys without Jenny as central character.

Once that pain was unleashed, there was no more need for Jenny to be center stage in her parents' life. In separate sessions they started realistically looking at their divorce, and were later able to heal the pain. They started going out on dates without Jenny. No longer the central diversion and focus for family attention, Jenny was now free to grow up and leave home. Within three months she moved out to live with a friend from school. Six months later her dad moved in with her mom.

Rod and Aggie had needed an honest way to face how they'd mutually hurt each other, and to admit they still loved each other. They needed to find a way to live a full life without their daughter between them. Mom had to face who she'd been and how she'd survived. She had to forgive herself and then she ultimately asked her daughter's forgiveness. A year later the couple remarried—on what would have been their twenty-seventh wedding anniversary!

EXERCISE 3

MOM'S SECRETS

In your journal, write about the secrets you kept for your mom and how you felt about doing this.

1. What secrets about your mother's life have you kept?
2. What secrets about your mother's life have you suspected?
3. What feelings are stirred up as you think about these secrets?
4. How did you feel about having to keep these secrets?
5. How did these secrets get acted out in your plate?
6. What secrets did you keep from Mom?

WORKING YOUR OWN SIDE OF THE STREET. You may now think that you want to see YOUR mother be as honest as Aggie. Focus just on yourself. You may be upset with her because of her own personal dishonesty, whatever it is. Be careful here of focusing solely on Mom. Remember, Jenny was seeking her own forgiveness from Dad. She didn't want anyone else to come clean. She wasn't looking for her mother to do anything. Each of us has to work our OWN side of the street. As you work yours, others may be inspired to come out too, but maybe not.

The Struggle to Separate

Recovery from destructive eating habits involves growing up emotionally. It means leaving Mom's house. Leaving home is a basic decision you will make for your own survival. You must develop the firm resolve to get up and go, to make the move, to separate. When you leave home you'll stop living Mom's life and start living your own. It often takes anger to give us the energy and motivation to get out. But staying angry is a way of staying stuck, of never truly letting go. Anger keeps us tied to someone else's apron strings. You must find your own home in the universe. If you must stay angry with parents for a time to get out there, then go ahead. But just keep asking yourself if this is getting you to your own home.

No one taught mothers how to help their children grow up and leave home. There's no manual to teach us about separation. The best we get is instructions from a "good parenting" manual, or even codependency literature that talks about "releasing with love." But what does that mean? How can mothers be expected to invest so much time, knowledge, effort, and love—and then just let go? It all sounds quite noble and easy. But let's face it—it's hard! It's heartbreaking.

At my seminars a well-meaning mother will usually ask me, "How do I help my daughter separate and grow up? I want to be the best mother I can. I want to let her know that it's all right to go. I want to help her in any way I can. How is a mother to be supportive?"

My answer is invariably the same. "There's only one way for a mother to effectively help her daughter leave home. You must lie down on the floor, grab your daughter by the knees, kick and scream madly, 'I can't let you go.' That's the truth of how you feel, and that's all that really needs to be said. With that truth, your daughter can do her own wrenching, struggling, and birthing. You helped her the first time around. This time, she's got to get born without your help. In fact, emotionally she may want to kill you in order to make the break. The last thing she needs is you helping."

Now you may be a daughter, or have a daughter who really doesn't want to go. Why should anyone want to leave a super-cushy trip of three to ten meals a day with attention, excess involvement, and support? Our fat says we have to go.

Truthfully, as hard as it is, mothers really do want their daughters to leave them. They haven't been schooled for it. They don't have a clue how to weather the pain. And somewhere they know they'll have to face everything they've been avoiding once their daughter escapes. With all that, and even though fearful, our mothers know we must go.

Ask Yourself:

- *Do you still live at home? In other words, do you still live with your mother emotionally?*
- *Do you still live with your mother's pain?*
- *Do you still live with your mother's anger or sadness?*
- *How do your mother's unexpressed emotions show up in your life today?*
- *Have you sensed any indication that your mother really knows you need to make the break?*
- *Can you tell her how difficult leaving is and ask for her help?*

NO BLAME. No one is to blame. Life is difficult. Living an authentic, honest life requires continual changing and adapting. It requires just the fluidity we fear by calling on us to stay open and flexible. We chose obsession over development.

Yet once mothers and daughters look at this clearly, there is a sweet, poignant honesty that opens up between the women that transcends mere sadness. We realize that recognizing Mom's dilemma is a way to recognize our own. No one has more to give than they are actually giving. Everyone is giving their all. If it's not enough, it's not enough, but it's all there is.

Seeing this clearly will help you stop railing at your mother. It will also help you feel the new space, the wonderful emptiness created when the fighting subsides. You will then have to face your own life. And you'll begin to see how the addiction has been your way of avoiding living your own life. Just as daughters blame moms, moms try to blame anyone they can. Feeling excessively and inappropriately guilty, they'll try anything to make it look like they're not involved in the situation.

An "Incest" Event

I was approached by a very thin but attractive woman after a seminar in the Midwest. She told me that her daughter was being treated for anorexia at a prestigious East Coast university.

She said, casually, "My daughter's psychiatrists have found that her anorexia was caused by an incest event with her father."

I am always suspicious when I hear the word "caused." It usually indicates that the clinicians are involved in an investigative process, seeking simple, quick solutions rather than waiting and listening. This mother spoke as if the answer had been found and the culprit labeled. Now she was done. She seemed relieved to blame her ex-husband. Somehow it didn't fit. I could sense the sadness in her eyes. Rage and fear seemed to shoot out of the top of her head. She seemed a very unresolved and pained woman. I suggested she come into our family week so she would have a chance to explore her own feelings about the situation.

I asked her to tell me more. She reported the following "incest" event.

"When my daughter was twelve years old, she came into the living room wearing a sweater and my husband said, 'My, you're getting some titties there.' " She stopped short to emphasize how horrible this statement was. She saw this as a most unthinkable, violating event. I waited patiently to hear what had further transpired. I wouldn't have called this incest. Of course, such a call depends on how the statement was meant and how the daughter received it. No violation seemed evident to me yet.

The woman gave me an accusatory glare as if to say, "Wasn't it great that she and the psychiatrist had discovered this carnage?" She knew by my gaze that I saw there was more there. She had suffered her own personal violations and was enraged, but she was able to channel all her hostility toward him into this event of her daughter's.

I stared back, softening my eyes, as I realized the terror she faced. She was afraid of her own rage. Her daughter lived out her rage with rigid starvation. There was really nothing I could say, and I invited her again to come to treatment. I knew that hunting for causalities would keep her stuck unless she and her daughter could renegotiate the rigid walls and boundaries they both use as defense.

I knew by the look on the woman's face that there was more work to do. Mom needed to face the subtle daily violations SHE suffered with this man. It did no good to blame the father for Daughter's problems if it helped Mom avoid listening to her own internal messenger. Feeling guilty and scared, Mom wanted her daughter's "incident" to get her off the hook. This would let her continue to focus on her daughter's problem and not her own. She never took me up on the invitation to treatment.

Leslie's mother, however, came to our treatment center long before her daughter. Evelyn had heard about the family intervention program, where we gather family and friends, and train them in how to confront an eating-disordered patient with "tough love," honestly recalling painful and scary events, in hopes of getting that person to ask for help for themselves. Evelyn first came to treatment because she didn't like who SHE had become. She was desperately controlling and nervous, seeking tranquilizers to calm down as she watched her daughter withering away. She found herself counting bread slices in the cupboard and was mortified at how sneaky and scared she'd become. She was highly motivated to look at her own behavior, and after a month, became very accepting of herself and her daughter. She realized there was a chance her daughter would not seek treatment, but at least she could feel secure that she had tried all SHE could do.

One of our main reasons for treating family members is so that they can see they have tried their best and done all they could. This allows them to let go and surrender to whatever happens. Moms desperately need to be reassured and told: "You've done enough."

Well, Evelyn certainly had. She worked night and day assembling friends and relatives, making all the appointments, getting them to our training sessions on intervention. Because this process gave her a strong sense of "doing something," she felt even more loving toward Leslie, less scared, less powerless.

The intervention sessions went well. Leslie defiantly agreed to come to treatment, although she sneered, "I don't want anyone bugging me to eat." We soon learned that her defiance was a case of "methinks she doth protest too much." Eating-disorder patients are sometimes like Uncle Remus's Brer Rabbit pleading to Brer Bear, "Please don't throw me in the briar patch." They protest that they don't want exactly what they DO want. Leslie wanted her mother to keep monitoring her food intake, reining in the eating disorder, taking responsibility.

In treatment we helped Evelyn to stop helping, stop watching, stop fixing, so that Leslie could feel responsible for her own life. Moms need help to kick their daughters out of the nest. In her own groups with other anorexics, Leslie was helped to see how much she wanted to start listening to personal signals, but that she'd been afraid of her own body. This was not something Mom could help her with. Because Evelyn had never felt scared of her own body, she kept trying to talk Leslie out of these feelings.

In her groups with other mothers, she was encouraged to see that her daughter's feelings were NOT her responsibility. That her daughter's fears of a demon body had been taught her by a culture, a media, that promoted such fears and had nothing to do with her. She was helped by other mothers not to offer suggestions to her daughter. The mothers exchanged phone numbers. Evelyn knew she needed guidance and support each time she wanted to "help." The best advice we can give mothers comes from an old blues song of the Forties: "Do nothin' 'till you hear from me." For a while, mothers will be instructed to tie their hands and bite their tongues and try to get out of the way every time they have the urge to help.

Evelyn was helped by some DOs and DON'Ts learned in her "mothers' group."

Dos and Don'ts for Moms

- DO face the pain of your own life.
- DO go to Alanon or Oanon.
- DO accept how difficult your life has been.
- DO acknowledge out loud to your daughter when you've felt inadequate for her.
- DO admit to your daughter that you've been ambivalent about your own role.
- DO spend some time alone each day listening to yourself.
- DO become more "selfish."

- DON'T keep asking her "What's wrong?"
- DON'T protest and minimize her pain.
- DON'T tell her about your marriage.
- DON'T expect her to save you.
- DON'T ask about or even hint you know how much she weighs.
- DON'T talk about her to your friends.

Evelyn was encouraged to see that any time she wanted to "advise" Leslie, she should view this urge like an alcoholic wanting to take a drink. Rather than acting out on that "compulsion," she was to bite her tongue and call another mother for help. She was to imagine masking tape across her mouth.

Evelyn used the phone a lot. She learned there was nothing for her to do but encourage her daughter to explore her own thoughts. She learned that her daughter needed to find her own way. Leslie needed to be left alone. She needed to be witnessed by other fellow sufferers who had felt similar feelings. She didn't need help, just a loving, watchful eye. Somehow, in getting that kind of attention, Leslie would begin to feel a gentle call to come out. It would feel like safe ground for exploring. That she could have a thought or a feeling and not necessarily have an answer. In time, she would find that there's nothing to do but ALLOW ourselves and our thoughts to exist.

Within a few weeks, both Evelyn and Leslie were laughing in the hallways between groups. Evelyn never asked about Leslie's food plan. And Leslie relaxed a bit, stopped acting waiflike, and even showed more energy. In turn, Evelyn, by talking with other mothers and encouraged by counseling staff, really came to believe that she had done enough. She felt secure that whatever the outcome, her work was finished. Leslie got the message and rose to the challenge of her own growing-up. When mothers like Evelyn get to see the value of the "do nothing" approach, they're amazed.

The Primal Shrug

I've found that I have to teach both counselors and moms to give their charges a "primal shrug" when reporting back that we don't have a clue what to recommend. Sometimes we shrug and say the situation seems too difficult, we just don't know how to proceed. Mostly, we're letting patients know that there are no simple answers or quickie shortcuts. The process of recovery will take a while, and the path will be a bit precarious. At first patients get angry, complaining the staff is worthless, and then they accept this lack of direction and find their own personal path.

Just like counselors, moms were busy doing for, being there, proving to your own moms, your girlfriends, your men, yourselves, what good moms you were. You had no chance to relax and let your daughters forage a bit for themselves. You needed comforting when times were bad, celebration when times were good, and more than anything, you needed to be left alone. You needed witnessing.

Being left alone is something you daughters long for and at the same time fear. It's a lot like your relationship with food. You lust for it and at the same time you're repulsed by it. You see it as a comfort, but then suffer terrible consequences. Finding your own answers, growing up to live your own life, feeling that lost, vacant, empty feeling like your skin is peeled off, is what all the excess food has been helping you avoid. Organically, cells are uniting and separating all the time. As a spiritual entity, you need the same fluidity. Now you need to walk away feeling fully, but not full. You're full, love it!

5

LEAVING HOME

SUFFERING FROM AN EATING DISORDER IS LIKE LIVING AS A RIPE FRUIT rotting on the vine. It's time to grow up, time to live your own true life. We've looked at the function your suffering served in your family. Now, we'll take a sideways look to see how we got this way. You need to understand consciously how this painful programming developed. We have to look objectively, without blame. We are going to begin with the way we denied our power and made ourselves objects. How mothers—how all women—for many generations, have been taught the same.

Those of us with eating disorders must take an honest look at all of this. Our programming to deny our power and fail in the plate started the minute we were born.

Many daughters can recount chapter and verse on how difficult their particular birth was on their mother. Was your mom sick? Did she have a difficult pregnancy? Did she labor long? Did she scare you about delivery? Were you ever consulted about how difficult being born was on YOU? We all assume the infant doesn't know. Did anyone ask how you felt about being separated from Mom's nurturing warm body? The birth trauma is just as dire a disappointment for daughters as it is for Mom.

Once you're born, you begin to experience loss. First there's that deadly feeling of "otherness." You realize that, alas, the rest of the world is not inside your skin. It's no longer as nice as it was in the womb. Inside, we got whatever we needed, whenever we needed it, without even asking. It was organic, pulsating, and immediate. When we were inside Mom, all our needs were met. That was clearly a bonded and functional relationship. However, in years to come that primal relationship would generate many deeper, perhaps unanswerable questions: attachment versus independence; loving and leaving; holding life, and each other, with a loose hand. You're now being asked to hold food, physical nurturance, with a loose hand. It's the same dilemma.

A WOMB WITH A VIEW

The minute we're born, we begin dying. All that time in the womb was spent growing, expanding, adding on cells, opening to new experiences, and surging toward life. Also, all our needs were met without much personal effort. That umbilical cord supplied whatever was needed at the exact rate and pace we could tolerate. Without any effort and without any consciousness, we got FILLED.

Then the birthing happens and everything changes. Now we're out and it feels as though our skin has been peeled off. Everything is raw, and new, and strange. Worse, we have to experience discomfort and find a way to voice our concerns. Feeding is no longer automatic. We have to ask for what we want. Then, worse yet, we have to wait an interminable amount of time from our first wail of hunger to the moment when Mom rushes over to feed us. "WHAT TOOK YOU SO LONG!" we'd scream, if we could. Facing this emptiness between self and environment, experiencing otherness rather than wombness, is so traumatic that many of us try to re-create that womb through our lives. We seek what anthropologist and philosopher Ashley Montague called, "a womb with a view." We search for nurturance without risk. Food provided all that. In food we could feel mostly merged, saved from separateness.

As adults we're searching for the same thing in relationships, either with food or folks with umbilical cord in hand. Whether we seek love with lovers, in the marketplace, or with women friends we love like old high school buddies, we hunger for that merged attachment. Only food can get that close. In a sense

compulsive eating is a suicidal wish for oneness again. That oneness existed in the womb. How we enjoyed that warm, dark, private, growing place. We could be true to ourselves and to life.
Now, merger is not an option. We must learn to live separate,
but still somehow involved. Who knows how?

To Separate or Not to Separate

Throughout feminist literature and the psychology of
women, a great deal has been written to support the theory that
women seek affiliation and bonding, while men seek to separate
and leave. In the work of Carol Gilligan at Harvard, and Judith
Jordan and others at the Stone Center at Wellesley, a powerful
case is made for women's need for affiliation. Jean Baker Miller
at Harvard has called for a "new psychology of women." Much
of this literature shows us that women think a lot about relationships, that we're the considerate, nuturing bonded ones.

Carol Gilligan and Lyn Mikel Brown studied the development of young girls. They noted that, by the age of eight, girls
show definite signs of separation and the development of dominant identities. But by age twelve the same girls had learned to
adapt, to compromise, to keep their mouths shut. They learned
to swallow their identities, to make no waves. They became
adaptive—at exactly the time they needed to become more assertive.[1]

Emily Hancock, in her superb book *The Girl Within*, gives
voice to very perceptive women who speak of having a strong
sense of themselves until the age of nine when they then gave it
all up. Many only reclaimed that awareness of who they were
through some tragedy or crisis, when they had to call on long-
forgotten resources. As the literature points out, this early adolescent period was when they were moving toward separation.

[1]In ancient Greece, little girls around the ages of eight or nine went to live as
acolytes in the temple of Artemis. Their service was to Artemis as "The Lady
of the Beasts," "The Wild Mother," and the little girls (just about the right age
for the Girl Scouts today) were called her "Bear Cubs." They remained in the
temple until puberty, when they returned to their fathers' houses to be married off. But for three or four years, they were able to grow up, leave home,
and seek their own true selves, their wild selves. In serving the goddess, they
were trained to listen for her messages, to develop and respect their Inner
Voices.

In our society, instead of individuating and moving away from Mom and home, girls became compliant. Boys were encouraged early on to separate from Mom. Because of this they would always see themselves as different and separate from their primary love object.

Many of those who are proposing a new "psychology of women" make the case that girls WANT that greater attachment and focus on relationships. They tell us that boys want separation, but that girls really don't. It is worth questioning how much of this is naturally true for girls, and how much is programmed by cultural conditioning. In our last chapters, you will read stories of women with eating disorders who had to admit to themselves and others that they really didn't desire or seek out relationships as much as the culture had programmed them to. They really preferred to be alone. Their food consumption lessened when they were alone.

What all this means is that it may be time for all of us to reexamine the almost kneejerk way in which we have made relationships "women's work." Just because we did it this way doesn't mean we wanted it this way. The assumption was that since girls focused on bonding and relationships, that we were the "nicer" people, who wanted closeness. Maybe.

In all my work with addicted women, I can tell you that they suffer and struggle when trying to give equal time to the side of themselves that chooses apartness, that wants to be alone, nonattached. Once they give themselves permission to honor this in themselves, they find that they no longer fear being alone. Quite the contrary, they cherish it. They're surprised to discover that they're more like "the boys" than they've ever been allowed to think. By the end of this book, you will see the value of being alone, by yourself, free. You won't have to use drugs to do it, and you won't have to psychologically kill off your mother to do it. You will discover how useful your mentors are in helping you birth yourself into a sweet, separated place of choice.

Object Again

Our first experience of feeling like an object centered around food. It was at the breast or in the high chair that feedings became a separation event. Eventually, the infant and the mom develop awareness of their separateness. The infant expe-

riences separation as food is PUT INTO her. What had once
been an organic ebb and flow now becomes a penetration as
boundaries are crossed. The baby learns there is ME and
OTHER. Sometimes the feeding rituals are fraught with fear, as
Mom panics that she won't have enough milk, or that her
daughter will refuse to accept nurturance from her. For many
moms, self-doubt and the power struggles that spiral around
their fears will continue for decades to come. The daughter's
acceptance or rejection of Mom gets fought out in the plate.

Many first notice this problem as they attend seminars
where, using the "Dignity Dine" video, I instruct them in feeding each other and then feeding themselves. They finally see
and consciously experience the boundary problems they didn't
negotiate with Mom. Many have no awareness of these boundary
struggles until, as adults, they discover they have sexual problems related to entry. The same relationship problems coincide
with being overly adaptive and too focused on other people's
needs and wants. It all began at the breast and spoon.

Those of us with eating disorders are nursing personalities
that are outer-directed and overly adaptive. We remain very
finely and exquisitely attuned to others' needs and wants—but
not our own. In natural development, healthy infants experiment with separateness and attempt to individuate. They get
into food fights with their feeders, usually moms.

When Dr. Hilde Bruch, an early researcher in eating disorders, interviewed mothers about the early eating patterns of
their later obese daughters, mothers reported feeding episodes
as "uneventful." All of the wrenching apart and negotiation
went unnoticed by the mothers. This may have been due to a
lack of sensitivity on the part of the mothers, or to an extremely
adaptive, compliant infant. Some of these babies were so adaptive, so sensitized to their mothers' needs that they moved toward
conformity and compliance, rather than fight through the pain
of separation.

Is that you? Have you carried this compliance into your adult
life? If you're rebellious, you're still just as connected as if you
were obedient. Substance or activity abuse might have helped
for a while. It kept you unaware that you weren't truly living
your own life. Maybe you were living Mom's life, or maybe you
and she were in a mutual suicide pact to avoid facing real life at

all. But now you will have to face reality and cut the ties or turn back to the sauce a few thousand more times.

Leaving Mom—The Personal Power Struggle

Leaving Mom is worse than going through a major divorce. A divorce may represent the ending of a relationship you've had for a quarter of your life, or even half your life. But leaving Mom is a relationship you've had ALL your life. In that respect, it's harder on the daughters because it involves your whole life. Mom had a life before you. You didn't have one before her.

If both you and your mom each have a sponsor or mentor for support, the road will be a little less bumpy. I now invite both of you to take a look at how this food obsession has kept you together, but prevented you from thriving.

This is not just a struggle to separate from Mom and her needs, but to separate from all the messages you got about disowning your power and avoiding your own voice. You came into this life fully conscious of your true SELF, your inner wisdom— what Emily Hancock calls "the girl within." At age nine, you probably lost that purposeful, initiating, choice maker and became what your culture demanded of you. In getting civilized, much of your sense of who you really are got buried. Unfortunately, since moms are given the major civilizing function, they get most of the blame for this. In less "civilized" cultures, a mother's job is to help us find the soul. Western culture convinces us to lose it. The arguments between mothers and daughters are life and death struggles for the survival of the Self.

For both mother and child, the conflict is about taking in and owning power. Maybe you both have to tell the world some things about nurturance and vulnerability. Did your mother encourage you to eat, or not to eat? This is the great issue between mothers and daughters. It determines what you eat, but more importantly, *how* you eat. Many of us find that we have rarely been encouraged to get nurturance and filling. More often we've been trained in deprivation. Were you encouraged to take in, to savor, to wallow in pleasure, to get your needs met? If not, you learned to eat with guilt.

You also learn to LIVE with guilt. Guilt, so that you wouldn't have too much effect on others. You had to keep ever vigilant to avoid being too powerful and possibly destructive. You were taught to limit energy, like tying up a bull.

Years ago I took my dear Aunt Hope to a bullfight in Tijuana, Mexico. I had to leave. It wasn't the killing that sickened me. It was the teasing. The bull was such a noble creature, full of such potential power and grace. To get the bull raging, men had to poke and jab with swords and noisemakers. They finally got the bull to fight, and then felt triumphant in the killing.

How many fat, powerful women are teased the same way? This juxtaposition of energies—getting us to fight, encouraging us to die—is the battle fought to live our own fulfilled lives, a battle our mothers disowned and passed on to us.

In recovery you will need to get very comfortable with your own power. You will need to learn to trust it, to celebrate it, and never to sell it—or yourself—short. You must be true to yourself. If not, you'll eat. In the process, you'll probably have to walk away from a lot of what Momma said. To recover, you must walk into life on life's terms, with the umbilical cord truly severed.

You were born eager and reaching out to life. But life's disappointments, yours or Mom's, shaved most of that away. Mom socialized you to see the world as she saw it, very likely with a depressive, pained lens. You were told to adapt and conform to your mother's life. With your super-sensitivity you may have been much more compliant and adaptive than most. Most studies of women's attitudes about themselves show that whenever we make a move to take care of ourselves, we label that SELFISH. Our mothers taught us that it's deadly to be seen as self-involved.

ASK YOURSELF:

◻ *How did your mother take care of herself?*

Nurturing the Self

The idea of being there for others, of anticipating the needs of others, of doing for them and not for one's self has been known in our culture as "women's work." Mothers teach their daughters to serve the same way they have served. In addiction literature much of this conditioning is labeled "codependency": attention paid to others in avoidance of self.

To give up food abuse, this behavior must change. Take some time now to consult your Inner Self about what you need to say to yourself to stop paying DISPROPORTIONATE attention to the needs of others. Think of yourself as a beast of burden and now is the time to take off the yoke.

■

EXERCISE 1

LETTER OF RESIGNATION

Pick up your journal. It's time to write a letter of resignation. You're officially quitting your job as Mother of the Universe! This is your chance to lay down your burden of excessive concern for others. This is not a personal letter— it's directed to society at large.

1. Write about the number of times in the past week that you've let others' needs come before your own. Include family, work, friends, strangers, children, pets, church, community organizations, et cetera.
2. How has this all-consuming focus on others kept you from getting to know your real SELF?
3. How have you paid the bill for self-neglect with FOOD?
4. Now it's time to write your letter of resignation. Spell out what you're sick and tired of, and what you refuse to do anymore.

Joanne wrote her resignation both to her stepmother Winny and her daughter Brandy, declaring she was done, finished, gone home:

I QUIT!

I'm tired of trying to make you understand. And I'm tired of trying to do it all right. It's over. The whole damn thing is over. I'm sorry, Mom, if you wanted me sweeter, more polite, folding napkins correctly, wearing the right set of pearls. These things have NEVER been important to me. I've been trying to satisfy your ego needs by playing out the role of "good daughter." But who were we dancing for? YOUR mother? Who cares? I want to live MY life. I want to wear white shoes after Labor Day, and I will from now on. Just because I wanna!

And I don't want to hear one more damn thing about your problems with Dad. If he won't fix the toilet, then hire a damn plumber and stop complaining to me. I really don't care. I can't advise you or fix it. I think you want to continue this power struggle with him. Well, enjoy it, but leave me out. I'm done.

I guess you think I should keep feigning concern. Well I won't because I really don't care.

Boy, I love how this sounds. DON'T CARE! DON'T CARE! DON'T CARE! I could make this my mantra if it didn't sound so naughty.

What's wrong with it being my mantra? It's the truth, isn't it? Why have I been wasting so much of my own precious time listening to people who don't want to change complain about their lives? Why should I invest so much concern and caring when they don't? This has really been depleting me. No wonder I stuff my face to try to fill up again.

From now on, I'm going to associate myself with people who do want to face their lives. People who want to grow up and change. I want to see progress and results, not this endless trickle of whining and complaining. It hurts me to hear you. Take it to your own sponsor, or a therapist, or anyone you like. Just not me. I'm done.

And the same goes for you, Brandy. Just like you always scream that you wish you had another mother, well I don't know how readily I signed on for this mother job myself. It was a lot messier than I thought it would be. I thought I'd get a lot more appreciation. I thought my efforts would be rewarded. I thought you would understand. Yeah, yeah, I know you don't owe me anything, but I finally see that I don't owe you EITHER. The ledger is clear. I've done enough and I am enough!

You may expect me to bail you out financially, but that's stopping right now. Times are hard for us all, and you'll survive. I also expect my needs to be considered when you're making dates with me. I won't wait while you're late, because you're so damn "busy." I also won't be available every time you drop in unexpectedly. And another thing, I don't want to hear about the latest new crisis in your life. You can manufacture them on cue, and there's always SOMETHING. I'm worn out. Like the wall plaque at work says: YOU MUST UNDERSTAND THAT FAILURE TO PLAN ON YOUR PART DOES NOT CONSTITUTE A CRISIS ON MINE.

From now on I'm going to walk a little softer, with less chaos in my life from day to day. I'm going to surround myself with others who show me respect, and quiet, and consideration. When YOU can do that, give me a CALL and we'll make a date. No more unexpected drop-ins and pleas for crisis intervention. You can take that to an AA clubhouse, local church or synagogue, or even a crisis mental health clinic. This one has closed her doors! Whew! Thanks. I needed that!

Joanne didn't realize how easily this would flow. She was shocked at what she wrote. She didn't expect what came out. At first, she felt guilty and thought we'd forced her. Later she realized that she had simply been given direction, permission, a pen in hand, and a few quiet minutes alone. It was all there waiting to be tapped. We all carry within us the keys to our own liberation and salvation. The treasure we unlock will be recovery from compulsive eating or starving.

———

EXERCISE 2

PROCLAMATION OF SELF-SERVING

Make a sign and pin to your chest the words:

SELF-SERVING

1. Now march around the house for a while sticking out your chest.
2. Look at yourself in the mirror. How does it feel to proclaim to the world that you can be self-serving?
3. The time has now come for you to be SELF-SERVING. Do those words create conflict within you? Why? How?
4. If you were being self-serving, what would you be doing for yourself? How would that feel?
5. If not you, who would serve you?
6. Now, complete the following proclamation:

    I, _____, on the _____ day of _____, in

the year 19__, do officially resign from my lifelong role of servant to others and Mother of the Universe. I declare that from this day forward I will courageously serve myself FIRST. I will use the word *"NO"* as a complete sentence. I will not apologize for attending to my needs. I will not lie about the fact that I have needs. And I will _____

_____

_____

ME
SELF-SERVER

Denying Your Own Counsel

Rabbi Hillel asked, "If I am not for myself, who will be? If I am only for myself, what am I? If not now, when?"

When did you stop taking time to listen to yourself? When did you walk away from your own internal home? Once you've accomplished this "swearing off," you will need to take active steps for safety without abusing food. Make use of your illness here. Your disordered eating now requires that you MUST take care of yourself. For pure survival, you must become more self-involved; you must become what others might label "selfish." This is why you're resigning from the job of helping others. It is your call to arms to a more personal inner battle. You have to get your food and your own life in order now. You have to be courageous enough to get to know and listen to your inner self.

Let your inner self know that you want to come home to take care of her. Tell her that you want to be aware of her needs and stop diverting yourself into others' lives. Let her know that you want to be aware. You don't have to know yet what awareness you're avoiding. Just write this as an affirmation about your intentions. Remember, INTENTIONS COUNT. You probably gave up this listening to yourself long before you were aware of what you were doing.

When in your life did you approach awareness and then sedate it? That's when you abandoned your *inner self*. This is when YOU left—not when others left you. For those of us with eating disorders, that awareness was present and was sublimated very early. Perhaps we were more precocious than most. After more than two decades treating addicts, I can attest that nearly all report some major awakening, insight, or traumatic event around age five.

When we ask patients to report their earliest memories, they will usually scroll back to events when they were five years old. Some remember incidents between parents, an argument, a coldness. Others remember something that happened to them while playing with a friend, eating a cookie, getting a spanking, sneaking out to pull down panties (for boys). These are very momentous events.

What happened when you were five? Whatever the event— getting beaten, watching parents fight, sexual molestation, verbal abuse, parents ignoring you—it seems that around age five, WE become more consciously aware. When we report what happened, we are reporting "otherness." Remember—the-alone-but-not-lonely feeling you had when you were able as a child to play alone and make up the world?

CAN I GET A WITNESS? By age eight, you were totally gone. Before you left your five-year-old self, you were getting very clear about feeling separate, individual, unique. You had clarity that YOU exist as an independent being, part of the world, but separated. With helpful mentors, that could have been the seed for future blossoms. Instead, most of us were cautioned to become more adaptive. It could have been a time when you liked to walk alone in the woods, ride your bike for hours, minister to your fish tank, read, read, read.

But without encouragement and support, many find this a terrifying time. We sense the aloneness, but have no training to appreciate it. The next few years are spent trying to maintain a sense of clarity and security in our aloneness while well-meaning adults insistently intrude.

I use the word "intrude" because as much as the involvement is meant for our own good, there is little encouragement for you to quietly develop yourself. Somehow, others, mainly mothers, have a need to help you. But you didn't need help—you needed to be left alone. The more you assert your independence, the more they interfere. You don't need their interference. You simply need their attention. If you could, you'd sing along with Marvin Gaye: "Can I get a witness?"

Most of us needed a lot less from parents than popular psychology would lead us to believe. If anything, moms are trying too hard. They didn't learn to let go. I have seen many patients in treatment who, despite being sorely neglected, even sometimes abused by parents, managed to develop a very strong and dominant sense of self. I've also seen many who were well cared for, even indulged, end up confused and ambivalent about who they are and who they want to be. They never had to fight to find out. Theirs were the truly "deprived" childhoods.

Now that I've developed a training center for addictions and family counseling, I find that counselors need the same directions as mothers. I encourage them all to stop working so hard. When staff at my treatment centers have a problem with patients, it usually stems from trying too hard, because they like the patient too much. But the patient is sitting back and judging rather than investing.

As a child, you needed a witness—someone willing to listen and to acknowledge your personal truth. Basically, that's what therapists do. And that's what Twelve-Step sponsors do. And that is what mothers who can let go and detach do. Even if they disagree with your solutions or decisions, they will acknowledge that you are responding to something real. They won't say you made it up. Many mothers try to help their offspring deny reality. But no one is asking them for judgments. They're just being asked to watch. Witnesses don't evaluate.

A little girl is learning to ride a bike. She exclaims with glee, "Mommy, watch me ride!" She's asking for a witness, nothing more. Mom watches, feels proud and happy, then reverts to her own inadequacies. "What do I say or do now?" she asks herself. Could it be that words aren't what's needed—that no one needs her to say anything? Maybe her job is just to be a warm body smiling, witnessing, being happy. But Mom never learned that could be enough or that SHE's enough.

In this culture, mothers are rarely encouraged to realize that they've done enough or that they ARE enough. In early psychological theory they were more often blamed than appreciated. They were accused of causing maladies, labeled the "schizophrenogenic mother." Later writers lightened up a bit, theorizing that we all needed "good enough" mothering. Every mother felt her's wasn't "good enough." So here you are, a mom, loaded down with inadequacy, plus your mother's directives, plus your own vows to be a "better mother" than your mother. And you take this all out to the playground with Janie. Instead of having your own joyful experience with your little girl, you're busy healing your own sense of inadequacy.

You resort to what you learned from your mom. "Good job, Janie," you call out. "You sure are a good bike rider. We'll need to see a lot more of that from you." You mean well, but it's deadly. Now Janie is mixing in performance expectations, requests to duplicate her past efforts, demands for more output, and of course internalizing your ever critical comparative eye.

It was a moment of joy! Can't we enjoy without comment? Can't you just BE there? Wouldn't that be enough? In joyous times, very little needs to be said. The smile says it all. Janie is so ecstatic anyway, she's just trying to share the gift of herself with her mom. "Watch me, Mommy." Janie just wants a witness. At that moment she doesn't need a thing from you or anyone else. Your role as Mom is to share in the celebration, claiming no credit or victory; making no comment. Can you weather that loneliness, letting Janie have her own experience?

This is difficult to explain unless you've lived it. Yes, we all do well with stroking and approval. However, what the daughter may actually become finely sensitized to is whether you're being honest about "whose actual needs are getting met"? On the surface, this scene seems idyllic and psychologically and emotionally correct. But you may be telling me, "Give Mom a break here. I'd love to have had an adoring, observant mommy giving me compliments, and oohs and aahs. What's the bitch here? Can't moms do anything right?"

This is exactly what happens to patients in treatment when they try to tease out what didn't quite work for them in the nurturing area. Those who had ostensibly adoring and perfect mothers are the very patients who have the most difficulty getting heard. The daughter of an outrageous and abusive mother has it much easier here.

If the patient is reporting her pain at Mom's caring, I have to believe that even though the behavior seems correct, it DIDN'T FIT for that daughter. That's not necessarily Mom's fault, but usually the intuitive daughter is picking up the mother's selfishness and self-concern, though the mother can't openly and honestly admit, "I want to treat you well so that I will LOOK like a good mother." There isn't a single thing wrong with such a position, if only the mother can say it honestly. The wise daughter picks up the mixed messages, and rebels against her mother's disowned selfish self. All would be so much easier if both mother and daughter could announce their own self-interests. But it's never been allowed. You will hear later about a mother who was able to tell her daughter she was playing "good mother" for her own sake. It was healing for all!

Even appreciative comments like, "Oh, you're such a good girl, so kind and thoughtful," can be condescending and controlling. What the daughter needs at this point is to learn joy in the celebration of her own gifts and delight in HER OWN EXPERIENCE. She only needs a witness, someone there to observe the experience. Mom is there to show that she's affected, that she's allowing her daughter to penetrate her. If Mom is truly joyous, her daughter will know it. It will sparkle in her eyes.

Those sparkling, witnessing eyes can heal whatever ails ya. Try to remember times when you got that witnessing. Remember that age five is important. Can you recall a difficult moment in your life when Mom was there with no judgment, no performance expectations, and no anxiety? I have a personal memory that is very simple, undramatic, and even boring for some. For me, each time I recall it brings tears to my eyes.

It was when I was five. I couldn't learn to read. I went to school every day and sweated, flashed hot and cold, got diarrhea, and trembled in fear that I'd be called on. I can still feel the heat in my body as I heard other students recite lines like "See Dick, Jane, and Spot run." I was amazed; I couldn't understand how they looked at those shapes on the page, and then those words came out and the teacher nodded. There was some magic formula, some secret code I couldn't decipher. I came home from school every day panicked. I so much wanted to learn to read. I had already memorized the Peter Rabbit story just listening to my mother read it to me so many times. The world of books was beckoning, but I couldn't find the key to its lock. I finally confessed to my mother the tragedy of this dilemma, that I was deficient in some way, that I just could not learn to read. She listened to my full story, all the heartache, fear, terror, humiliation, helplessness. Then she very quietly answered, "Oh, don't worry. You'll learn."

More important than learning to read was the other messages my mom's simple, nonworried, confident response gave me. Her simple instruction echoed the words of the grand-mother in the sweat lodge outside Santa Fe—a simple message to let go, wait, relax, let life happen. It helped me develop an ap-preciation for life's struggles, that some things would be difficult to attain, but worth the effort. I gained a sense of timing: tena-ciously sticking to a difficult project, and awaiting results. I also was subtly imbued with a strong sense of personal confidence. She never doubted my abilities. She trusted herself, so she trusted me. Mom's eyes knew I could do it. I DID!

ASK YOURSELF:

- Would your mother feel she is a "good enough mother"?
- How did she try to prove herself?
- Did you think she was a good mother? Why or why not?

Your Truth Is Your Truth

The stories of Janie on the bike and Judi with the book can be interpreted many ways. Some would say Janie's mom was per-fect and Janie is just "too sensitive." Some might say my moth-er's simple confidence was too haphazard and uninvolved, that she didn't worry about me enough.

It doesn't matter what anyone says, and it really doesn't even matter what "reality" is. What matters is how Janie and Judi EX-PERIENCE the situation. What matters is how YOU saw your childhood and your mother and your moments of truth. The *truth* about your life is within you. That is the truth that you are living today, or avoiding today. Reality has nothing to do with it. This is not a court of law, and no Perry Mason is needed. Your work is to stay abstinent, so you can trust your instincts and trust the messages from your own body. Your abstinent body will sig-nal your own truth. As we'll see, it was when that body started growing into a woman that you began to tell your own self some of your greatest lies.

ADOLESCENCE: RAGING AT WOMANHOOD

In adolescence you become aware that often Mom is there for you, but not for herself. You pick up her self-abandonment. You get a strange inkling that this is a woman's lot and you may not like it. As you grow out of childhood and you start to become more like Mom, you become very conscious of her sadness. You could avoid it until you start growing into that woman's body. Disordered eating often flowers in adolescence as daughters watch themselves growing into women. Many are railing at Mom for the "curse" of being born female. They don't see positive prospects for growing into womanhood. They've been taught for so long to devalue the feminine that, rather than seeking guidance from Mom, they sometimes reject and judge her.

The "Curse"

Your worst fear is that you'll grow into that demon female body which has to be shaved, sanitized, limited, and kept in check. You were never taught to celebrate womanhood.

Take the case of Sarah, whose story is not unlike many modern women's. Sarah first learned about menstruation by finding her mother's bloody Kotex on the bathroom floor. She had no reason to believe it was blood, since it was darkish brown, almost black. She brought it to her mother, who, embarrassed, shooed her away. Mom was enraged at this "curse," and so rebelled by staying dirty, keeping secretive, leaving telltale hostile tokens around the house. She never learned to express her anger openly, so she just took to bed for six days during every episode.

Sarah woke up at age twelve with blood running down her leg, so Mom was forced to explain the dirty doings. Sarah only felt revulsion and a firm resolve never to end up like Mom. There was the stench, the bother, the inconvenience of it. Mom explained, all the while complaining that this was something women had to go through. She cautioned Sarah that she'd better just accept it. Her own bedridden behavior, however, signaled her rebellion. Everyone knew how she suffered.

Sarah vowed she'd never allow herself to feel a menstrual cramp. Whenever there were rumblings from her abdomen, she ATE her way through every month's discomfort. For each month of her senior year in high school she stuffed herself all through her period, then dieted diligently getting ready for the senior prom. Unfortunately, she went to the prom fat. That's when she decided, "Enough of this! I'll starve."

College started with her anorexic phase. Anorexia suited Sarah well, as it allowed fastidious attention to detail as well as cleanliness. She had vowed from her first period that she'd never let anyone know, never let anyone smell, never let any trace of that animal ooze escape her. She was quite successful, keeping eternally vigilant, sniffing herself, checking pads, withdrawing into bed with sweatsuits and ice cream. These outbursts were "medicinal," staving off those cramps she wouldn't let herself feel. That would be too gross, too failing, too like Mom. Finally her periods ended completely. O happy day! She could feel pure as driven snow, free of secretions, mucus, anything animal or alive. It was a vague death wish, a wish for ascension to purity, rising above the animal. She hated how much she was like her mother. Thank God she'd finally exorcised her!

As Sarah floated into our hospital, she felt sure everyone knew she was pure and didn't menstruate. Like many other anorexics, she tried to be like an angel to leave the planet, leave the body, leave Mom. Her recovery work involved gaining weight, getting grounded in the body, and eventually making friends with Mom and menstruation. Because many daughters blame their mothers for birthing them female, they project their self-hate onto Mom. Any attempt at intimacy on the mother's part can produce tremendous rage from the daughter who is embarrassed by her.

Wendy could never forgive her mother the grossness of her mother's body. Here is what Wendy wrote and later read in group:

"I remember she tried to tell me about starting my period and I stormed out of the room. How dare she tell me anything. She was gross and I hated her. I told her nothing about myself. I never wanted her to know things about me.

"I remember the night I started my period I was really pissed because I couldn't figure out what to do and I finally had to tell her. I was crying, mostly because I needed her help. She said she was glad because it meant I was growing up. Oh, how touching. I never asked for her help again. I remember how gross she was with her period stuff. She left it laying around in the bathroom and it smelled so bad. How could she be so gross? She didn't shave her legs or under her arms or wear makeup, and her hair looked like shit. When she did wear makeup it was the wrong color and gross and she always, always had sweat running down her face. I hated her.

"One time she started her period and bled all over her dress. I saw it and wanted to tell her, yet I was so embarrassed. As she walked away I felt vaguely guilty but only for a fleeting second. Mostly I didn't care. Later she asked me about it and I told her I hadn't seen it. I didn't care that I lied to her.

"I never felt like my mother was a female. I didn't care that she was embarrassed. I hate when I feel any compassion for her. I do remember one time when my dad left to go fishing and she didn't want him to go and she cried. I felt sorry for her, I was about ten. I think we ate hamburgers together and it was all okay."

After reading this to others, Wendy cried for three days. She felt great regret that instead of compassionately allying with her mother's pain, she had instead absorbed it and hit out at her mom. It's often easier for daughters to stay raging than to really face the pain of their mothers' lives. Wendy's tears were both for her mother and herself. She regretted how much she'd not "been there" for her mom, and also how Mom had not "been there" for her. There had been such possibilities for closeness, for sharing common experiences and sensitivity. But instead of uniting, these women became adversaries.

Wendy actually disliked most women, preferring the company of men. She had many men friends, but had great sexual difficulties trusting men, or celebrating her body around men. She was so embarrassed about every part of her that was powerful and female.

Wendy had come to treatment and was already quite aware of her personal dynamics in this area. She explained it all to us quite well. She needed to take some action to begin re-owning her own feminine side. She had to see her feminine aspects as not negative and dark, but as joyous and filled with light.

As her period approached, Wendy agreed she would use pads instead of tampons. We wanted her to see and EXPERI-ENCE the flow of her own juices. In our new age of greater efficiency and absorbency, it was difficult to find a pad that would actually let her SEE the blood. Most were made to quickly absorb any traces.

Wendy came to group walking taller the next day. It was as though she'd learned a great secret, that she was somehow in touch with nature in a way that was different from everyone else. She almost resented another group member who was also menstruating at the time. At first she was sheepish, and then critical, about what was going on in her body. "I'd rather NEVER have to go through this mess. I don't see what all the fuss is about menopause. I can't wait."

But as other patients talked about their "secret" that only other women know about, Wendy began to cry. She recalled all the abuse she'd hurled at her mother for "smelling," even for living. Other women in the group shared stories about the pains and joys of childbirth too, and how that again duplicated their mothers' experience. Their common experience was that mothers warned them about the pains of being women, but rarely celebrated the joys.

It would take further work with mentors for each of them to make best friends with their bodies. Many had found loving men who were very helpful with this experience. There are many men who love a fleshy woman. There are many men who like the smell of women. There are men who like intercourse with menstruating women. All those men were lovely for our patients. The greatest healing, however, is to be in the presence of other women who are celebrating the flow of these juices.

It's so important in this kind of treatment that we have six weeks to work with women. Because women are different at different times of their cycle, we like to work with them through one full cycle and then have a few days to discuss the experience. Unfortunately, the health care system wants them diagnosed and then treated consistently each day. This is almost impossible, not to say unnatural.

Finding a New Lover—Yourself!

Wendy's rejection of her womanly juices was a part of rejecting her womanly wisdom and thus in effect her womanly voice. She saw her mother's voice being lost to the demands of fishing trips or whatever her dad found more important. And after enough years watching that model, she lost her own voice as well. She didn't even allow herself to get to know women better, suspecting them, judging them, leaving them as she'd left her own mother. Wendy really had nothing to say. She starved trying to diminish herself.

When we eat or starve to excess, we are muting our inner voice. We don't want to know what we know or see what we see. Now, why would anyone want to stay blind? Why keep struggling so hard not to hear? Why continue to seek out a substance that seems to be the bane of your existence? Are you crazy?

No, you're not crazy. You're just in love. You've refused to attend to yourself, often because you were busy focusing on your mother's pain. Food became a substitute lover to replace legitimate self-love. You didn't know how to love yourself when you saw your mother hurting, so you shut up your own inner voice. Now you're in love with a lost part of yourself you know you need to find.

That attachment to Mom's pain is similar to your obsession with food. Both are love affairs that have outlasted their usefulness. They have to be treated like any other love affair gone sour. Even though it's not working out, there will still be a terrible wrenching and longing when you really break up. That breakup with food will precipitate breaking your attachment to your mother's pain. But instead of hanging on tenaciously, when you detach from food and Mom, you'll be available for a whole new way of loving and a whole new lover—yourself. You'll learn to truly listen.

When we want to stay in any love affair gone sour, we remember only the good times. That holds true for a handsome devil or a piece of cake. We want to deny what we really know—how we're killing ourselves, killing our body; even more importantly, killing our Soul. Compulsive people DO listen to medical warnings. We're not deaf. You may even believe, "Yes, it WILL happen to me." However, when the compulsive urge comes in, all reason goes out the window. The rationale is "This time will be different." It's like going to bed with an ex-husband.

We also want to believe we have all the time in the world and won't have to do what is put in front of us. *At least not yet, anyway.* But when orderly eating becomes your primary agenda, you will have to attend to whatever is put in front of you, and pronto! You developed a love affair with food because it did great things for you. So did your love affair with Mom. Both relationships helped you make it through a half life.

Passing the Spear

You express your mom's unspoken fear. This fear is about a world changing too quickly, with new roles for women. We all have inadequate training. In a way, you've been engaged in and victimized by Mom's difficulties with this. Your recovery will involve leaving her to fight her own battles. By staying emotionally joined at the hip, you're helping your mom's wounds remain unhealed. Daughters too often serve as therapist, confidante, dumping ground, and salve for Mom's pain. With those jobs filled, Mom never really has to do anything about changing her situation. When Mom and Daughter stay close, Dad (or other men) stays safely distant. Many complain, not much transpires. Someone eventually dies of obesity, but we blame it on the food. Mom has made her daughter her best friend. Consequently, Dad is triangled out, abandoned, related to as an object of scorn.

Mom doesn't tell her daughter the advantages she gets from staying in the relationship. Instead, she sets the daughter to battling the father, protecting her from her own work. And yet, on a spiritual level, Mom chose this mate to do this work. Now she's copped out and handed her battles over to her daughter.

In family groups we have to practically bind and gag the daughters to keep them from attacking Dad on Mom's behalf. Typically, as we ask Daughter to mind her own business, Mom pipes up with "Let her speak. She sees how mean he is to me."

I'll usually counter with "Perhaps that's true, but it isn't HER job to tell him. It's YOUR job to fight him." I then get up and walk over, handing her a symbolic spear. "Here, get to work."

She'll answer, "Hell, no. I've given up on him!"

This is when I look her straight in the eye and tell her: "If you've given up on him, then get rid of him." I state it so graphically it hurts! "Stop sleeping with dead bodies. No necrophilia here!"

Mom and the group will look at me stunned, but the message is clear. After a short silence, I drive it further home. "Even if you've given up, your daughter's life is at stake! You've got to do your job or refuse your job; but you can't afford to sit on the fence any longer. You married him, you deal with him."

By then you can hear a pin drop. Every mother in the room knows she's played this out to some degree. All have tried to avoid the fight with various compromises and accommodations. All are sitting in that very room because their daughters in some way have been forced to the front lines. They sat back, as generals in a distant command post, fueling the front line mortars, but relatively safe, secure, and often fat.

As long as a daughter continues to see herself as Mom's sole protector and helpmate, she won't set about her own work of emotionally growing up and leaving home. Mother and daughter are allied in anger and resentment, which passes for love and closeness. Dad as the enemy keeps these two united at the hip. Daughters, rather than flowering, are staying home emotionally, festering and rotting on the vine.

Our moms often teach "how rotten men are." They're teaching about their own anger and disappointment. Worse, they're shunting it into their daughters in a way that may appear protective, but is really irresponsible. It's Mom's unfinished business and should not involve the daughter.

You see, if Mom takes care of business, gets her life and love in order, then Daughter can safely and securely leave home. She can feel she's done her job. She will grow up, leave home, and find her own guy to fight.

ASK YOURSELF:

- ☐ *Did you ever act as a stand-in or referee in your mother's fights with your father? How did it make you feel?*
- ☐ *What did you learn about power in relationships?*
- ☐ *How has that affected your current relations with men?*

Healing the Present

Some mothers are on a blame hunt against Dad, but there are other mothers who totally ignore and excuse Dad's truly inappropriate violations of daughters. Neither case is simple; the bottom line is finding how the information can be used to heal the present. It's not about the past; rather, it's about healing the present and future.

Take Mary, who actually had been sexually abused by her father. Her mother was fearful that Mary would tell the truth in treatment. SHE DID! Mom showed up drunk, banging on the doors, insisting that Mary was a liar. She kept screaming, "Mary has nothing to say." Mary, shy and reclusive, had until then lived out her mother's dictum. Our work in recovery was to help Mary acknowledge what had actually happened to her, and to acknowledge her anger at her mother. *We helped her find her voice.*

Mary's early violation was actually a double-edged sword, as it made her very aware and more perceptive than most. She judged others and herself quite unmercifully. She was hypervigilant and uncanny in her evaluations of others— especially our staff. She was a difficult patient to treat because she spent much of her time outer-directed. In most cases, her scathing and incisive criticisms of staff and other patients were correct, but in focusing so much on others she had failed to develop any true insights into herself. That same rapier sword of judgment she used on others she used on herself. All of this made it hard for Mary to go public.

Many of our patients suffer this fear of coming out, and allowing themselves to be seen, to be vulnerable. This is another reason we strongly recommend attendance at OA meetings. The meetings offer a gentle invitation to come out. As others talk honestly about themselves, our patients become less self-judging and sometimes take the risk to speak and be seen.

Mary was especially fearful of speaking at OA meetings. Our staff gave Mary a definite prescription: "Speak up at a meeting." It wouldn't matter what she said, just that she came out. That SPEAKING was a necessary part of her recovery. It was even more important than recounting the sins of her father or her mother!

Mary argued back, "The anxiety of speaking with people gives me a great excuse to eat. I'm scared to death of other people knowing anything about me." What Mary learned in treatment is that we walk through our fears. We acknowledge our fears, but proceed anyway.

Even though Mary has countless issues to address about her incestuous father and her drunken mother, what she actually CAN CHANGE today is her own ability to come out. She will test that and practice by speaking at OA meetings. This is her first baby step into recovery and her most important ongoing recovery assignment. Twelve-Steppers recite the "serenity prayer," asking for the power to change the things they CAN, and the wisdom to know the difference. In this case therapy teams or sponsors serve the purpose of helping someone like Mary see what she CAN do about healing her present. It is pure and simple. She can start speaking up today, without ever investigating, blaming, or "working through" her unhappy childhood.

Each time Mary overcame her fear and spoke out at a meeting, she gained strength in the present, and thus minimized what her abusive parents had done to her. Each time she held back from talking, remained reclusive and withdrawn, she was swearing allegiance to her dysfunctional family, maintaining the status quo of the family system. It kept her the "problem child" and kept family secrets hidden. However, her childhood trauma began to take on a different perspective as she faced present ACTIONS. In speaking up, she has begun walking the road of recovery no matter what her parents do or don't do.

IT'S IN THE TIMING. When and how to emotionally leave Mom always involves a difficult negotiation. There will be times when you're ready but Mom isn't. Be careful not to expect your mother to operate on your timetable. You want her to have seen the impossible. You want her to admit she's been kidding herself, that her game isn't working. Why? Why do you want that? Why should she ever have to acknowledge to you what she sees or doesn't see about her own life? What's it to ya? Why is it important?

You've probably told yourself that if Mom could only get honest, then you could grow up and leave her. Well, you'll probably have to wait a long time for that one. Why would she want to let you go so easily? You may be enraged that she plays games because she disowns her power. But as much as you wail, wish, and try to escape, isn't there a haunting inner awareness whispering to you that you're just like your mom with a slightly shinier suit of armor?

This may be doubly difficult to hear if you're doing megadoses of therapy and raging at Mom. Many find mom-bashing easier than self-examination. You hope that you'll get to see that you didn't do it like Mom did, so why are you suffering now.

Sorry. By the time you're ready to take an honest look, it's too late to exorcise those demons. Obsession is now woven into every cell of your being and has to do with denying your power, and also an unwillingness to live up to your potential. You learned this at Mom's knee, watching her suffering on a daily basis. Mom mercifully was generally more unaware. As the daughter, picking up on Mom's pain, you've tried to overcompensate by eating or vomiting, raging at the dirty deal you both were dealt. You may even have created yourself a more miserable life, to provide further distraction for her.

Blaming and self-hate don't help. The time has come to develop compassion and understanding for yourself and your mother as well. Life is to blame. Even though Mom is ever ready to take the guilt, you need to forgive her and yourself for lost time. It is now your job to bravely stumble forward with baby steps and enter into your own, true individual life—fighting your own battles, living by your own rules.

You may have developed an eating disorder as an angry martyrlike stance, wanting to prove to Mom how much you've suffered. Since your mom's suffering was probably worse, you may fear no one will believe you.

Is this your drama? If so, unfortunately, the one who doesn't believe how much you have suffered is *YOU*. You're the one who needs convincing. You need to truly fall apart and cry—not maintaining the affectation of pain, but actually experiencing primordial personal pain. It is yours, no one else's. Carl Jung said, "Neurosis is an avoidance of legitimate suffering." The time has come for you to suffer legitimately. The best results come from slow and painful recoveries. In many ways, dying of malnutrition is less painful than facing the real pains of living.

Ask Yourself:

☐ *How is your pain identical to your mother's pain?*

☐ *How is your pain different?*

☐ *What pain do you avoid by keeping focus on the pains you know?*

As you face your own pain now, you will separate from your mother's. When you do, you'll be more motivated to ask for help from a mentor/sponsor—a more distant surrogate parent who can help you find your SELF and your separate identity.

6

SPIRITUAL MIDWIVES

*A*S YOU SEE HOW TIGHTLY YOUR PROGRAMMING KEEPS YOU STUCK IN a failing groove, you can begin to admit to yourself how much you've needed help. It's clear by now that your mother has been just as much a part of maintaining the status quo as you. You need some directions from people who have been where you are and who walked OUT of the addictive cycle. If you want to birth your SELF into your new life, then you need the help of a skilled midwife who's been there before. You don't have to do it alone.

If you're already limiting your food consumption, your body is probably crying out for your aches to go away. Not only that, but your psyche is waking up. Your spirit wants to be attended to. You need help and support. Addictions have been called "diseases of isolation," and you may actually prefer to be alone.

OPEN, TEACHABLE, AND VULNERABLE

However, keeping the food in order requires that you stay open, teachable, and most of all, vulnerable. You can't afford the luxury of anxiety-ridden isolation. You'll need to find a healthy mentor, someone who will care about your progress but stay detached enough to guide you effectively. I've found that the most readily accessible and cost-effective source of such guidance is from a "sponsor" in Overeaters Anonymous. You may choose any surrogate you like, but I strongly recommend trying the Twelve-Step route first. Choose anyone, but begin at once.

Your earliest programming kept you outer-directed, looking for how you could be of service to others. But now your Inner Voice is calling. That means you are ready to RECEIVE and be in a position where someone has something TO OFFER you. This is the scariest kind of relationship. In all your previous relationships you were the giver, the helper, the mommy developing a caseload of friends. Well, that isn't really intimate. You didn't receive as good as you gave. You were in charge. You probably felt more like a mommy than a baby.

In many OA groups, newcomers are referred to as "baby" by their sponsors. This is not to disempower or overpower the newcomer. You may have political, philosophical, and personal objections to this word, but please hold those in abeyance for a while as you read. This direction is not meant to harm or insult you. It is simply one way to reinforce the importance of being teachable so that you can RECEIVE.

Surely if you are reading this book, you are admitting that despite all your other successes in life, food still brings you to your knees. So, for this one aspect of your life, let yourself assume the vulnerability of a baby. Intuitively and spiritually your baby self is often wiser than any adult, any mommy or any sponsor. For a while it will help to be a baby, to crouch down and crawl. As a baby you'll learn how to let go and get.

ASK YOURSELF:

□ *Do you object to being regarded as a baby? Why?*
□ *What do you fear most about being a baby?*

You can start out with very basic "baby" questions. At first, those will be about your food plan. "How do I know what four ounces of protein will look like at a restaurant meal? How do I call in advance to the banquet to special-order a salad? What should I say when they insist I try the birthday cake?" These are all worthwhile questions. And they put you in your proper role of being a "seeker"—not having it all fixed and finished.

Your later questions will move from your outer periphery into your inner core. Some of the questions you'll be asking are: "How can I be sure this is the job I want? How do I know if my feelings have really been hurt by HIM, or if the real wound is from something in my past?" Above all, you'll ask your spirit, "Why am I here?" Getting your food in order inevitably leads to asking the hard questions that help you get your life in order.

Your sponsor will be very involved at first, giving specific directions for dealing with your food plan—the map of your journey. Then she'll begin to direct you inward. She'll suggest you begin to take travel notes—spend quiet time alone writing—to listen for your own INNER VOICE. She may give you writing assignments similar to those you've undertaken with this book. She may give you lists of questions to respond to. She may suggest you make some free-floating journal entry each evening. She may direct you to specific pages in AA literature that explain how to write your own inventory. Each sponsor works differently. But you can be sure that she won't suggest you do anything she hasn't done herself. Check her out on this. Ask her to verify what she's done. It's important that she has walked the path before you!

Can I Get a Witness?

It's essential that you choose someone who has suffered the same illness as you. Don't try to consult experts who haven't been there. They have a lot to offer, but not enough of what you need right now. You need to surround yourself with like-minded women. Only those who've lived through and transcended similar experiences can truly understand. Your sponsor in a Twelve-Step group can serve as a more extended family; a distant guide who offers caring, but more importantly, PERSPECTIVE. This new form of mothering offers distance, clarity, respect, and separation. It is a more healthy intimacy; as much as you can stand at the moment. It lets you "take" with no obligations. You will re-own aspects of yourself that are like your mother—the disowned baby self you threw away with the bath water. You will reclaim these for Mom's sake, and your sake.

You'll see that gaining guidance from a more distant mom, a sponsor, will help you learn about a more separated intimacy. It is a sisterhood you've sorely missed. This will feel very awkward and hard to take, but ultimately teaches you about being vulnerable and open to help, as well as being strong and responsible for yourself. Later you will see that the only relationships worth having are those that foster your own personal growth. You'll seek that in all your relationships.

The simple prescription for choosing a sponsor is, "if they have what you want and you are willing to go to any lengths to get it," then that person is for you. You might at first be attracted to someone's weight loss, her career, her clothes, her relationship with her husband, or her home. Later you might seek more spiritual values such as clarity, honesty, compassion, or humor. It really doesn't matter. We all choose what we are ready for.

At first you may only be able to stand the distant intimacy of attending speaker meetings. There you can hide and remain invisible while witnessing someone else's sharing in a large, crowded room. You may just want to sit and listen for a while. That's quite all right, your sponsor awaits. It may be a long while before you feel comfortable enough to say anything about yourself. Because you will hear others sharing so honestly, you'll probably be afraid that they can see straight through you. In some cases, they CAN. Don't let that stop you. Remember, they've been there too. You don't go to OA to impress anyone. It's actually a gigantic walking outpatient program. Who are you there to impress? If you are trying to win friends and influence people, trust me, there are better clubs!

■

EXERCISE 1

IN SEARCH OF A SPONSOR

If you now want a sponsor, it pays to advertise. Write out a "personals" ad for the mentor of your dreams. Focus on what you do want, not what you don't want.

1. What qualities do you want in your mentor?
2. How do you expect to be treated?
3. What does the job entail?

4. How will your sponsor be benefited or compensated
    for the effort? In other words, say how interesting it
    will be to get to know you and work with you, and grow
    with you.

Once you do this, you'll be amazed at how quickly the right person will appear. As the Hindus say: "When the student is ready,
the teacher appears."

For example, Alice, a tough-minded journalist who fought
coming into the program tooth and nail, advertised for her
sponsor this way:

HELP WANTED

In search of a sassy program veteran who's heard it all and
seen it all. My dream coach is a highly stressed career woman
who has the proven endurance of a marathon runner and the
speed of a sprinter. A woman who's looked relapse in the face
and keeps coming back.

Sense of humor mandatory! Must be willing to laugh at a few
bad jokes daily. "Healthy relationship" certification crucial. (I
need a role model—fast!)

Belief in mysticism and love of God a must. Membership in
the Rainbow Tribe a plus. Must share a deep commitment to
psychospiritual revolution.

What's in it for you? A relationship with a woman whose job
keeps her in the know. A more current event than me is hard to
find. I've been described on occasion as "almost delightfully entertaining." Beneath my rhinoceros hide and my hard head beats
a heart of gold.

Only genuinely abstinent night owls need apply.

When you get a sponsor, you have taken the first step in getting yourself teachable. Food keeps you teachable. Despite all
you know and have accomplished, you have found at least one
aspect of your life you can't control: FOOD. Food brought you
to your knees. Thank God! This illness will be your ticket to
ride, to a gentler life.

At my clinic, patients are asked to start calling a sponsor
from Day One of treatment. With a short inpatient stay, we don't
have that much time. If you go to a meeting, no one will push

you to get a sponsor, and no one will MAKE you call. In treatment, we will strongly suggest it, and ask why if you don't.

It doesn't matter whom you pick, though we suggest that men sponsor men and women sponsor women. It also doesn't matter what you discuss. Just start calling. You will get into the automatic habit of telling someone on a daily basis what you are going to eat. You'll begin to gain clarity and discipline, but best of all, you'll be allowing yourself to be vulnerable. Telling someone your food plan is one of the most intimate, vulnerable things you can do. You might prefer reporting on your sex life, homicidal fantasies, anything other than your food plan!

ASK YOURSELF:

- *How do you feel about giving up control?*
- *How do you feel about reporting every meal you eat to your sponsor?*

HOW TO FIND A SPONSOR

You'll find a sponsor by attending a Twelve-Step meeting. If you don't feel ready for that right now, then pick a nonrelated confidante, preferably NOT a close friend. Remember this is the time it's important to "try something new." Instead of—or in addition to—OA, you could use a therapist, a member of the clergy, or a new group of friends you've assembled just for the purpose of working through these issues. For example, if you don't go to OA, you could ask someone from your Weight Watchers or Jenny Craig meetings. It might work to use someone in your life who's not in OA, but I have definite reasons for suggesting an OA member. She will have the support of all the rest of the group as she takes on the difficult task of working with YOU—the newcomer on the path. I know you don't want to be a burden, and you really won't be because the sponsor wants to help as part of helping herself. She needs to carry the message to others so she can hear her own echo. It helps her continuing efforts to heal her own woundedness. As a newcomer, you will be difficult at first, because you won't have the same hopefulness. You may still be carrying a great deal of negativity. Don't worry; remember, your sponsor has her sponsor as well as the group's support behind her. You just pick what is best for you.

Getting Honest

Even some long-term OA members refuse to get a sponsor. They think they can do their own sponsoring. One oldtimer told me, "God is my sponsor." Those who refuse to find a sponsor may not yet be ready to be that visible; or they may be refusing to grow up spiritually and leave home. They're not yet prepared to enter the growth lane with a like-minded fellow survivor who can share equality and a more detached wisdom and experience.

That detachment is very important. It's a more distant intimacy. It gives you the freedom to talk about things you'd never share with anyone else. There's an excitement, but also a reverence about this sharing. This is because the sponsor is not in your family. She's just distant enough so that you feel safe to come out. Your sponsor cares. She's involved. But since the Twelve-Step programs are basically a "save your own ass" endeavor, sponsors are always taking care of themselves at the same time they're working with you. That is actually the saving grace. This is what lets you feel free to call. Knowing your sponsor is doing it FOR herself TOO gets you off the hook.

This was the problem with Mom's help. She kept saying it was for YOUR own good instead of HER own good. The sponsor heals that wound. She's doing it FOR herself, for her own healing and spiritual growth. You may not like that idea, and prefer guilt games. But when you really see that help can be given for fun and for free—no strings attached—you will take it.

One newcomer, sobbing and depressed, said to her sponsor, "I feel I am burdening you with my problems." The sponsor replied, "Oh, don't worry, honey. I'm not burdened. The only things that burden me are MY problems. Yours don't bother me at all."

You may not like such a response. You may feel it's cold or uncaring. But it's exactly this rigorous honesty that you've sorely needed. *Your fear of burdening a sponsor may have more to do with your fears of getting honest with yourself.*[1]

Your ongoing recovery will involve becoming and remaining teachable. You will now learn about surrendering in order to be helped, by others. You must LET someone help you. It keeps you teachable. The Chinese say: "One day with a teacher equals a lifetime with parents." It doesn't matter whom you ask, and it doesn't matter what you ask. The healing ingredient is THAT you ask.

You've been on a treacherous journey to make friends with your body, your mother, and your SELF. You need a guide to help you stand up to see yourself, hear yourself, celebrate yourself. You need to see strong, confident models who can tolerate staying open. Women's bodies are built for penetration and when we can't open up, our psyches starve, becoming insatiable. Our souls know we are not doing what we were sent here for. We need other women to help us learn welcoming, opening up, and letting go with dignity. Where in our lives were there models on how to be strong yet penetrable? This is women's work, being fluid while staying strong. Trying to affect a rocklike male model of strength is totally off the mark. You may someday be grateful that the food obsessions have required you to become vulnerable and open to help.

At first, though, you don't have to like it. You may still be balking at being called a baby—and you may feel you're too grown-up now to need a mommy. This journey requires giving up heady intellectual rationalizations and restrictions, and demands that you become more attuned to your inner voice of the spirit; this voice carries your strength, your vulnerability, and your empowerment. It is the voice of healing.

A New Primary Relationship

Once you face how you've used food to cover up your soft side, you'll see that you must be vulnerable in order to survive and stay abstinent. In this relationship, you are "the seeker" and your sponsor is guide. This guide–seeker relationship parallels

[1]For more on this, see Hazelden pamphlets by Dr. Hollis, "Resisting Recovery" or "I'm Not Ready Yet." Also tape series "Hope for Compulsive Overeaters." (1-800-328-9000)

the mother–child relationship. And yet it's quite different, because you have a specific purpose for being together. This relationship is created for the distinct purpose of healing. It is medicinal—there is a specific project at hand, based on a mutual commitment. There are skills and a body of knowledge to be taught. We get together to avoid self-abuse and to learn how to live in a new way. The sponsor offers you a model of success since she's been able to overcome similar difficulties. Her expertise is not theoretical—it's experiential. She will only recommend and ask you to do things that she, herself, has done. And she's worth listening to, because she has achieved a semblance of sanity in that primary love relationship—EATING.

You may, at this point, ask if you could instead use your friend, Sally. Of course, if it works, go for it. But I'd like to suggest starting with someone totally new in your life whom you've contacted for just THIS purpose. Have this be an area of your life where you are really taking care of the food business. Keep it separate from the rest of your life. For now, it is best not to confuse the relationship.

When you ask someone to be your sponsor, you're taking the risk of asking for help. In that act you make an important statement to your innermost self. You're acknowledging your inner war and asking for reinforcements. You're letting her know you are on the way to open up and listen. You are telling her that YOU are willing to do all you can, that you are willing to make an investment. You are stating your intentions. Your inner self is listening, watching, and waiting.

Please don't be discouraged if you find yourself balking at this suggestion. You'd be surprised how many current members of OA find it difficult to ask a sponsor for help. They attend meetings, but don't take the next critical step. The difficulty of involving another person in their plate or their lives feels like too much to ask. Many stay obsessed because they keep trying to do it alone.

ASK YOURSELF:

▫ *Think of a time in your life when you needed the help of an experienced teacher—and you had to ask for it! Was it "for fun and for free"—no strings attached? Or did you have to pay through the nose for it?*

▫ *How did you feel about asking for help? How did you feel about receiving help?*

▫ *What comes up for you now as you contemplate being that honest and vulnerable?*

Don't Ignore Your Spirit

Asking for help means taking this process seriously. It means taking yourself seriously. When you start, others will follow. If you use this book as a way to ignore your own inner messenger, your wise and perceptive body will again rebel. Read with a wary eye. Scout your own answers in the depth of your being while you listen to mine. Your answers are already written and recorded by your own spirit. Respect your answers first. And then use this book to enhance what you already know.

Whatever you read here is only a model. Remember, categorizing, labeling, and objectifying is exactly what most of us are running FROM. In fact, the very act of organizing the material and categorizing the subjects in this book can lead you to mold yourself into similar limiting categories. What we're really hungering to find are our own meanings in life. Living by others' labels has created a desperate emptiness that we keep frantically foraging to fill. Be careful not to inadvertently re-create the initial wounds that got you here.

We eat to stuff our emptiness, to ignore personal, disowned power. You've been bingeing and purging to quell the rage. And because you know it, you are very angry. Your anger is not about the body, it's about the booty—a life unlived, prizes unclaimed. It's about a longing for connection with self, for a connection between parents and children, life partners, associates, colleagues, and friends. You feel free floating and lost. You've lost your heart connection. You're eating to ground yourself because relationships with people haven't stabilized you enough. Instead of making those necessary life connections, you've resorted to stuffing, deadening your senses. Such connections have been long ignored; connections between our bodies and our spirit and the power of life. Without facing these issues more directly and consciously, we are doomed to continue in the same failing groove. It's very serious.

People with disordered eating have a hearing problem, an inability to listen to their inner wisdom and then act responsibly. You have always known on SOME level that curtailing food abuse meant changing your whole life. That's why you've waited so long. You know how difficult the task is. Even doctors' threats didn't work to keep you resolved. Medical warnings just don't work with the food-obsessed. Those warners don't realize what we are facing when they say, "Just cut down on your eating." No matter what may have happened to others, when we want to run away TO food, we don't even consider consequences.

Without a cookie by your side, you won't have a clue how to act. You won't know how or who to be. Without a bag of Fritos you may not know how to be a sweet little girl subduing your rage. Without the control and false bravado—the chutzpah—you managed with cupcakes, you'll have to go inward for deeper strength. Rather than a warning about death, this book is an invitation to claim a full life.

Compulsive people are wonders to medical science. Internists who warn, "Drink and you'll die!" don't believe alcoholics returning to their offices vomiting. When a surgeon cuts out half a woman's digestive tract and she loses two hundred pounds, how can he accept her returning obese after two years? She experienced all the ill effects of the operation, but ate herself back into oblivion anyway!

In 1964, researchers at Baylor University found that the only people who were successful subjects with bypass surgeries were those who had been in excruciating pain every day of their lives. They were so nauseous that they didn't want to eat. A daily hammer blow to the frontal lobe might have been just as effective, and much less costly. These patients could have found sponsors in OA for free.

Your Sponsor and You

Since the service is offered for free, you may tend to devalue what you're getting from this somewhat distant form of intimacy. A leap of faith is needed here. You won't know the inestimable value of this relationship until you're farther down the path. For now, just trust that this is the most serious decision of your life. This is how you're going to birth yourself.

In giving up either compulsive eating or starving, you found you had to renegotiate your space in all your relationships. You had been hungering to be heard, to have attention paid to you, to be validated as a unique individual. *The phenomenon of modern women hungering for their true selves has fed the greatest addiction epidemic of our age.* Some of that hunger can now be filled with the help of sponsors in Twelve-Step groups. Once you've experienced this noninvasive form of peer guidance, you can no longer pretend it's unavailable. You have many basic needs that need to be met. You can't expect them to be met continuously, regularly, and always from one primary person.

You need someone who hears you on a deep level. Not only are good ears needed, but you also need wise souls that can further your journey. This individual must be trustworthy, have a spirit of investigation, and also know how to take a leap of faith when answers aren't clear. An OA sponsor who is willing to act as your spiritual guide or mentor is willing to take her/his own leaps of faith.

You will notice that there are very few "how to" solutions offered in this book. I would not demean your noble effort by presuming to offer some quick-fix solution to your complex problems. Those solutions kept you hungry. You must first take a risk and participate, and then you will be able to mobilize your own resources, finding your own answers. Healing comes from personal, specific adventures.

Daily dilemmas in your own life will cause you to ask for guidance and wise counsel. You'll be open to hearing the impressions of another about YOUR behavior. You'll be asking for feedback about minor daily occurrences. How you talked to the sales rep, how to sign for the UPS delivery, which drawer to clear out first, are all opportunities for growth. The little things mean a lot. You don't have to embellish. Many at my seminars ask general global questions rather than risking the specific. One of my most influential mentors, Dr. William Ofman, says, "God lives in the details." The specific is actually much more personal.

If you make a commitment to yourself to work with a sponsor on a daily basis, your life will begin to unfold. Your own answers will begin to rise to the surface to be explored individually and respectfully. This is not a book to get you to adapt, conform, or label yourself so that you are then packaged, categorized, and sent off to eat. Its purpose is to open you up to the difficult task at hand of living a full, unpredictable life. It's an invitation to get started on the path. You may find yourself feeling a little more scared than when you tried past packaged solutions. You are now left with all options open. You decide. Quickie prescriptions may soothe in the short run—just like cupcakes—but they don't help in the long haul. Try looking at your fear or temporary anxiety as a source of excitement. You're writing a new script, creating your own life.

Going It Alone

CAUTION: THIS BOOK MAY BE HAZARDOUS TO YOUR HEALTH.

If you set out by yourself to take on the exercises proposed here, you may think this book is all you need. That may make things worse instead of better. You won't feel the necessity to consult a mentor. But this means you're buying the answers of others instead of teasing out the more personal, intimate answers you and your sponsor can uncover. Going it alone can often be destructive. AAers say, "An addict alone is in bad company." Left to our own devices, we make decisions harmful to SELF. Please use this book as an invitation to turn to another human being for guidance. Then, together, the two of you can take the first step on the path. The answers are already within you. Listen!

Finding some form of mentoring along your chosen path helps you take yourself seriously. You're neither a fat buffoon nor a waiflike incompetent. You have a powerful life to live. You may have previously minimized this, not facing the seriousness of living an authentic life. Some of your relentless search for medical diagnosis and validation has been an attempt to be taken seriously. We search for new diagnostic categories to prove to ourselves and others that our pain has validity. Some people die with labels but no awareness. When you find a spiritual mentor, you may not have to enter the medical system to get the needed attention.

The lovely singer Karen Carpenter had to die before her anorexia was even recognized by her public. At her funeral, fans said, "She didn't die of anorexia. She died of heart failure." Yes, the death certificate read so, but she died during the dangerous refeeding stage of anorexia where she appeared to be doing better, gaining twenty-five pounds; but her heart could not stand the strain. She died from complications of anorexia. A year later, reports surfaced that she'd also been making herself vomit. Did this keep her anorexia diagnosis pure? Or should she now be labeled bulimic? Who cares? Certainly not Karen.

You've probably never considered your disordered eating to be this serious or deadly. You may still make little-girl jokes about yourself and your dieting. But disordered eating is much deeper than food choices, and much more personally abusive. It goes far beyond simplistic definitions and categories. That is why being diagnosed can be deadly, because it promotes an attitude of simple labeling and we are so sensitive to this violation.

Women are more sensitized to the labeling issue than men, and that may be partly why "eating disorders" have been so predominantly a women's problem. We have been brainwashed that the only way we can get serious attention is to be weak and helpless. For many centuries, women's concerns were honored only in sickbeds. If "sick," we're taken seriously. In the nineteenth century, women were diagnosed with "hysteria," from the Greek word for uterus. They were then labeled and treated in manmade categories. In the twentieth century, our hysteria has become "eating disorders" and we fill psychiatrists' offices seeking that same serious attention. Now is the time to go for attention where it will really do some good.

Taking Your Sponsor's Time

Can you take their time? Some people balk at choosing a sponsor because they're afraid to bother someone, or feel their needs and desires are too minimal to be discussed. This is where the addiction model helps. If you keep remembering that people at those meetings treat this problem seriously and with respect, you will realize that calling a sponsor is like getting a medical prescription filled. *It's not about ego or making nice.* It's an absolute necessity.

These sponsors wouldn't offer themselves unless helping you helped them as well. The whole system of choosing sponsors is set up to guard against the exploitative need situation. You attend meetings and find someone you feel you can relate to. Then YOU ask THEM to be your sponsor. They don't ask you. You make the initial overture, you make most of the early phone calls, and basically, you need them more than they need you.

This is the opposite of the situation with your real mom. She was the one who initiated your birth.

Have you ever heard a snotty teenager sneer, "I didn't ask to be born?" That's right. They didn't. Mom was totally in the driver's seat in terms of wanting the relationship, the contact, the involvement.

With sponsors, this is totally turned around. You are directed to pick a sponsor for guidance, to ask that person to be your mentor. They don't ask you, and for the most part, they don't call you. It is YOU who wants the relationship; YOU who have something to gain and only misery to lose. It's a whole different investment, and it creates very interesting interactions.

Service is Slimming

Sponsors take on the job to ensure their own recoveries, by passing on what they've learned. WE ALL TEACH WHAT WE MOST NEED TO LEARN. Therefore, don't waste a moment with guilt or even appreciation—and certainly not shyness. Use 'em. Chew 'em up and digest them fully. Sponsors are trained in self-care. They learned it from *their* sponsors. An AA slogan regarding this twelfth step, helping others, quips, "You'll be successful if YOU come back sober." It's difficult to be out on the firing lines with newcomers who are still negative and hopeless. Sponsors will be careful to keep themselves motivated so they won't be pulled back into the abyss.

Are You Ready?

The question is, like the Fifties song asks, "Are you ready to fall in love?" Are you ready to meet and fall in love with yourself? You don't have to feel in love *continuously,* nor ready *continuously,* nor motivated to follow this path *continuously.* That's what sponsors are for—they help you regain your willingness and readiness when you're falling away. You looked earlier at all those diets you gave up. It's the nature of this journey that you can't stay eternally and continuously on the path. You will fall off the horse and want to lie still. Let someone else hold your stirrup and give you a leg up again.

Readiness is an elusive condition that you have to face on a daily basis. One morning you may wake up absolutely convinced that you have to face your life and follow this path. And the next morning you'll wake up telling yourself that you really don't need to be so fanatic, that all those "helpers" are just bleeding deacons trying to brainwash you. Either way, you'll be absolutely convinced of your position. But how do you know if this reaction is healthy? Maybe your self-destruct button has been pushed again. This is where your sponsor comes in. She's there to help you maintain your readiness on those days when your resolve weakens.

From the first step, you will see both the terror and the value of going public with your food plan. Letting someone else stare at your plate—being visible in this most intimate area of your life—gets you ready for even more visibility later on. As you allow yourself to be seen, open yourself up to feedback, and negotiate the rocky path between wanting attention, getting it, not getting it, wanting involvement and not wanting it, you will be gently training yourself for other kinds of intimacy later.

Ask for Help

It doesn't matter who, what, or how you ask. The healing ingredient is *that* you ask. You're asking a sponsor to be your witness. You're asking for attention and it is freely given. It is the ATTENTION that is so healing. The sponsor pays careful attention, remembering your important issues, and she cares that you should succeed. She encourages you to survive. She wants to watch as you change behavior patterns. She's not grounded in the past, and has no vested interest in keeping you there. She's much more attuned to the future. Your guide doesn't have to have brilliant advice, helpful slogans, or prissy platitudes. The whole point is *that* you asked, and she's there, watching. That detached, nonenmeshed WITNESSING is what you've hungered for all your life. Now let's look at what the sponsor actually teaches that heals the hunger.

ACTION IS THE MAGIC WORD

Until you invest some effort, you can't properly evaluate the results. If you offer your judgments before trying something, the sponsor will say you're practicing "contempt prior to investigation." Your real mother probably didn't expect you to try something first before she allowed you to complain and reject. But your new parent figure will keep telling you to "try working the program." She'll want you to get busy and then seek her guidance. She won't do it for you. Remember, it's all about AC-TIONS.

In his hit song "The Gambler," Kenny Rogers advises, "You gotta know when to hold 'em and know when to fold 'em." You and your sponsor will carefully monitor and negotiate *when to take action and when to sit back and await results*. It's never an easy call. Sometimes she'll advise you to do nothing other than attend an OA meeting and listen to others. In that witnessing, you will actively absorb recovery.

Walk the Walk

When you are actually living the program, you find out more about what others are doing and you learn to listen attentively to those just ahead on the path. *Doing* it requires more diligence than talking it. If judging others has been getting in the way of your recovery, realize that it stems from your need to reject any group that would accept YOU so easily. If, as OA declares, the only requirement for membership is an honest desire to stop eating compulsively, then maybe they may not be discriminating enough for a person with your standards? Some of this competitive, striving critical assessment is a carryover from earlier programming toward self-hate.

It's important for you to pause a minute to look where those standards have brought you—right to the doors of Overeaters Anonymous.

I recommend Overeaters Anonymous so highly because I

feel there is tremendous value in receiving help from fellow suf- ferers. When you're being helped by someone who has never suffered the illness, you think they just won't understand, think- ing "normies" have it all together and never act out compul- sively. At OA, you will see others who've walked in the same shapeless flowered muumuus.

Any "suggestions" offered will come from an experienced person who says, "This is how I handle that." Directions aren't given from someone who hasn't experienced your struggle. This direct approach helps you listen while your argumentative, "No- body tells me what to do" inner kid wails. She gets to see well- meaning people who are themselves struggling with abstinence. No one will ask you to do anything they haven't done them- selves.

Wounded Healers

You may prefer to pay for help. That lets you stay more in control, and it also allows you to keep fooling yourself that real healing comes from OUTSIDE your SELF. Sometimes it's hard to face that you can be helped by people *just like you.* Other cul- tures put much more faith in the "wounded healer"—someone who has suffered also. *They are* better able to prescribe for those who share the same problem. In the West, we tend to trust more to intellect and the scientific method. In OA you will become willing to accept help from fallible human beings. Your sponsor will teach you about Twelve-Step principles, and what she walked through to get where she is today.

Oh, yes, your sponsor will fail you countless times. Some- times you'll telephone and she'll have "call waiting," and you'll be put off for another caller. You'll scream, "Doesn't she see what it took for me to make this call? How can she be so insen- sitive? Doesn't she know who I am?" Sometimes she'll want to finish her lunch. Sometimes she'll be having her own bad day and just won't have anything to give. Sometimes she'll want to bring up her own interesting stories right in the middle of yours.

All that will eventually happen. If not, you're not dealing with a real authentic human being—you're operating with a phony who has already failed you. She has failed you by not let- ting you weather reality. Real people fail us from time to time. We survive. If she's worried about being a perfect sponsor, she's teaching a lie. She's taught you inauthenticity. She may fail you in the same way that Mom did. However, if she's failed you in the same way—but you both hang in there and walk through it—an even greater healing can occur. You will have been with someone who could own up to her own stuff, seen clearly and discussed intelligently. She will be willing to make amends. The sponsor–baby relationship is one of the most intimate we can experience, and it allows both sides to heal many wounds. A Twelve-Stepper must remain open to making amends, admitting wrongs. This will be a crucial factor in allowing mistakes and slights to be healed, so they don't grow into major catastrophes. As the sponsor models how to clean up errors quickly, you will gain perspective. If you can forgive a fallible sponsor, you can also later forgive a fallible mother.

Weathering Disappointment

Sponsors WILL disappoint you—this is called "life." The sponsor must keep her own priorities in order. She will not take on martyrdom, helping you at her expense. When you need to talk to her, she may be otherwise engaged. You'll have to spread your neediness around among other companions on the path, so you can be assured of getting your needs met. You'll have to have more than just your sponsor's phone number. You'll need help from a lot of people.

Some days, you may feel abandoned if no one is home. You'll want to return to the old empty wells. You'll even call home to Mom. But what if Mom is having her own bad day? Of course moms judge themselves by trying to be perfect and available whenever needed. No one can be there for you forever, even though moms surely try. Even a paid therapist will only be available at a specified, appointed hour. Crises rarely occur so neatly.

If you spread your support system among a group of people, more than likely you will find someone who can be there when you need them. In an actual family situation, there is often a push–pull between mother and daughter about being either "too much" or "not enough." If you are a mother yourself you know you wanted to be always available, but couldn't possibly. Putting all your needy eggs in one basket, even if it's Mom's, is a sure way to make yourself too much of a burden. When you spread the neediness, you can trust you won't be abandoned.

You'll find there will be enough support to bolster you up. You really won't be "too much" for anyone.

ASK YOURSELF:

- *When people let you down, do you give them a second chance?*
- *Do you give bad-tasting food a second chance?*
- *How do you feel when people let you down?*
- *What do you do?*
- *When people let you down, do you blame yourself as "not enough" or "too much"?*

Terminal Uniqueness

As you get help and listen to the needs of others, you will see clearly that your needs are NOT excessive. It is important that you get your witness, but ALSO that you witness the ongoing struggles of others. The most powerful learning often occurs by listening to the solutions and struggles of others. By attending the Twelve-Step meetings, you will hear some of the problems others experience—but won't take on their burdens or feel in any way responsible. Because you share a common addictive illness, many of the personalities present will be like people in your family—but not so close as to smother. Most importantly, you'll see that you are not alone and that others feel as you do. You'll see that others have walked the recovery path and made it. They are neither better than nor less than anyone else. Most of all, they are not terminally unique.

A great deal of guidance is offered just by tracing the paths of others. Newcomers may at first reject what they hear, declaring, "I'm not that bad yet," or "That'll never happen to me," and then surprisingly they find themselves in the midst of what they swore they'd never experience. It is important that we all witness each other on our individual paths as well as walking a mile in someone else's moccasins.

Rhea was listening at her afternoon meeting to women declaring they were deciding to give up on sex and become celibate. She left each meeting muttering, "These women are fruitcakes. Giving up food and sex at the same time. I can't imagine anything more abusive." She knew she'd never have that kind of resolve, and actually felt it was a dumb idea.

Slowly, however, she began to see how she'd become as obsessional in her sexuality as she'd been with her food. A month later, she got to make her own big swearing-off speech. She decided to try celibacy for a while. Be careful what you judge. All judgments come home to roost . . .

"First things first." Your new surrogate mother will not help you waste idle hours in that old "what if" or "if only" game. Instead she will move you into action with direct treatment of a symptom. The symptom is compulsive overeating or starving—and the agenda is first and foremost to stop that behavior. When your house is on fire, you call the fire department and do what you can to put out the blaze. There is no time to evaluate how the fire started or to investigate the nature of the flame. Diagnostics, and searching for the underlying reasons why you do this, are best left for those freer minds who have time to ruminate—the pathologists with dead patients to cut. Theoreticians can operate like the fire marshall examining smoldering embers. We'll be content to be alive and as little charred as possible, thanks. If you are the person in the fire zone, fighting the flames, take all precautions to secure your perimeter. SYAS: Save Your Ass, Sweetheart!

Willpower?

Willpower with food is just as ineffective as willpower with diarrhea. As we listen to OA members in varying stages of recovery acknowledge difficulties with their illness, admitting to periods of control interspersed with relapse and some random outbursts of bingeing, we begin to accept the tenuous nature of recovery, and stop pushing and beating ourselves. We see long-term members who have stopped struggling and evolved to a healthy neutrality with food and eating behavior. We get to see that abstinence is something that will happen to US. As we give up all that rah, rah, firm resolve, we can hope that soon our relationship with food will improve. Recovery is something that happens to us by osmosis. It is an inside job that we can't work at too directly. It happens sideways as you do your best.

U R Responsible

Doing YOUR best is the key ingredient here. Your job is to suit up and show up—and not to quit before the miracle. Your personal path will unfold on your own personal timetable. It won't be Mom's and it won't be a diet doctor's. It will unfold organically along with your life. Each of us learns about our own personal and individual recovery. No one is more expert about you or your life than you are. Others are helpful guides, that's all. Your actual mother felt too responsible and in charge to teach you this vital message. With the OA sponsor, you will hear compassion and support. But she will insist that even though you didn't ask to have this malady, you are totally responsible for following prescriptions in order to recover from it. We may all be on a similar path and can offer torches along the way; but each of us is also sure-footed enough to walk alone.

One Day at a Time

Hey lady, can you spare fifteen minutes? Most research shows that an obsessional urge lasts approximately fifteen minutes. A sponsor helps you get your priorities straight in your life so that you can keep choosing "abstinence no matter what." As abstinence becomes your first priority and agenda, you will need help and support during those brief fifteen-minute temptations so you won't have to give in or act out. It's during those obsessional periods that you need help. A sponsor will ask you to hang in for "one day at a time."

The following story shows clearly that one-day-at-a-time aspect of recovery. Susan, an OA member, was fired on a Friday. Filled with future projections of doom and gloom, she complained to her sponsor that she'd never work again, probably lose the house, be better off dead. Her sponsor listened attentively and then comforted her with "Well, don't let it ruin your weekend." With that, Susan relaxed. On Monday morning she went out interviewing for a new job. Tuesday she was called back for a second interview. By Wednesday she was notified that they'd like her to start the following Monday.

Susan called her sponsor, elated and very appreciative of how the sponsor had helped her stay calm and wait-and-see, how she really helped her out of the fear. Now she had to get her clothes together for the exciting new job. "Just think," she said happily, "I was out of work only one week and now I start back next Monday."

Her sponsor listened to all the excitement and then comforted her with "Well, don't let it ruin your weekend."

CAPTAINS OF CHAOS

You may think of yourself as "needy" when you have crises and problems. It is most often the good times which make us eat. Therefore, you will need help handling the good life. More dangerous than having a crisis is the time when crises stop occurring. That is why I so strongly recommend OA; because you will certainly need help a few years farther down the pike, when things get better. As ridiculous as it sounds, you are going to need more help weathering the GOOD times. Your sponsor will model for you how to celebrate joy, how to have a good time, how to walk away from a long-suffering life without any guilt whatsoever. Your mom wants that for you. Despite her own pains, she wants you to be happy.

You can gain perspective from a sponsor. She can help you sort out splinters from logs, pebbles from cannonballs, and molehills from mountains. You'll find you have greater need when you stop having "problems." What happens when there is nothing to cry about? How do you handle the good life with gusto? What if your whole reason for being was to ride as a "captain of chaos" into the next fray? How do you retool?

Many people lament, "Serenity is boring." Many treatment programs are geared toward relieving pain and solving problems. Just as we have few practitioners and teachers in preventive medicine, we have even fewer experts at teaching new skills for savoring life without self-abuse. Twelve-Step sponsors have been offering guidance with new adjustment problems in recovery for many years. They know perfectly well that most relapses occur when times are good. You'll need help enduring your blessings long after traditional therapies have stopped.[2]

Risk It

To lose the fat risk, we must be at risk. We have to live more on the edge. Past episodes of high drama may have been our attempts to avoid risk. Were you re-creating the same old scripts, the ones where you'd rehearsed the blocking and dialogue so often that you could play it in your sleep? This may be exciting, but it isn't as risky as really letting go, as listening for direction about a new way to live. If life doesn't feel risky, it could mean that we're regressing.

Here's where your sponsor can be more helpful than your real mom. Very few mothers can whole-heartedly encourage their daughters to take on a risky life. Once they've locked the daughter up somehow, got her penned down for the night, they breathe a sigh of relief and feel they've done a good job. Mom teaches you to hold on—your sponsor teaches you to "let go."

Why not?

As you grew up, you rejected some of what your mom proposed because you could see that it wasn't working in her life. As a result, you may have developed an overly discriminating rejection factor. However, as you observe a new authority figure, your mentor in OA, and hear her advising you to follow her path, you might try lowering some of your fear barriers by realizing there's no reason NOT to try what she is proposing. In medicine we refer to "iatrogenic sequella." This means problems that were caused by medical intervention: for example, a sponge left in after surgery, or infection from incision. These things happen, even in the best of circumstances. But it doesn't happen with OA's prescription. What your sponsor advises has no negative complications. A few relationships may be shaken up a bit, but people quickly return to the status quo if they choose to.

[2]See Dr. Hollis's Hazelden pamphlet, "Relapse."

For Fun and for Free

At OA you'll be advised to try out new behaviors for fun and for free. And while you're witnessing and absorbing, no one expects a single thing from you. Whatever is offered is given, "for fun and for free." If you're dissatisfied with the results, they'll refund your misery. But in the long run, you'll find that it's definitely worth the price.

You may find yourself wanting to help, to offer advice, to DO for others. This is part of your great inability to receive—a pattern learned at your mother's knee. She couldn't receive from you. Now you can't receive. In fact, you would have loved to be able to give to her, to help her change, to make her happier. She couldn't take you in, and now you have the same difficulty taking in.

Remember, no one at OA needs anything from you. When you first begin going to meetings you may think that the people there really need your help. But this probably has more to do with your need than theirs. In other words, like Mom, you're more comfortable giving. Be careful of helping others when you haven't been in the "receiver" seat long enough yourself. You may be one of those overzealous newcomers who decides, "I've got a problem," and then help someone else with theirs. You'll waltz from Step One to Step Twelve, without doing the necessary ten other steps in between. We call this the "OA two-step."

There is a reason the AA founders kept Step Twelve for last. You can't give something you haven't got. You must do your own footwork—the work of the eleven previous Steps—before you have something to give away. You'll learn about a fantastic new form of personal self-care, where everyone takes care of their own needs and everyone seems to benefit. All come to the meetings needy and most get what they need. How does that happen? There just seems to be enough to go around.

God?

Where do we get all that extra energy to meet everyone's needs? It doesn't seem possible. It isn't. Here's where your sponsor may want to share with you some of what she's learned on her spiritual path. This surrogate mother will help you access another form of power beyond your own control.

Many balk when they hear OAers mention something about a "higher power." They quickly reject this "God talk," insisting that the program is "too religious." If you feel this way, try to suspend judgment for a minute. Wasn't food a false god? Consider where your own personal, driven, willful efforts have taken you. There just may be another way. There may actually be a power that transcends understanding.

Scientifically a bumblebee shouldn't be able to fly. It has none of the properties of an airplane—there's very little pressure differential between the upper and lower wing surfaces. It has no sleek aerodynamic shape, no smooth, drag-free surface. All it has is one tiny pair of wings to lift its fat and fuzzy body. But the bumblebee accesses such tremendous POWER that those tiny wings beat the air into submission. And by some miracle, it flies. It doesn't question the aerodynamics of the situation. It's too busy flying! That same power speeds us along on our flight path. All you need to know about God is YOU AIN'T IT!

See the Big "C"

It's all about control. About allowing yourself to receive. Maybe it goes back to your struggle not to be controlled by your mother. She had struggled not to be controlled by hers. Those struggles were lost in the plate. And the minute you agree to follow directions from a surrogate mother, all those struggles for control will resurface again. You'll unwittingly draw up similar battle lines. It's nothing personal between the two people involved. It's about that lifelong battle to get nurturance without getting killed.

Remember, in Mom's efforts to get you civilized, you were nurtured and punished by the same source. You are now conflicted about whether you're being helped or harmed. On the path to recovery, you'll watch yourself battling paper tigers, rejecting and defying without even knowing why. This behavior is automatic. It was easier in caveman times when it was a mammoth you battled. Now it's not a mastodon but your own masticator.

Slowly, by trial and error, you'll come to see that your sponsor has nothing to gain or lose by offering this help, or by your rejecting it. This is your own personal battle for control, and you'll be allowed to win it. This couldn't come in the battles with your real mom because she has her own power struggles. It won't come out as blatantly with a therapist either, because as long as you're paying—controlling the purse strings—you get to feel some power in the situation. With the sponsor's advice, freely given, and your reaction of it, you gain great awareness about your own personal battle grounds. That awareness is very healing.

Cat Dance

Some of the battling against sponsors is because we long for but actually hate being SEEN so clearly—especially when we're moving toward self-destruction again. The sponsor can smell out self-abuse, whether you're getting ready to do it, or you're already into it. Fellow travelers know the personal con game. We've all played it. We can watch ourselves at it. We know that when we're playing those little mind games, we're absolutely convinced of our own self-justification. The sponsor just sees it all so clearly. To her, you look like a little kitty in a sand box kicking to cover up doo doo. You'll probably offer elaborate "explanations" for your behavior and your position. But it's all fancy footwork to those who see clearly. And the reason it's so obvious is because they did it themselves.

My Story

Early in my own recovery I was on a very strict food plan, weighing and measuring my food, calling my sponsor each day to tell her in advance exactly what I would eat that day. One Friday I had committed myself to an apple for my breakfast fruit. When I looked in the fridge, all the apples were little green ones. I was very hungry. I decided I'd have two and tell her about it the next day, feeling for sure it would be okay. The next morning I forgot the extra apple and instead proceeded to tell her my Saturday food plan.

That whole weekend I was a raving lunatic, acting out toward everyone in my life, finding fault, giving orders, totally externally focused. I didn't want to look at myself. By Monday I was sick of my own behavior, but I was still complaining to my sponsor about all the intolerable people in my life.

She let me rant for a while and then gently queried, "How's your food?" I felt like I'd been punched. I'd had the wind knocked out of me. I started to cry. I remembered that extra apple. I'd been so foolishly scared and covering up a very innocent extra apple, that I'd compensated by finding fault with everyone around me.

When my sponsor saw past that and asked me about my primary agenda, my abstinence, it gave me the clarity I needed to sort through the situation. It's not that there was anything good or bad about an extra apple, or even an extra doughnut. It was the cover-up that caused the pain.

When we're running scared and trying to get away from OURSELVES, we hit out, often at those we love. A sponsor, someone separate from our personal lives, insists that we be rigorously honest in the plate. She sees past the cerebral cortex right into the scared little kitty. She sees more clearly than any cat scan.

The little kitty is doing a cat dance. She's dazzling herself with fancy footwork as she scurries to kick up enough sand in the box. She knows she has to cover up what she did there; she knows her thinkin' is gettin' stinkin'. The sponsor smells it and knows how useless this fight is—but she'll wait and watch quietly for as long as your cat wants to dance. Eventually you'll gain enough clarity to see your own cat dance and you won't need the watchful eye of another. You'll be able to monitor your own con man.

Sixteen years into recovery I had given up most of my favorite binge foods, especially my two favorites: pistachio nuts and bittersweet chocolate. Those were two things for which one bite was too many and a thousand not enough. Just as with alcohol, I didn't want to be bothered with a minimal dose. I wanted a vat of chocolate, or a duffle bag full of pistachios! If you saw the movie *Naked Gun*, there's a scene where Leslie Nielsen and his sidekick are on a stakeout, eating red nuts in the squad car, waiting for the bad guys. The next scene shows them red-mouthed and swollen, and when they try to open the car door, the empty shells are piled so high on the curb that they can't get out. That, to me, is a *moderate* dose of pistachio nuts.

Well, I was giving a seminar in Boston, and in the hotel gift shop, displayed oh, so nicely, was a product I'd never encountered before. It was a cellophane package of BITTERSWEET-CHOCOLATE-COVERED PISTACHIO NUTS! I thought I'd died and gone to heaven. I couldn't imagine anything so scrumptious. I wanted to meet the brilliant mind that had concocted such a delight; my mind raced into high gear to justify buying some. I first assured myself I wouldn't eat them on this lecture tour. I had too many presentations to give and wanted my mind clear. I told myself, "Just pack them in your suitcase and have them when you get back home." Then there were further questions:

"How many bags should we buy? We may never pass this way again."

"Let's look at the package and see if we can write the factory for refills."

"Why should it hurt just to have a few while still on tour?"

"Look, sugar is only the *fifth* ingredient on the label!"

But all the while, a deeper, quieter voice kept pushing a question up from within me:

"Who is SHE talking to?"

This gave me just that crucial moment of clarity I needed to observe the situation from another perspective. Someone was asking about the chatter. WHO was she talking to? Who was doing all that talking? I saw clearly that it was my little "I wanna" self arguing the merits of this package to my larger, more nurturing Inner Self who knew I didn't need it right now. I stepped back and saw clearly that one bag would only be the beginning. It was a new product I'd never tried. It was better to never know. I was giving it too much energy and too much importance. I was lusting. I gave the package "one lust look" and marched away. When you want to eat, first give one lust look.

ASK YOURSELF:

▢ *Think about your equivalent of "bittersweet pistachio nuts." Are you in like or lust?*

▢ *Are you worried there won't be enough? How do you feel physically?*

▢ *Do you feel panic?*

▢ *How are you planning to get and have enough?*

Staying the Course

After all my years of recovery work, I had incorporated that watchful, reasonable, more distant perspective into a quiet part of myself. For that incident anyway, *She* showed up. Please know that this lusting *never goes away*. It's just that after you've practiced enough with a sponsor, you will develop an ability to observe it more clearly and step back. You'll tell yourself, "When in doubt, leave it out." I still think about those nuts, and know that BECAUSE I think about them is exactly WHY I can't have them. They're too important. I can't hold them with a loose hand.

With a sponsor you will learn about letting things go, surrendering, holding them with a loose hand, instead of clawing them to death. This letting go and surrender has to do with more than what or how much you're eating. It may have something to do with HOW you are eating, and how you are living. The sponsor understands the subtlety of how you behave around the substance. It's about your RELATIONSHIP with the plate.

Do you approach food with a moderate, middle-of-the-road willingness to take it as it comes? Or do you get into a ravenous feeding frenzy? Are you working up a sweat like a compulsive gambler, telling yourself, "This roll will be different!" Ours isn't a roll of the dice, but we bargain for jelly rolls. A sponsor will smell the burn if you are talking too much about food. She'll know you're talking yourself out of listening to your inner self.

No matter how far along in recovery you get, there will be those times when you think it's okay to self-destruct. It's not the cookie you're after, but the flight from awareness. No matter how smart, powerful, successful, insightful, helpful, or generally okay you are, periodically the feeding frenzy will light up and you're gone.

You will find yourself in baffling situations, wondering how you ended up there again. Your only answer will be "It seemed like a good idea at the time." Compulsion has nothing to do with reason. It is absurd to ask "why." The only answer is BE-CAUSE. We are addicts, we are self-destructive, we want out of life. Left to our own devices, we will make decisions harmful to self. . . . This is why we need sponsors. Hopefully they can be there when that death wish beckons.

Attitude of Gratitude

As OA suggests, you choose a sponsor because of her success—"You want what she has and are willing to go to any lengths to get it." Your honest sponsor will probably remind you that recovery is difficult. Instead of giving credit to strong will and determination, boasting of weight loss, thanking Jenny Craig, Weight Watchers, or Slim Fast, the sponsor will instead warn you that the illness you share is "cunning, baffling, powerful—and patient." It looms up when you least expect it. Your sponsor will help you develop a sense of relief and gratitude for those times when food is NOT a problem. Your mother will be more hopeful of getting you out of the mire and will want to believe that eventually you'll be perfect and problem-free. However, with the more realistic parenting you'll get from your sponsor, your orientation will be toward lifelong prevention rather than fantasies of eventual cure. You'll be prepared for the bad days and grateful for the good.

Humility

With such an attitude of gratitude, you will move toward a humble respect for your obsession. You might have initially scoffed at OA's Step One, where you were asked to admit to being "powerless" over food. You will now learn to take evaluations of "good" or "bad" out of the dining room. You will see what a gift it is when food is in order. Compulsive people have been de-scribed as "egomaniacs with inferiority complexes." You will come to appreciate that ego has nothing to do with it. We are

not bad people trying to get good, but humble, sick people trying to get well. After acknowledging that this is an area of your
life that you can't conquer with willpower, you'll begin to develop a compassion for all who must accept human frailty—even
your mother.

Giveaway

Even though the sponsor may not NEED you, helping you
helps her heal HER own wounds. Helping will help you later
too. It helps you re-own your disowned self. In the past, you may
have taken on some form of dieting, recovery, or growth, declaring that you never wanted to return to that old self. You swore
you'd never be a fat girl again. Well, that was very disrespectful
to the person who brought you so far and through so much. She
rose up in rebellion. Sponsoring newcomers allows you to continually welcome your former self into the new life. That means
there's no one left behind to pull you back.

In order to stop dying you just need to stop, listen, receive.
Your sponsor will love you and give you what she can for fun and
for free. That love will be unconditional because it will be honest and clean. Everyone will be getting needs met.

Unconditional love doesn't mean acceptance no matter
what, but it will mean, I DON'T CARE IF YOU LOVE ME BACK.
It is freely given, with no obligation. You don't have to love back.
It's just there for the taking. This is the exact healing ingredient
addicted daughters need. Poor Mom needed to be loved in return, but she didn't know how to receive. It became a battle-
ground.

You may want to give back to your sponsor. DON'T! Stay in
the receiver role with her. Since the sponsor's needs are getting
met through HER sponsor, most of the time she'll tell you her
best thanks from you will be if you "pass it on." Your helping
others helps her.

> ## ASK YOURSELF:
>
> □ *Do you know how to receive? Can you recall an incident in which you were happy to receive? How do you think the other person felt?*
>
> □ *What's the scariest thing about receiving?*
>
> □ *What do you fear in people who need nothing from you?*

What Has Love Got to Do with It?

The problem for most of my patients has not been lack of love, but lack of opportunity to GIVE love. They had a lot to offer. Naturally, they wanted to spread their wealth of love and kindness to their closest love object—Mom. But Mom was too scared, too closed off and too concerned for her own performance to let you in. The ability to be open and penetrable while still remaining strong was a skill moms couldn't teach. This is what addicted daughters struggle with today. We needed an opportunity to give love, but Mom was closed off, addicted, scared, so our instincts were thwarted. The precious present of ourselves could not be received. We ached at this loss. And we began to devalue what we had to offer. OA gives a new opportunity to give, and to have our gift received and appreciated. Whatever we do have to give will be ENOUGH.

Sponsors, however, give with some expectations because the relationship is based on a teaching model. Sponsors are teaching life skills; they expect their students to take action steps and practice. If you don't follow directions, she may suggest you try someone else. In OA, you grow or you go!

When you begin working with your sponsor, read her the writings you've done thus far while following this book. You've catalogued your previous unsuccessful attempts to control your eating disorder. That was a form of the first step. You've written a fantasy of your own mother's expectations while pregnant with you. You've written a letter of resignation from the "caring" society. All of these writings are part of moving you away from the old role of daughter, and into your new role of "self-creator."

Your sponsor will act as your midwife, helping you through the narrow birth canal.

The following capsulized chart will give you an idea of the value of a sponsor's more distant intimacy versus the overly involved intimacy you got from your own mother. Not to say that your real mother was "bad" or wrong. It's just important to point out that now, you need this new kind of guidance. Remember too, we're looking at extremes here—an ideal sponsor and an all too real mother. Not all sponsors are detached saints, and not all mothers are enmeshed, but by blatantly presenting the extremes, you'll begin to fashion some form of moderate, helpful relationship.

SPONSOR'S DISTANT INTIMACY	MOM'S ENMESHMENT
1. Relationship founded on healing.	1. Relationship founded on love.
2. Detached.	2. Smothering.
3. Acknowledged agenda.	3. Says, "All for you, dear."
4. Self-care.	4. Self-sacrifice.
5. Rigorously honest.	5. Blindly self-deceptive.
6. No image to protect.	6. Fulfilling cultural expectations.
7. For fun & for free.	7. Needs appreciation.
8. Models success.	8. Illustrates suffering.
9. Has overcome same problem.	9. May not have, or denies.
10. Promotes risk.	10. Plays safe.
11. Walks the walk.	11. Talks the talk.

After you've worked with a sponsor for six months, add more to this list. You'll find that you begin to appreciate both your own mother and your surrogate. You'll find that you're finally getting enough. Then it will be time to start forgiving your own mother.

■

EXERCISE 2

I DON'T NEED ANOTHER MOTHER

Take out your journal and write a letter to your prospective sponsor.

1. Outline all the reasons why you don't need or want a mother. Explain why your interactions with your mother left you hungry and conflicted. What do you know that you don't want to repeat in another close relationship?
2. Explain what having a sponsor, rather than a mother, will mean to you.
3. How can this time be different?
4. How will you let in without letting down or giving up?

Your sponsor is an ally. With her guidance you can now go farther into yourself and into your mother's life. The Beatles sang, "All you need is love." Your mom wanted love she couldn't receive. You suffered the same way.

As your food obsession forces you to open up to receiving, it also opens another channel of looking at the pain both you and Mom weathered. Seeing this clearly moves us on to forgiveness.

Chapter

7

FORGIVING MOM

*E*ATING MODERATELY AND ALLIED WITH A SPONSOR AS A GUIDE, YOU will find that you're now strong enough and supported enough to let yourself cry a little. You will be crying for you and your mother and all women, and for the future. It is worth crying over.

Big girls DO cry. That means fat girls and adult girls and basically human ladies. There's a lot to cry about. Here we're expected to have answers, and we don't even have a clue to the questions. Just realizing how long you've shut yourself up hurts a lot. Life is hard. We are asked to take on phenomenal tasks but are given very little comforting ourselves. We've all heard that little boys weren't allowed to cry, but little girls weren't supposed to cry, either. Oh, we're allowed to cry about skinned knees, lost boyfriends, broken tea cups, and some hurt feelings. But we're not encouraged to cry about the bigger issues, the failure of modern culture, our lack of grounding in self, and the myth of security and permanence. We have to keep up pretenses about these things, we have to pretend even more than the men. After all, we're the birthers, we bring beings into this life and we're the ones who are supposed to teach them to like it.

We get tired, and sad, and despairing. Our society avoids that sadness at all costs, encouraging us to be plasticized and sanitized. What happens when real life shows up and we want to live it? Sometimes we have to eat, starve, or vomit to make it through the day. Sometimes that animal behavior is our only sense of aliveness. No wonder we have to cry. The crying must be allowed. This chapter will not offer a path out of the pain, but a penetration deeper into it. We must face how hard life is.

You may now complain: "Why get more into it? I bought this book to get out of it!" Good question. I can only respond by saying that avoiding your pain is what got you here. Fighting life gets us fat. I'd certainly get quicker buyers for some new enlightenment that teaches how to shout three "hail to me's" at a mirror. I just haven't found that effective. Positive affirmations may be all well and good as far as they go. Self-talk IS important. And yes, we can accomplish new things through some positive thinking. But, for you and me, such talk wounded us further. We need crying time. Otherwise, it's feeding time.

Some things are worth crying over. Sometimes mothers couldn't let themselves cry about their real hurts, so they used their daughters to cry over and with. Sometimes moms have punished daughters when they didn't know how to take care of themselves. If mothers are not resolved about their own assets and liabilities, they may rail at a child for expecting too much from them.

If Mom feels bad about herself, you may feel endangered and degraded around her. She may be too abusive for you right now. You may need to stay away for a period of time. She may be acting out an ancient script written long before your arrival. Because of all she's ever known or expected, she has to see you as a disappointment. Of course you can't help but take it personally.

JEALOUS MOMS

This changing world has offered you many more opportunities than your mother had. As happy as she may be for you on one level, you have many more options than she did. She's jealous as hell! With all the promised possibilities of closeness between you, it is hard to face how truly distant you are. Maybe Mom doesn't even like you. Although you have suspected it, you may be trying to prove it to yourself and to your mom. You might want to believe that if you behaved better, Mom would like you better. Be careful. Perhaps you'll get proof of what you knew all along—no matter what you do or don't do, Mom just doesn't like you.

Gotcha!

"GOTCHA!" said Jody, snapping her fingers to emphasize the clarity and awareness she'd found in a recent bout with her mother. "She's always complaining that I don't make time for her. She has no awareness of my schedule, never learned what it means to be a woman out working in the world. And she always takes my necessary scheduling to make a living as some kind of personal affront to her." Jody is a fashion designer and buyer for a large chain. Her work involves competition and concentration. She has come far. She also fights her body diligently to maintain a fashion consultant's "appropriate shape."

Jody worked with me and two sponsors to get her eating behavior clean and true, and then asked her mother to join her on a four-day break she'd be having in Miami Beach. After countless excuses and misunderstandings and confusion over the arrangements, her mother finally refused the invitation.

Jody was hurt and tired of all the excuses. She came back with "Mom, look, you just don't want to be with me. You don't have to make up so many elaborate excuses. I told you we'd do whatever you wanted and keep it open-ended. You just don't want to go. You don't have to make so many excuses."

Mom answered quietly, "Oh."

"But she does have to make excuses," I countered. "Don't you see how hard it would be for her to accept that SHE really doesn't want to be with you. You want her to say the unthinkable."

Jody pondered a moment and tears welled up. "In a way I've been protecting her from admitting that. I stay busy."

"That will only work as long as you DON'T deliver, or convince yourself you haven't done enough," I told Jody. "Unfortunately, as you're now farther along the recovery path, you find that you ARE enough and have done enough, and still she's disappointed and withdrawn. Now what you get to learn is that it has nothing to do with you and your efforts. This is about your mom. She never got the loving she needed when she needed it, and neither will you. It's unfortunate for you both, but enough is never enough. Mom wanted to get the love she craves from you, and you wanted it from her. But it will always be too little, too late. Give it up."

I needed to help Jody see something even deeper than this, something that would be healing for her, her mother and her own daughter as well. "When you said, 'Mom, you don't have to make excuses,' you were wrong. That is what you have to get. Mom DOES have to make excuses. She has built her whole life around finding ways to justify to herself why she is unhappy, empty—and they're usually related to you and your efforts. Then she does whatever she wants to do. She won't own it directly, but will say other circumstances are FORCING her or making her feel or act a certain way.

"You want her to admit directly that she DOES what she wants to do and GETS what she wants to get. She's not there yet. She's not where you are. You're expecting a level of clarity and self-awareness that only comes after years of taking honest looks at yourself in recovery programs."

Jody sat quietly, and then a slight quirk of recognition appeared in the corner of her mouth. "Poor woman. I guess she really doesn't like me."

"Not as much or the way you would like," I said. "She only likes you as much as she does and can't like you any more than that. You either accept what she can give and how she can give it or you'll be railing at the whirlwind of how things should be for the rest of your life!"

"I wish she'd just admit that," Jody insisted.

"She can't. It's too much for her to take. If she can convince herself that you're the runner, she can feel abused and deserted. It's the role she's chosen for herself in life. You've filled in your part to make it work for her. But now you're changing the rules, and she doesn't know how to do this dance. It's too much for her to believe you love her, and too much for her to face that she doesn't love you as much as she'd like to."

The room felt peaceful. There was little more to say. Then Jody continued with gentle sobs: "You know, I really forgive her for not liking me too much. She really couldn't help it. She told me once that she'd never really wanted to have kids. At the time I saw that only in terms of me and my feeling rejected. But now I see it as her. She was a woman carried along by circumstance, not too aware or empowered to go for what she wanted. I became a sweetheart, working my ass off to get loved. She couldn't help being her, and not loving me."

ASK YOURSELF:

▫ *What part of your mother–daughter wound—your unresolved pain—are you afraid to cry about?*

■

EXERCISE 1

FORGIVING YOUR MOM

Take out your journal now and write a letter to your own mother. This isn't a letter to send—it's for you, for your own growth. Read it to your sponsor-mentor and reap your own rewards.

This is daughter-forgiving-mother work. Even if your mom hasn't asked for your forgiveness. Even if you're waiting for her to apologize to you. Let it go. She can't. This is truly your work.

This is something you're doing for you, not her. What writing this letter will do is help you transform yourself from an abused, neglected child into a forgiving, accepting adult. You need this much more than your mom does.

Be careful not to fall into extreme black-and-white thinking. It's not that Mom didn't love you at all, it's just that she might have been more focused on her fears for you, or on her own personal resentments, than on really watching you flower.

You obviously got some of what you needed, or you wouldn't have matured enough to be reading this book and doing this work now. You wouldn't have developed as successfully as you already have. It's just that Mom couldn't deliver more than she had.

Take up your pen now, and write about forgiving your mother.

1. Forgive your mother for not loving you as much as you both would have liked.
2. Forgive her for all the big hurts—and the small hurts. List some of the most painful ones that you remember.
3. Forgive her for not being there when you needed her, for not understanding who you were, or what you were asking of her.
4. Forgive her for being there too much when you needed your privacy, when you needed space to be yourself, to think your own thoughts, feel your own feelings.
5. Forgive your mother for not giving you the freedom you needed to discover who you were—freedom to separate from her into your own unique self.
6. Forgive her for being fearful for your welfare, and for not consciously understanding that this was the hidden motivation for her controlling acts.
7. Forgive your mother for not owning her own anger or sadness and for unconsciously passing it on to you.
8. Above all, forgive her for all the mistakes she made with you. If you're a mother yourself, you know how easy they are to make.

Here's what Jody wrote:

Dear Mom,
    I see how hard it must have been for you. I was a lot to handle. I was so intelligent and had those big eyes all the neighbors marveled at. I know you were terribly starved for attention, being a middle child and all. It must have been hard when I came along and everyone made such a fuss.
    I know you were looking to get your identity from raising me well, and when I ran away so young, you missed out on a lot of credit. I know you were resentful and jealous of me, so needy of attention, and I forgive you for it. I know you found things about my behavior to explain why you were so unhappy. Even though I went through great pains because of your being such a rigid taskmaster, your discipline has molded me into a fine and responsible adult.
    I spent much of my life trying to find the reasons you didn't like me, hoping I would change myself and mold myself as you

would want. That has made me insecure in many areas, always longing to be liked, feeling I was "never enough." I used to over-eat to dull that voice of inadequacy. Now I see how "okay" I really am. I also see how much you need to feel okay about yourself too. Maybe some day you will. Don't worry about the damage to me. I am getting out of this and doing much better today.

As Jody began the work of forgiving her own mother, she was moved into assuming more responsibility for her mature adult self. She could then heal her own woundedness in being a mother to her own daughter, Lydia.

Lydia had been anorexic for two years. Remember, Jody worked in the fashion industry. It has been suggested by some research surveys that daughters of parents who deal with looks and fashion expectations develop more eating disorders than most. The research is too flimsy to rely on, but it offers some interesting points to ponder. Sometimes it seemed the daughters were purposely rebelling against what the parents found important.

I twice spoke to the International Society for Food Media Writers. This group encompasses food editors for major newspapers, magazine editors of *Woman's Day, Family Circle, Ladies' Home Journal,* all well focused on food and nutrition. There are also cookbook writers, restaurateurs, and weight-loss experts. More than in any other group, many women called me aside to discuss a daughter's eating disorders. Daughters seemed to be rebelling against the parent's attention to the topic, the focus on food and body image.

Lydia fit such a pattern. As she entered adolescence, she picked up Jody's attention to fashion, and styled herself as an anti-hero caricature of everything her mother valued. She was emaciated and slovenly. This drove Jody "up the wall." However, as she began resolving her dilemma with her own mother, she became more accepting of herself, and compassionate about what it must be like for her daughter. One day they sat down to talk.

"I've got to tell you that you probably don't feel loved enough by me," Jody told Lydia. "The truth is I really don't have a lot of love to give. I'd like to, but I can't give out what I never got. I don't know how to do this mother-love thing. It's hard to figure just what I want, and what we can have together. I really get a lot of satisfaction from my work. Truthfully, I prefer to run around the country on trips and do what I'm really adequate and competent with. The mother deal just stumps me. I'm sorry if you feel cheated. You ARE. This is all there is."

The room filled with heavy silence. No one spoke for a while. Finally, as usual, Jody interrupted a silence that always fell between them with "I guess I'd better get to work." She never got any response from her daughter, except that Lydia's eating became more regular. When Jody finally admitted that she just didn't want to give her daughter attention, Lydia faced the truth she'd always known. Now she could stop demanding what she'd never get. A mother getting that honest is a rare gift.

Some readers have told me that Jody comes across here like a mean bitch. They say that my sharing such truths smacks of Mom-bashing. I don't see it. I see Jody's loving honesty as healthy and healing for her daughter—who knew it all anyway! The bottom line was that after this conversation, Lydia's disordered eating cleared up. What better criterion can we use?

For those of you who focus on the "hateful mother" image, I'd like to ask—"Why can't a mother be truthful?" In writing this book and speaking to these issues, I found that no matter how sweetly and quietly we tiptoe around the topic, people take offense at the idea that maybe some mothers can't love as much as they're "supposed" to.

As a mother, are you afraid to say that you gave all you could, but your daughter needed more? What's wrong with that? Does that make you a "bad mother"? If we don't break through this kind of excessive judgment and expectations of mothers, we'll never be able to talk about the subject. Isn't there any way that a mother can honestly and safely say, "I gave it my best shot, but it just wasn't enough for you. Sorry."

Having a sponsor is a special gift during these times for both mother and daughter. Mentors can play a powerful role, once you begin to realize there just wasn't enough to go around. Everyone was needy. You needed more than was there. In recovery, you can spread around some of the neediness and you won't spend so much effort taking your bucket to wells that need their own filling. There is no blame here, just reality.

ASK YOURSELF:

☐ *What clear but unspoken messages have you been unwilling
to receive from your mother?*

The Rotten-Daughter Syndrome

When mothers aren't allowed to express their ambivalence,
jealousy, and disappointment, some of them need to live out the
"hateful mother" image. They don't do it all the time. But when
they do, those are the times daughters remember and carry to
the plate. Even if daughters aren't blaming, there are moms who
blame. Some of them can be very offensive and abusive, and we
have to face their ravings. Mom may actually need to see you as
a "rotten daughter." She may need to heap all the disappointments of her life on you from time to time.

"A rotten daughter" was what Heather's mom called her.
Heather defined that phrase by eating defiantly and compulsively for three decades. Her top weight had been over 350
pounds. She came to me after she'd lost weight and wore a size
twelve. Her head was still obese with "rotten daughter"
thoughts. After being in treatment with me for a few months,
Heather stormed into my office one day, seething with rage and
disappointment.

"I don't get it! I just don't get it! Whatever I do, whatever I
say, however I am, no matter how well I think it's going, her rage
and venom are just waiting under the surface, waiting and ready
to pounce."

Then Heather sat down, took a deep breath, and continued.
"She got me again. She rants and fumes and phones her old
biddy cronies and complains about her 'rotten daughter' who
messed up again. Why does it always come back to this? Why are
we always fighting? Does she really hate me so much?"

I wanted to smooth it over, tell her it wasn't really "hate" but
fear. I wanted to explain how mothers see their daughters making the same mistakes they did, and out of an overprotective and
vain hope that their daughters won't follow the same path, they
keep a hostile vigil, hoping to forestall the inevitable. While that

was part of the story, it didn't include this hateful, vengeful, spitting, beating mother Heather had struggled to understand all of
her life. Trying diligently to understand her own self-
destructiveness, Heather had become an eating-disorder counselor. This work kept her weight off, but didn't help her exorcise
her self-hate. That took mother work.

For eight years in Alanon, Heather was guided and supported to "release with love" as her mother kept overdosing on
drugs. Relatives called long distance, berating Heather for not
"fixing" her mother. "If you're so smart, why is your mother in
the hospital? Aren't you coming home to help? Your mother is
going to be found dead one day and it will be ALL YOUR
FAULT."

They were mouthing all the ravings she'd heard for more
than three decades as her pained and lonely mom claimed a
miserable life. Mom somehow felt her pain paid for her daughter's happiness. Heather was constantly stumped. All she'd ever
heard was that mothers were happy for their daughters and
wished them well. The idea that her mother might resent her, be
jealous, and actually wish her ill seemed too sick to swallow.
There must be some more reasonable explanation for Mom's
ragings. "Maybe I really am too selfish," she'd suggested to her
sponsor. "Maybe I am supposed to do more to help her?"

"It's not your job," answered her sponsor. "All the times
you've tried to help ended up the same way. Your mother is raging about her whole life, and you just happen to be a willing, re-
ceptive ear. Nothing you try will make her happy."

Her mother painted a pretty grim picture for anyone who'd
listen: "I have a terrible daughter who won't help me. She
doesn't care and never will. She only cares for herself." Heather
stayed trapped in this picture. She attended regular Alanon
meetings, learning about separation and how individuals needed
to work their own side of the street. Reviewing her own addiction, she'd known there was no way to force her mother to accept the new way of life she'd found at Alcoholics Anonymous.
She'd taken her mother to meetings, hoping some recovery
would rub off. But her mother left scowling about how "sick and
screwed up" those addicts were. After all, her drugs were doctor-
prescribed, and just for "help with a little nervousness, to cope
with 'the change.' " Nothing could get her mother to look at her
own behavior. Mom's explanation for her depression, addiction,

and miserable lifestyle boiled down to one glaring, uncontrollable enigma in her life. "My life would be fine if I just didn't have such a rotten daughter."

That was the message emblazoned on Heather's forehead when she first came to see me, eight years after she thought she'd "finished with" her mother. She'd gotten a call from Uncle Morris that her mom had been admitted to the hospital again. It was a dramatic turning point, as Heather announced, "I won't be coming home to help," and hung up the phone. She immediately called her Alanon sponsor for support. "Did I do the right thing?" she screamed frantically. Despite all her expert training, and all the "letting go" speeches she'd made to countless spouses, siblings, friends, lovers, and parents of other addicts, this was HER mother. Knowing the proper thing to do doesn't always ring true in the heat of battle, when everything within you cries "rescue" one more time. "Isn't there something I could do? Don't you think she needs me now?" Just like every compulsive gambler, Heather convinced herself again, "Maybe this time will be different. Maybe this is the time she's ready to hear what I have to say."

Her sponsor responded gently with the same advice she'd voiced hundreds of times before. "Heather, you've done enough. Heather, you are enough. You can't say any more if no one wants to listen. Now is the time to let go and pray. There's nothing for you to do. Your mom doesn't want to hear it from you. Let it be. You've done enough."

Hitting Bottom

Between Heather and her mom there was some strange, unmentionable animosity just butting the surface, which no amount of therapy or personal growth and awareness could quiet. It wasn't like they'd never tried. Heather had attended all manner of growth workshops, group therapy, sensitivity training, private therapy, and professional seminars. She'd gone to mother–daughter workshops, studied family therapy, had a few sessions with her mother. The pain she brought to my office that day was the same she'd carried to countless other therapists and counselors.

Heather had benefited from the best of sponsoring, followed the guidelines, and let her mother "hit bottom." After two more hospitalizations her mother got off drugs. She did it without ANY help from "that rotten daughter." Heather later conjectured that this could be a message from Mom: "Even in the deadliest of times, I'll do it myself and don't need shit from you." This was an old tape from childhood. The double message was, "give more, leave me alone."

This was the paradox that kept Heather trapped. Her mom's failing life, drugged and depressed, called out to discredit Heather's wellness. As long as Mom continued to suffer, Heather couldn't soar. Heather always felt guilty about her recovering life. It was a trap for them both.

But when her mom got off drugs, it was time for Heather to soar. A major pain had lifted. With the focus off Mom, she entered therapy to look even deeper into herself. Mom's continuing problems had helped Heather avoid the work she needed to do on herself. Just as no addict can honestly describe his drug use while he's still using, a codependent, overly responsible daughter cannot see her excessive attachments to Mom until she stops the behavior. It is a form of addiction, and it develops the same denial patterns. With Mom drug-free, Heather had a quieter opportunity to look back and wonder.

She mostly wondered why she was still so attached to Mom after all these years. A great motivator was guilt. Mom was off drugs, and despite a transfer to compulsive overeating, she had developed a somewhat more conscious and healthy lifestyle. At least she stayed out of hospitals, paid all her bills, and functioned. After she became drug-free, however, Heather's mom constantly berated her each time she visited. It wasn't "Thank you for releasing me and letting me hit bottom." It wasn't "I know it must have been difficult for you to see me that way." It wasn't "Would you like to go to an AA meeting together?" Instead it was "I'll never forgive you for how you treated me that summer. You were really going to let me die!"

When Heather told me of these confrontations, she sobbed and heaved not so much with anger as with desperation and humiliation. "How do I get through to her? How do I let her know I love her? I write her notes, I send gifts, I've explained countless times about my program, my life, welcoming her into recovery. She just kicks and resents me."

For years Heather had told herself that her mother loved her. "Mom really loves me. She just doesn't know how to show

202 FAT AND FURIOUS

it. She has a different way about her. She has trouble being direct and she's afraid to be hurt." I would soon learn over many more years of working with addicts what a phenomenal amount of care and consideration daughters put into understanding and explaining their mothers. It's as if they believe their efforts to make sense of the animosity and ambivalences will pay off in diminished hostilities. I've never seen it work; but they keep trying.

With women like Heather, we have to deal with the complete inappropriateness of Mom's response. I tried as gently as I could to help Heather allow in the painful reality that perhaps what she saw was the truth—that her mother didn't like her. I shielded it with "perhaps" and "maybe" but the message was clear. "What you see is what is. No whys or if onlys. Just what is, is. Now what?"

Heather quickly responded with "I think that's because I've grown up different from her, that my values are alien to her, that my success threatens her." She had quite a few ready-made answers. She worked in counseling, after all.

"Whoa!" I cautioned. "Please, try not to 'understand' your mother's position. Try focusing more on your own instead. Allow in the magnitude of what I've just said to you. Can you let life penetrate understanding? Try to sit quietly and let reality ooze over you. Your mother doesn't like you."

"Well, sure. But don't we want to find out 'why'?" she countered.

"Why find out?" I probed.

With that the dam broke. She screamed and heaved and glared at me as if I'd brought her the dead body of a long-lost love. She couldn't understand why I didn't care WHY.

"If we figure out WHY, we can do something about it. Isn't that your job, to help me gain in understanding? Why should I waste my time and effort if I can't get it fixed?"

"EXACTLY!" I answered emphatically. Her crying stopped. Her face took on a strange calm and her eyes seemed to float wider apart as that scornful, contemplative, "figuring it out" scowl left her face. In an instant she appeared much younger. She stared at me without saying a word. For a long time, we looked deeply at each other and no one spoke. She knew and I knew that there was nothing more to do.

Rather than ending our therapy, that became a starting

point. It became a rallying cry for Heather and countless other women. What difference would knowing or not knowing make? Continuing to look at the trauma of your relationship is a simple way to avoid seeing the big picture, not to face the fact that perhaps there really is nothing to work on. This idea is so strange that it is rarely mentioned: "Some mothers don't like their daughters. Some mothers are incapable of having relationships with their daughters." These mothers DECIDE not to like these daughters for their own good reasons, and there is nothing the daughter can do or not do to change that. End of report.

ASK YOURSELF:

□ *Have you ever wanted to divorce your mother? Why?*
□ *What grounds would you give?*

Ally, Confidante, and Image of Self

Your mom may have been promised more out of motherhood than any child could ever deliver. Birthing a daughter was supposed to heal some of Mom's woundings. The whole prospect of being a mother was supposed to make moms feel better and fulfilled. Birthing a daughter, an image of self, an ally, a confidante, was supposed to make moms happy. At least that's what their moms told them, anyway.

So what's a mother to do when she delivers a sweet little girl, and instead of joy, she feels regret? Instead of longing to nurture the infant, she becomes painfully aware of her own gaping need that was never filled? Many mothers felt ambivalence about their pregnancies and had nowhere to take it, no one with whom to share it. What if Mom secretly resents the child for getting and taking so much? With no allowance or opportunity to voice that disappointment, Mom's frustrations and disappointments go underground and daughters end up bingeing and still puking the rage twenty years later.

A rarely mentioned eating problem is rumination disorder, where infants spontaneously spit up whatever food is given to them. In recent years more and more adult women have been diagnosed with this disorder. They teach themselves how to vomit and then can't stop. Research about rumination-disorder infants found that they were "unwanted babies," delivered late in the mother's life, often unexpected.

By the time the child was born, the parents were quite resolved and wanted the baby. But the infant had picked up the earlier ambivalent signal in the womb. It was almost as if the infant sensed it wasn't wanted and thus refused nurturance, in order to leave the planet, remove the problem.

As we work with daughters in our "Dearest Mom" workshops, many find they imagined their mothers didn't really want them. As they confront their mothers with this in family groups, many are blessed with a truly honest mother who admits, "Well, you are right. At the time, I was scared and insecure and actually a little depressed to be facing motherhood. Everyone told me to feel happy and elated, so I did. I'm sorry you picked up the truth of what was really going on for me. I'm happy now that you are here, but at the time, I wasn't sure." When this truth reverberates between these two brave and honest women, tremendous healing occurs.

Unfortunately, this kind of breakthrough is rare. Why? Because there are no models, and few opportunities, for mothers to explore their ambivalence about motherhood. But the hypersensitive daughter picks this up from her mother. She always knows. What she needs, what she's always needed, is someone to validate her perceptions. It's the ambivalence and lack of clarity that fuels both the mother's and the daughter's depression.

Babies Don't Do It

Each year in the United States 4,000 women are *hospitalized* with postpartum depression. Countless more function as the walking wounded, depressed, with no voice and no one to listen. Profoundly depressed mothers make headlines for abandoning or killing their babies. Often new mothers are prescribed Valium, Prozac, or Zanax to quell the depression motherhood can trigger. Combining these medications with eating and drinking eventually gets some of these mothers admitted to addiction treatment centers where, hopefully, the underlying depression, disappointment, and disillusionment will be addressed.

The mothers feel terrible that they aren't joyously celebrating the "blessed event." The babies clearly sense something is wrong. Mom's disappointment, coupled with no permission for discussing it, is dangerous for both mother and child. Had our culture allowed such talk, we could accept reality and move on. Instead, Mom's legitimate disappointment is deadly because it feels like such a major betrayal. If only there could have been more mothers allowed to speak the truth.

There is now an organization that provides an extensive support network for mothers experiencing postpartum depression. Hopefully, the depressions won't have to become extreme before more mothers can share their ambivalence with each other, and later, honestly, with their daughters.

Moms wanted to believe the myths they were taught, despite their own evidence to the contrary. And so the myths go on. For thousands of years women have had very few choices they could make about their lives—marriage or a life at the perimeters of society. The myths about motherhood were invented to help us hide from our inevitable disappointment with marriage.

The shared experience of women has also taught us that men often leave us in the lurch. As a result mothers teach their daughters that marriage isn't really about the man. He's just a tool to get you to your primary purpose—having babies. Generation after generation of women have gone through nine months of pregnancy and into labor and delivery desperately trying to pretend that they're not alone or afraid.

Until recently, very few women considered these issues carefully before having children. What was the point? Before the pill, before the women's movement, before legal abortion, such decisions weren't as complex. Women were thrust into motherhood—like it or lump it. Once lumped, we usually sentimentalized the journey. There was no one to help us explore the downside of motherhood.

Confronting Mom's Ambivalence

Mom's unconscious ambivalence went unchallenged until "choice" became a real option. At that point, when moms tried to pass along the myth of the joys of motherhood that they'd fooled themselves into buying hook, line, and sinker, their daughters clearly sensed the pain beneath the words. And that's when they began the battle to make their mothers get honest.

Mom's honesty is crucial. Daughters need it desperately. Their disordered eating is a clarion call for Mom to come out and be seen.

As you read this book and look at your own life more closely, you're likely to become much wiser in these matters than your mother. She may never be able to own up to the possibility that she wasn't happy mothering you. She just can't face it. But for your own recovery, YOU must!

Remember the letter you wrote, forgiving your mother for not loving you? Now, if you feel you've had a mother like Heather's—one who resented or abused you in some way—you will benefit by writing her a letter and telling her how you felt about all this. Write to her with no thought of actually sending it. But do show it to your sponsor—she's been here before and can be of great help and support to you.

Despite Mom's inappropriate ravings, there's another reality here that you're going to have to face. Perhaps you couldn't fill your mother's needs or heal her woundings—no matter how hard you tried. Yes, I know—it wasn't your job. Be careful of railing at your mom here. Because, in reality, she couldn't fill your empty well any more than you could fill hers. So, instead of protesting about what you didn't get, instead of yelling for her to stop demanding so much, why not just stop a minute and calmly, quietly, face the truth.

This has nothing to do with any inadequacy on your part. It was too big a job for a little kid—any kid. We can't fix our moms. They have to do their own fixing. It's a monumental task. Mom has to accept life on life's terms. She has to acknowledge and play the hand she was dealt. It wasn't your job to make things up to her, and it wasn't her job to make things up to you. You were each given a life to live in your own unique way, to enjoy in your own particular fashion.

EXERCISE 2

YOU'RE THE WISER

Open your journal now and write your own declaration of independence to your mother. This is not to be a guilty or self-condemning letter. Write this as a factual acknowledgment of what you know, what you've seen, and how aware you are.

Here are some things you may NOT put in this letter:

1. You may not apologize.
2. You may not make amends.
3. You may not show this letter to your mom—only to your sponsor.

ASK YOURSELF:

▫ *How was your mother broken? Write about all the ways in which you tried to fix her. Did it work? How did you feel about this?*

▫ *What kinds of mixed messages did you get from your mother? How did they make you feel? What did you do about them?*

▫ *How did your anger, failure, and fear show up on your plate?*

Emily resigned from mothering her mom like this:

Dear Mom,

I'm resigning from being your mother. I needed a mother, not a child. Now I see that it wasn't my job to fix you. I kept trying to salve every wound the world dealt you by becoming all you dreamed I could and should be. But Mom, I can't be a new, improved version of you because I'm me, not you. Even if parts of me are you, I want to pick and choose those parts myself.

Don't you see that I couldn't have been prettier, smarter, or happier than I was? I kept trying to get what you told me straight:

"—Be seductive and appealing, but don't be a slut."
"—Marry a doctor, but never tell the truth that I think doctors are mainly shits and certainly don't want the kind of woman I am."

"—Get straight A's, get a good job, win lots of rewards, but don't ever confess the bingeing and the starving and the lifelong self-abuse it takes to make the grade."

I tried to heal the wounds of your life by being a better you. And I ended up not even being ME! No one is big enough to fill the holes in your life but you. Your life, your unresolved pain, your fear, anger, and sadness are just too much for me to swallow. I can't feed you any more with my life's blood.

I'm resigning my role as your mother because I can no longer protect and take care of you. I have to take care of my SELF.

THESE AREN'T AMENDS! If you're actively involved in a Twelve-Step program, you'll note that the steps about "making amends" are down at numbers Eight and Nine. This is because you're not ready to actively make amends to anyone until you've done a certain amount of preparatory work first. Many newcomers show up feeling terribly guilty, wanting to apologize for their existence. Remember, you'll be tempted to apologize to your mother for failing her in ways she expected. DON'T!

Be careful here. Don't take any action yet. This letter is about your gaining clarity about your own human fallibility. It's about seeing how much more was expected of you than you could possibly have done—how you were dished out much more than you could swallow. This is not to blame your mother or yourself.

If you're working with an experienced mentor, she may advise you that "the best amends are a change in behavior." In other words, you need no elaborate speeches or proclamations of future intentions. If you recognize behavior toward Mom you'd like to change, then just begin at once and do your best. Like the Nike ad says: Just DO it!

———

EXERCISE 3

TELLING MOM WHAT SHE MISSED

Sometimes Mom's ambivalence prevents her from participating in some of the most meaningful events of your life. Often at these critical times Mom's own stuff comes up and interferes with her being in the here and now. She's too busy battling ghosts from her past. It's not that she doesn't want to be there for you; she gets overwhelmed by all the old feelings.

Think about what she missed because she was blocked. This will help you develop the compassion you will need to see her clearly.

So now take out your journal and share with her the important events that she missed. Begin with:

> Dear Mom,
> I'm writing you this letter to share with you some of the things you've missed out on in my life . . .

> –Tell her about some of your major adventures, accomplishments, and trials by fire, and how they made you who you are today.
> –How did you feel about not having her there? How would you have felt if she had been there, sharing your life with you?
> –Tell her how much fun the two of you could have had together if only she'd been available. Think of some things you could have done together.

■

EXERCISE 4

THANKING MOM FOR THE GOOD THINGS

When you write this letter to Mom, it will help heal your own wounding, remove your own guilt, and thus improve your outlook on life. This, in turn, will help you act differently around your mother. Remember all that teenage rebellion stuff? You may actually still be in that phase. It keeps you close to Mom.

But remember Mom needs a few "there, there's" every bit as much as you do. So you might want to start off:

Dear Mom,
    I'd like to thank you for all the things you did that made me feel happy, whole, and loved . . .

> –Tell her how much you appreciate her efforts on your behalf—tell her what they were and how you felt about them.
> –Tell her that you know what a difficult task she had in raising you, what a handful you were at times. List some of those occasions.
> –Tell her you wish you'd acted differently sometimes. List several of these events, remind her what happened, and tell her what you would do now if you had the opportunity.

Writing such a letter, seeing your own part in the struggle between you, creates a more humble acknowledgment within you. It's not humiliation. It's true humility. And there's a world of difference![1]

Writing this letter will help you stay a little less sure-footed. Remember, we need to stay open to new answers instead of being solidly and righteously adamant about our own position. Writing this letter also helps us get our focus off our own pain for a while. It's very enlightening to see how these woundings have been handed down through many generations. We often say, "Humility is not thinking less of yourself, but thinking of yourself less."

LIFE SUCKS. You already know that life is hard. Our task is to find the precious pockets of joy or serenity within a difficult life. The single most common characteristic for all addicts in any state of obsession is an overpowering depressive attitude that life just doesn't work. Food abuse was our attempt to "treat" this depression.

This attitude goes hand in glove with an absolute insistence that life must be fair! We keep railing at the unfairness of life, and how disappointing it is. This inevitably leads to resentment. But it's exactly the demand that life be different that keeps us tied emotionally to Mom's apron strings.

In fact, it was probably Mom herself who taught us how hard

[1]See Hazelden pamphlet "Humility vs. Humiliation."

life is, and that we have to keep on struggling. She showed us how to go about living a difficult life. She showed us how we had to keep pushing and yet hold on at the same time. Even more confusing, she told us that showing our strength would scare the guys away.

She taught us to understand and "mother" others—always to think of others' needs before our own. She taught us to be hyper-vigilant. She taught us the uses of fear. She showed us how to worry. In fact, she came close to convincing us that worrying was worthwhile—as though it would yield some beneficial result. She showed us how to suffer, but not celebrate. And she never taught us to let go.

Befriending Women

The recovery path is threatening to the entire structure of beliefs and expectations that our mothers instilled in us. Changing that belief system means growing up. It also means befriending other women.

Women have a great deal of experience in dealing with life's disappointments. It's made us strong and resilient. You may try to escape into the "man thang," but in time you'll discover that women can offer you much more comfort and support. In order to heal your own wounding, you must make a connection with others who've been through all this themselves.

Many patients come into treatment suspicious of other women. They report they much prefer the company of men— usually men they can manipulate. They "don't trust" other women because they're "game players." It's difficult for them to realize that all women recognize manipulation, because they themselves are masters of the "game," too. That's where and why we need other women in our lives.

A young television starlet entered treatment with us after seeing a male psychiatrist for two years. Under his care, she developed a burgeoning drug habit, and was so emaciated that the producers of her hit series demanded she come to treatment. Despite the doctor's help, she was not able to stop starving or vomiting. He'd prescribed both Prozac and Zanax, and didn't find her marijuana use a problem, though it usually precipitated some raucous episodes with men and food.

When she came to us, she lied about the drugs, but our drug

screen turned them up. As we discussed curtailing the drug use and sharing herself more with women than with men, she balked. Despite extensive interventions from all our staff and her strong female costar, she checked herself out Against Medical Advice.

She didn't want to face women head-on, especially her mother. She resented her mother's feigned weakness. She wanted Mom more honest. She'd hated her mother's manipulations to try to make everything "nice." She described Mom as manipulative and passive-dependent. Her child stardom had become the family's sole source of income as her stepdad became agent and manager, while Mom passively put her daughter out for hire. She both relished and resented the power she wielded in this family. With everyone dependent on her, she was able to win for herself and for Mom—despite her mom's wimping out.

She longed for a strong woman to meet her as an equal, but she also fought it every step of the way. Her rationale for leaving treatment was "I can handle things better as an outpatient." She didn't like the vulnerability of hospital admission, partly because she didn't like being SEEN so clearly. She assured us she'd find an eating-disorder specialist. Of all the warnings I gave her before she left, I was most emphatic about her need to be seen by a strong woman.

She ran from me and that concept like the plague. She hunted throughout Los Angeles, and hooked up again with another male psychiatrist. As predicted, he gave her more drugs. She stayed away from OA, and continued to obsess with food. She lost the show. She continues to starve herself and has still not connected with any strong women.

If that female closeness does not occur, her chances for recovery are slim. She won't find a way to truly emotionally and spiritually grow up and leave Mom. She will not find a safe haven within the Twelve-Step programs. She may never bond with strong women who can meet her head-on. She will then judge that all the weaker women in her life are like Mom. She'll never get to befriend all the strong parts of herself, the parts that could be modeled and mirrored by a successful sponsor in OA. A common slogan in AA is "The men will pat your ass, but the women will save it."

Is That All There Is, My Friend?

In recovery, we will get a little more depressed at first. We will come to realize that we've wasted a lot of time and have not been fulfilling our destinies. We have not been, as Joseph Campbell advised, "following our bliss." Yet, never before in recent history have women been so close to claiming the prizes of the culture. And never before have so many women developed eating disorders. It seems to be high time to ask ourselves if these are the prizes we really cherish. Before these past few decades, women provided a balance in society, when acquisitiveness and meaningless endeavors took us far off the human course. Now the entire society suffers as women don the same suit of armor as their men. But men are starting to see that the whole enchilada hasn't been such a good deal for them either. Women used to know this. But we forgot our own strengths. We settled for winning at boys' games because we hadn't learned the girls' well enough.

Facing Disappointment

Disappointment is our number-one killer. AA wisdom tells us the number one killer is resentment, but resentment comes after the disappointment. Oldtimers in AA will advise newcomers that their expectations and attachments to what they want to gain or fear losing are what will get them into trouble. We expect so much from life. Rather than give up the wanting, our ongoing recovery will involve staying true to the longing while weathering the disappointments. All have to be acknowledged and cried for. Moms tried to talk us out of disappointment. Sometimes they thought they could distract us from our pain if they complained theirs was worse. If your mom couldn't face her own pain, how could she help you with yours? What if one of her major disappointments is YOU?

The Moms Can't Help It

Recently there has been a resurgence in pregnancies, especially among baby boomers. Women are now giving birth in their thirties and forties. For some this is creating new negotiations between mothers and daughters. When mother and daughter are in a recovery program, the project is easier.

Maxine had been in OA eight years when her own daughter became a mommy. Maxine had taken great pains to ensure that daughter Beverly never had to be trapped in a marriage she didn't want. Maxine had trapped herself in an abusive marriage to an alcoholic gambler. But she enjoyed the wealth, and had supposedly made her compromises with life. She encouraged Beverly to attend law school, where she graduated first in her class. She also encouraged her to put off childbirth until she was forty.

Immediately upon delivering her baby, Beverly felt there was nothing more important in her life than her daughter. She turned to her mother expecting support and, most of all, help. Instead, her mother felt left out and confused. She knew very little about infant care. She'd had maids and governesses and had been laid up for two weeks after delivery. Most of all, she didn't have a clue how to deal with Beverly's wanting to breast-feed, or spend hours alone with her baby. She worried that Beverly might not return to her law practice. Her daughter was too happy being a mommy. She also didn't like the weight Beverly had gained, and she recited the poundage to me on a daily basis. In this case, the daughter bought into the baby boom and left her mother out.

However, Maxine had been in recovery for quite a while. She saw the value of honestly recognizing her feelings and calling it as she saw it. She sat down with Beverly one afternoon and told her daughter, "Dear, you may really need me to be a different mother than I am right now. Quite frankly, I'm out of my league here. I really don't know from infants. Quite honestly, at this stage of my life, I'm into more play and less work. I don't really want to help you or to hold the baby much. I'm just not there. For a few months, you may need to hang out with other new mothers and I'll be more in the background. I'm also finding myself monitoring your eating too much, so I think I'd better keep some distance. If you want to go out to an OA meeting, I'll lend whatever hand I can, because I know my own agenda now is to see you get back to fighting weight. I'm sorry these are my concerns, but I've got to be honest."

Beverly loved it! She saw clearly who her mother was, what could and could not be there between them, and she quite honestly appreciated how much her mother was concerned for her even more than for the infant. Mom turned out to be the only one who really attended to her needs over the next several months. Everyone else was only interested in the baby. Even though her mom showed the weight arena as her primary point of interest, it was still interest. She took what she could get.

She accepted what her mom could and couldn't deliver. That's because Mom was straight and resolved about who she was. She was in her own recovery. She talked it out with her own sponsor first, and then was able to realistically play it as it lay.

Another straight-talkin' mom was Catherine, who worked two jobs to send her daughter to college and got out to the campus once each month to take her to dinner. Her daughter, Winnie, was not only unappreciative of this effort, she was actively resentful and hostile. Their dinners were always strained. As they returned to the dorm, Winnie confronted her mother with "I really feel guilty about you putting me through school and all. But the truth is, I don't really like you. I'm mad that you divorced my dad and I hate taking your money for my education. It makes me feel bad to use you this way."

Hurt, but proud of the honest daughter she'd raised, Catherine replied, "I'm putting you through school for MY sake, not yours. So you don't have any cause to feel guilty. And you don't really have to go out to dinner. I understand."

Winnie slammed her mom's car door and stormed back to her room with tear-drenched cheeks. In the following weeks she thought more and more about her mom, the honesty of their exchange, the guilt-free relating. She appreciated how her mom had responded. It didn't make her run to Mom's waiting arms, but over the next few years she remembered that incident and developed a softness toward her mother. She also stopped starving herself and pushing herself so much at school. She graduated—without honors—but with her mother in attendance.

FORGIVENESS

I know a lot of us don't like to hear, "She did the best she could." But in most cases, it's true. You have a right to feel disappointed or cheated, but railing about it won't help your own cause. You need to acknowledge your disappointment, cry with those who want to hear about it (in most cases, not your mom), and then forgive. Mothers also have to cry because their daughters didn't "do it" for them either.

You must forgive your mother for your sake—not hers. Her self-forgiveness is up to her. She can't afford to wait for you and you can't afford to wait for her. If you don't forgive her, it means you're still expecting her to fit your expectations. You may be hoping to make her feel guilty enough to change. If you keep believing she can change, you keep demanding something other than what is really there. This binds you to her and keeps you from finding other ways to fill the need. It is better to find alternatives and let Mom off the hook.

Leslie was in a double bind, both hating and loving her mother's behaviors, and thus hating and loving all the women in her life. Her mom was a hell-raiser, bitched a lot, and made many enemies. Leslie wanted the luxury of being as angry as Mom, but she didn't want the price Mom paid, an extra 150 pounds.

"Sometimes I envy my mother because she gets to be just as mean and hateful as she wants. She says whatever she feels. If she feels like calling my dad an idiot in front of his friends or our family or whatever, she calls him an idiot. I have never heard my mother say anything nice about my dad or show him any affection. I believe she probably hates him and the part he played in making her a housewife and mother. She has alienated herself from anyone who might care about her.

"I'm a lot like my mother. I don't know how to be the other kind of woman. I have difficulty understanding these sweet, giving, loving women. They are pretty. They fix themselves up for men to adore, they flirt and are giggly and talkative. I don't know anything about these women. They scare me, they appall me. I dislike and distrust them. So the best I can do today is realize that I accept as normal what is really abnormal and do not accept what is normal."

Now, where did Leslie get her concept of "normal"? It wasn't her mother's style. Who said what was normal? If this raging mother is what she saw every day, then who was giving her instructions in "normalcy"? Both she and Mom were victimized by cultural dictums on how to act. Mom lashed out with "I don't give a damn." Leslie conformed, playing nice girl, but her problems with food gave her away. Despite all her resolves to the contrary, she and Mom both came into treatment at the same weight. She had more of Mom's rage than she ever wanted to express.

Defiant Eating

Not all fat daughters are acting out with fat mothers. Fat daughters are sometimes slapping out at thin moms. They see a thin person as doing everything that is expected of her; being well groomed, well dressed, and desirable to the world. Fat people see thinnies as lacking inner qualities. To them, thin equals cheap and superficial. They believe fat people are deep. After all, they endure belittling remarks and ridicule, and even "understand" their abusers. This makes them much more worthwhile, and long-suffering. They believe, "I suffer, therefore I am."

No one can admit this until they see it. Often a daughter's eating or starving is an indirect rebellion not to buy into Mom's expectations. Disordered bodies are defiant screams at Mom's efforts to get you packaged and thus mated. Staying fat or emaciated may be announcing to Mom that you will endure and be strong. You are resisting the call to be displayed and chosen.

Estrellita, weighing over 600 pounds, really exemplified this spotlight defiance. What was really unusual was that she asked to participate in a TV special I was making. Most people that big don't want to be that visible. Estrellita was very honest. She chose to flaunt rather than hide her obesity. Her sisters were slim and blonde, her mom was a rail. Estrellita was the family problem. Her weight became the focus of all family discussion and interaction. Everyone could mobilize anger at her obese body.

She sneered defiantly at her mother's fruitless attempts to stop her eating. She felt that her mother and sisters secretly liked her this big—it kept her out of the competition. When she was around, her bulk was all-consuming, sucking up the air in the room. Her center stage took performance anxiety off everyone else. Keeping that fat out there in view also helped protect her secrecy and her privacy. She liked people talking about her hulk so they wouldn't be discussing HER.

Early in treatment another patient asked her, "Why are you hiding behind all that fat?" Her answer was quite simple and confrontative. She knew better than anyone the rage her fat suppressed. She knew it helped everyone stay contained. "I'm not hiding. I'm making a spectacle of myself. I have made the decision to become fat and ugly for the best of all possible reasons."

Seeing is believing. Estrellita's honesty and vision are what most obese or anorexic daughters have to offer—a truth that terrifies their mothers. Her 600 pounds is just as clearly defiance as Marsha's, a thirteen-year-old punk rocker with nine stud earrings on one lobe. They both came through treatment together and both confronted their mothers about that incessant pressure to find a man.

Their mothers were initially defensive and protested that they only wanted "what's best for you, dear." Later they had to own the fears they had that their daughters just wouldn't measure up to find a mate. The daughters were quite successful at not mating. They were acting out a disowned part of Mom that really thought the mating game wasn't all it was cracked up to be. But the moms continued to play the game, while daughters failed for them.

Whip Me, Beat Me, Make Me Write Bad Checks

Many with eating disorders unconsciously seek out punishment. Sometimes it's a way to feel alive again, close to Mom. No one can get those veins sticking out on your neck the way they do when you're screaming and pleading at Mom. It's convenient to shuffle your depression onto an abuser, because then you don't see that you have already incorporated your own demons. You don't see how much of this is YOU creating the abuse. You don't see that the message you picked up from Mom was that it was our lot to suffer. The best thing you can do for yourself is to bring more of this into consciousness. That means you must not look at the person who is causing you pain. They ARE doing it. I believe you. THEY are nogoodniks. THEY are mean. THEY don't understand. THEY may even be purposely hurting you. Since you already know this, you won't benefit much from learning more about them.

The Underlying Commitment

Instead let's learn more about you in this situation. Write answers to a few questions that will help you learn more about

YOU. Whatever you're doing, you came by it honestly. Don't try to understand why you choose this abuse. That's the past. Instead focus on TODAY. Ask yourself how you choose this situation today. How many times have you been here before? How did you teach this person how to push just the right button to cause you pain? How does your response reinforce abusive behavior? These are questions between you and your inner self. These are not intended to "blame the victim." You must answer these for yourself in order to move out of the victim role. You can only sweep your own side of the street. These questions are to help you do that.

You may balk and protest that you've already been too hard on yourself, that you always take the responsible role and blame yourself when you get hurt. Well, I understand that position, too. It's easier to blame than to change. You're still avoiding taking a good, hard look at your underlying commitment to suffering. You've got to make that conscious, because then you can begin to change the pattern.

Feed Me or Starve Me

I see this avoidance of personal responsibility all too often from patients who beg us, "Lock me up and keep me from eating." They want our staff to watch them, monitor them, and force them either to eat or to stop eating. Many eating-disorder units today use nurses as monitors to check plates and count string beans to make sure anorexics are eating all that's put in front of them. I train new nurses to wash that mentality out of their minds. Our job is to point out self-destructive behaviors. But counting string beans? What does that prove?

Though many treatment centers still do this for the patient, I find it quite counterproductive. Worse, it reinforces the idea that controls will come from outside rather than from within. Unless you orchestrate your own discipline, you'll never be able to get along without guards. You'll be like the prisoners who, unable to make it on the outside, keep ending up in jail.

Most of us find our own way to rebel when we're damn good and ready. We'll return to imprisoning ourselves in mounds of fat to create enough motivation to try once more. But once we have participated in our own recoveries, once we've seen "how hard it is," we don't want to go back so easily. I don't understand why professionals buy into this monitoring role. Do they need the power?

I once worked as social worker in a methadone maintenance clinic where one of the patients tested positive on his urine sample—he'd been using heroin even while on methadone. This was grounds for immediate dismissal from the program. In a clinical staff meeting the doctor in charge ordered me to "Counsel this sucker!" I asked, "What do I do? There's no such thing as counseling in this situation. He knows and we know that he broke the rules. There is nothing to discuss."

What would he come up with other than elaborate explanation, rationalization, and basically manipulation? Nothing needed to be said. When you're hot you're hot, and when you're caught, you're caught. Danger arises when someone wants to personally put themselves in the way of consequences. A social worker seeking power and control might enjoy reprimanding and punishing this patient.

Instead I chose to bring in the facts, and let him participate in the outcome. "You've got a dirty urine," I reported. Then I asked, "What do you want to do?" Sensing the honesty in this no-bullshit approach I presented, he looked at me straight and said, "Close the case."

That's all he could say, and all I really wanted to hear. Who needs to quibble with details? Do we need to hang the worm up on a hook and watch him squirm? No, throw him back gently, and proceed with your day.

ASK YOURSELF:

- How have you made others your guards?
- How often have you hung on tenaciously in situations you knew had to end?
- What does this struggle help you avoid?

When eating-disorder patients come in wanting to be monitored, it's often because they learned that scenario so well with Mom. Mom kept the worm on the hook. I give patients the bad news that we don't bait hooks in recovery. If there are problems with following our food plan—behavior we expect, by the way—then they'll have to consult their peers, their fellow patients.

The patients help each other in living up to and honoring their own personal commitments. Others will confront them in group about why they want to be there and what they are doing with us. They will mostly be confronted about wasting time. The responsibility will be toward self, rather than others. "Is this what you want to be doing with your day? Are you getting something out of cheating or getting away with something? Who wins? Who loses?" Sometimes patients complain that we SHOULD be monitoring them, that they pay us to police them. Our staff responds, "We're not paid enough to take on that work. That's jailhouse time, and we're clinicians." Rarely have these patients known someone in authority who didn't want to use it for control and power.

A LARGER PIECE OF THE PIE? For people with eating disorders, life is sad because you feel deprived. You'll probably continue to feel deprived most of the time. Therefore, you'll have to welcome that deprivation and make friends with it. You feel you deserve a larger piece of the pie? Well, even though you deserve, you may not get. That's life. You got what you got. Others got what they got. Everything has its price.

In accepting your life, your work will be to take more charge of your own choices about where and how to be deprived. You've been seeking your just deserts in the plate instead of in life. Until you turn that around, you'll always feel like there's never enough to eat. That's because you are using food to satisfy a hunger of the SPIRIT, not of the body. What you're really hungering for is to be closer to yourself, to live a conscious life.

This philosophy sharply contradicts those writers who tell you to eat as you like to "avoid feeling deprived." I've found there's no way we can avoid feeling deprived. When our natural state is guzzling, when all we've ever known is to plug up the holes in the dike, how can we not feel deprived?

The value in this case, however, is that *you* will prescribe, orchestrate, and commit to weathering the hurt. You will decide how to hurt, how long to hurt, and where you will take your tears and sadness. You will be in the driver's seat, acknowledging your discomfort every step of the way. This, believe it or not, is so empowering that it takes away some of the sting.

In time, even food will become a major disappointment. It just won't fill the emptiness. Sometimes, for brief interludes, "stuffing" keeps us from feeling the emptiness. That emptiness is something we must experience to keep on track. Continual avoidance of that emptiness is what has kept us on the merry-go-round called denial—looking for love in all the wrong dishes. Without excess food, we can begin to tolerate our feelings, face realities we'd formerly found too painful. Slowing down and listening to the quiet, the emptiness, the void, will awaken many new sensitivities and a new depth of meaning in our lives. You'll see the wastefulness of bingeing or starving. You'll realize that they're meaningless diversions from life's really important endeavors. You'll also admit to yourself that you've been living in a low-grade subliminal depression all this time. You were committed to it. Now you will bring it fully into consciousness so that you can embrace it.

We've got to cry or eat. Perpetually avoiding that depressive voice has kept us depressed far too long. Let's first cry about our powerlessness. From childhood we're taught a lie—that we can change things if we work hard enough. We start with little doses of this myth, and move on to believing we can control the universe. There is so much that happens in life that we are absolutely powerless over. Not filling your emptiness can feel like death.

IF IT COULDA, IT WOULDA. The poet John Greenleaf Whittier believed, "Of all sad words of tongue or pen, the saddest are these: 'It might have been!' " I say, "If it could have been different, it would have been." Considering all the ingredients in the equation, it has all happened exactly as it had to. Your depression is justified because on some level you know you're damaged goods. You were given insufficient tools to get the job of life done, and you don't have a clue whether you'll be able to retool at this late stage. This is not a fatalistic, karmic conclusion, but an honest recognition that we chose our paths for the best of reasons, but that sometimes life is simply a question of blind luck or coincidence.

Whittier was facing regret at lives unlived. Modern women are facing unfulfilled, empty lives, cluttered with busyness and rhetoric, but little substance. We have to face that we're not quite as tough as we thought we were. We've been attempting superhuman endeavors, career woman, wife, mom, with time for everyone and everything but ourselves. We've been racing all over the earth as well as shooting ourselves into outer space, but the inability to live a truly human existence has rendered us terribly depressed.

Daughters Pass the Torch

Some things just won't get figured out and some things you won't get over. Your job is to accept reality, even if those around you are losing theirs. You will have to accept and live with the idea that it just may be too late to win your mother's approval, to have a happy childhood, to grow up healthy, self-actualized, and problem-free. Your mom may have been angry or depressed with you because her own life wasn't working. You may someday have compassion for her about that. In the meantime, the best you can hope for is that you can separate out whose pain is whose.

Your life's work is to constantly separate your own pain from your mother's. As you take on this project, you will begin to see how you've been reliving her unresolved pain. If she comes from a long line of women who have suffered abuse from men, you have very likely written yourself into the same scenario, trying to fix it. If she battled hard and long to avoid vulnerability, you've probably taken a similar stance. Even if her fight was passive, with personal sickness or making others guilty, you'll either relive her way or rebel into its opposite. Either way, it's all about avoiding your own reality.

ASK YOURSELF:

- ☐ *How many times have you tried to "teach your mother" how she should live? What was the result? How did it make you feel?*

- ☐ *How will it feel if you abandon your mother and start to live your own life?*

- ☐ *What will it mean if you stop suffering, but your mother doesn't?*

Let Go of Mom's Pain

Mom's message about pain and suffering has now been incorporated into every cell of your being, but you've found no way to acknowledge those messages. Making these messages conscious helps you live your own reality. Uncovering events in which you were hurt may help you get in touch with the pain, but identifying your abuse doesn't make it go away. At this point, there is no sense in uncovering more childhood "incidents." Instead, let's acknowledge that it was the entire gestalt of all home life that created the damaged being we each have to accept in recovery.

This work is getting you ready to come home to yourself. You have to get launched out of Mommy's nest to get launched into your own life. Whether you identify yourself more as a mother or a daughter, this is your work to do now.

Your own mother can rarely be the one to help you get out of the nest. The attachment is too great and there is too much to lose. When the wrenching, growing, separation time comes, Mom will not be strong enough to let you or herself separate easily.

I have treated a number of mother–daughter teams who were so enmeshed they could not allow in one ounce of separation. We watched moms completing sentences for their daughters, practically breathing for them. Daughters fought to maintain the myth that they could work out their addiction problems with Mom's help. It never worked. That neediness must be spread around.

Sometimes if we were lucky, years later the daughter called after Mom had died. She would be so devastated that she was finally able to allow in some other nurturance. Unfortunately, by then it was too late for Mom to learn about her own separate non-mom identity.

It's Worthwhile Pain

Saying "ouch" helps. Some pain is worth having; especially if it moves you toward more clarity and honesty about your life. You've known this pain all your life. It's just a question of whether you want to live with it consciously or unconsciously. *Unconsciousness promotes food abuse.* Still, we need some acknowledgment of our pain and someone to complain to about our suffering. You need to get a tad more depressed as a way to truly accept your fallible human condition.

In that acceptance lies tremendous power and energy. You're probably great at not feeling pain. During a crisis, are you hard as driven nails? Do you do what it takes to get through it all? Have you found that months or years later, when you're feeling secure and on safe emotional ground, the pain and sadness wells up from nowhere? Do you tell yourself, "I should be done with this already. Why is it bothering me now?" The answer is, the pain is welling up now because you ARE safe and strong enough to allow it to emerge and to look it in the face! Your strength enables you to experience your weakness. After all, you were strong enough to buy this book.

No Pollyannas

When you're ready to face your pain, you'll have no time for people telling you to "pull yourself up by the bootstraps," "stiff upper lip," "make lemonade out of lemons." That stuff is fine for motivational seminars or making real estate sales, but we're talking about REAL LIFE here. As intelligent as we all may be, our lives are still physical and organic. That which is not allowed to organically ooze through a system will eventually fester and burst. Some things we just don't fix and don't get over.

That doesn't mean we throw away whatever power we DO have. Your life's work will be to find the gentle, moderate path toward personal action. When you allow the oozings without soothings, your emotional experience is more immediate. In time, the gap between moving through a life experience and actually feeling it begins to be bridged. Eventually we'll be able to live and feel at exactly the same time. What a concept! This is why we need to allow all our old hurts to surface according to their good timetable, and to just let ourselves cry for as long as needed.

A word of caution is in order here. Be careful of people who can't stand to see you in pain (namely mothers), who might try to divert you or at least bandage or sedate you for a while. Many Twelve-Steppers are guilty of this—pushing for fellowship and camaraderie, encouraging newcomers to just hang out with the gang while healing. They are suggesting the people-fix. It's really not a bad idea, as long as the group will let you cry if needed. But if there's an expectation that everyone must act excited, enthused, and happy, then there is no safe place to mourn.

Where do the mourners go? When do they get a chance? Why be fearful of the pain? Are they afraid that allowing themselves to feel pain causes eating and drinking? Au contraire. It's *not* crying that causes eating.

You need to allow yourself to cry and seek out others who will allow you to cry. You need a warm, friendly face as witness. What you don't need are reassuring platitudes. Often a witness will feel inadequate and feel a need to do something. There is nothing to do. When anyone is truly facing the pain of their lives, there is really nothing you can say to make it better. Why should you? Let people have their experience. For some pain there is no medicine.

WAKE-UP CALL. That pain is a call to awakening, a call from your highest Self to make changes. It's like the painful signal from your fingers when you first put out a hand to the fire, and pulled back with an "ouch." If you don't feel the pain, you'll let the flesh burn. The same is true of psychic pain; you must feel it to know where and how to make a move. You must listen to your inner messengers. If you medicate this pain, you'll silence the still voice and find no direction for action. If you don't sense the burning flesh, then nobody's home, you're out to lunch.

A pill won't improve your hearing. It won't help you listen to that inner voice. You'll soon start to recognize how difficult the way will be. It is an inside job, and thus a journey that each of us must travel alone. But now that you have allied with a mentor for the journey, she will help you learn to recognize some of the boulders and pebbles in the road and you'll learn to sort them out from the pebbles in your shoe. Your guide is someone who has walked into and out of her own dark forest and can alert you to common pitfalls. Still there are no signposts along the way for your individual, unique life. It becomes a matter of trust and faith for you to follow yourself into your life.

Many patients get angry in treatment when we won't give "guidelines" and prescriptions. Most of our patients are such compliant people-pleasers that they would love to be handed a prescriptive formula, so that they could dance for the staff like they danced for their mothers. It is hard for our staff to sit back, wait, and not give directions.

A number of treatment programs today, in order to justify their fees or to meet criteria from insurance companies, do offer a packaged formula. Psychologically, this works along the same guidelines as the storefront weight-loss centers selling prepackaged foods. The basic philosophy is that you don't know how to choose for yourself, so someone else will handle that for you. From my perspective, such treatments actually re-create the initial wounds that brought the patient to us in the first place. Your dilemma is not lack of knowledge, but lack of paying attention to what you already know.

Let's now move on to examining what you've always known.

8

FORGIVING YOURSELF

*A*FTER MOURNING YOUR MOTHER'S LIFE, AND THE LIFE OF ALL women, you also need some time to compassionately mourn for your own life. In the Twelve-Step programs, it will be suggested that you admit your shortcomings to people you have harmed and ask forgiveness. Many sponsors advise that the list should start with ourselves. Unwittingly we have been our own worst enemies and have harmed ourselves more than anyone else.

A QUESTION OF RELATIONSHIP

As women, one of the most painful ways we badger ourselves is in the area of love relationships. In this chapter we will take a look at this very crucial issue. Ultimately, we have to ask ourselves, "What has love got to do with it?" The purpose of this exploration is so that we can operate from a position of choice rather than on automatic pilot. As each of us becomes more willing to see that we also have the option of NOT mating, we will begin to seek more authentic relationships that satisfy both us and our men.

This chapter is about forgiving yourself for all the lies you played for love. It's about you getting honest with yourself and giving yourself a rest. You must honestly face what you have been doing with relationships—the "R" word—so you can let go and really have a fulfilled life with or without a relationship.

My first book began with: "We are as fat as we are dishonest." This area of relationships is where most of us have been the most dishonest with ourselves. We owe us an apology. But we don't need to DO anything. We just need to STOP and wait and watch.

Owning Your Real Life

The whole journey of this book has been about owning your real life, finding out who you are now, and who you're meant to be. And then going out and living your life to the fullest, with integrity, style, and personal grace. For a while you'll still need mentors to keep you on the path. Part of your work as a daughter has been to differentiate, to separate yourself from your mother's problems.

Your work now is to separate from your own false programming. You will eventually be able to tolerate quiet time with yourself and appreciate the emptiness. Doing this requires your negotiating the difficult pathway between staying vulnerable, searching and open to feedback, while at the same time trusting your own instincts, knowing how perceptive and aware you are. You will also be negotiating about contact: how much or little contact to have with your mentor, your love relationships, or your work.

For women this is a much more serious problem than for men because we seem to give ourselves away, to give up the farm, and melt into other people's needs. We're even more likely to do this if we're obese. The "jolly fat person" image comes from behavior that is people-pleasing, outer-directed, sacrificing self for others. We spend so much time entertaining the troops that we lose our own counsel.

It's very important that we now begin to consider just how that kind of relating affects our soul's intentions for this life. This requires a cool, clear look at the idea of whether we do or don't want to have intimate relationships. Since you're probably on automatic pilot, you'll answer reflexively, "Why, of course I want a relationship. Doesn't everyone want to be loved? Don't we all seek companionship, a partner, a soul mate?"

Well, maybe. It's certainly worth investigating and questioning both sides of the issue, just so you can be clear and sure. If being apart is what you want, this close examination of your deepest reasons and motivations will help you become a little more accepting of who you are now. Such a choice is tough in this culture—especially if you're a woman. Remember, this whole relationship thing is woman's work. You could be putting yourself out of a job!

Is This a Relationship?

"I don't know how to have a relationship!" I hear this cry constantly, whether it's in my office, at the treatment center, at seminars, or out on the street. My answer is: Who does? Unfortunately for us, women are supposed to know all about this one. We take the quizzes in the monthly women's magazines, and they tell us we're supposed to be more sure that we want to mate. This sureness overcomes the man's ambivalence and helps us snare him to home and hearth. Well, maybe we don't know how. Even more shocking, maybe we don't want to!

Relationships require so much ebb and flow, melting and stabilizing, that it may just get to be too much to bear, too much work. Every relationship is unique and fashioned out of the chemistry of those two people. Despite great treatises based on the experiences of many others, we really can't tell anyone how to do it. Actually, it's when you try to fashion your life according to the rules of those treatises that you usually get into trouble.

Love requires a measure of action and commitment. Women still seem the more invested half of the pair. One of the first rules of chess is that the king never moves: That's why so few women play it. "Working on relationships" keeps us at hard labor instead of having a good time. But recovery is about being happy, joyous, free, and definitely having a good time. The issues of sex and relationships are critical to our recovery. When they go wrong, the plate looms large. More than anything else, a crisis in a relationship pulls many addicts into relapse. At Twelve-Step meetings, you'll find most discussions center around either finance or romance.

If we think we want relationships so much, why do we leave them so often?

You may balk here, declaring you've been in a committed,

monogamous relationship most of your life. Just because you've stayed physically present doesn't mean you've been in relationship. Your excess weight testifies that you've been out to lunch! Were you related or sedated? If you're in a food stupor, you're not really here. You may even have been using your "work on yourself"—therapy and growth—as a way to not be here. Do you find more meaningful relating in your therapist's office than in your home? How long would your relationship last if it wasn't being supported by that third leg of the triangle, the therapist?

CHOOSING ABUSE? Why do so many relationships need therapists? At any hour of the day and most nights you can hear a woman in a therapist's office describing herself as "sensitive, caring, feeling, and aware," but she's involved "with a man who is a stone and won't relate." She will say he is "uncaring, self-involved, a manipulative user."

HELLO. Mommy's home! Daughter has chosen this relationship to heal her mother–daughter struggle. She's banging on the door trying to get through to Mom. Mom didn't allow her daughter in either. That's why the daughter keeps choosing a closed-off guy. She's trying to rework the unworkable.

We then complain that our job is to change this rock into a feeling fish. We say we want to convert his stored-up, disowned pain, get him "in touch with his feelings." Our myth is that when he becomes as sensitized as we are, then he'll be perfect and our job is done. Then the job with Mom is done. As you work the suggestions in this book, you'll find yourself more motivated to self-care, to listen to yourself. Then, ultimately, you'll be able to choose a style of relating that nourishes you and furthers your spiritual journey. It is not your job to fix Mom or to fix men. You're here to fix YOU!

Women focusing on fixing their men is an extremely important issue because it serves to divert you from your primary purpose, getting home to yourself. A few years ago I attended a workshop headed by a leading feminist writer. It was titled: "Women Attending to Their Spiritual Selves." The room was packed with seventy-eight women and ONE man. It didn't take five minutes before a woman in the audience raised the question of "how fine and good all this is, but how can we get our men to go along?" This generated a lively discussion among all the women about how they'd tried to get their guys to be more open—and how THEY couldn't be open if their menfolk weren't. I saw the hour quickly passing with all this discussion about men.

Finally, I got so angry I couldn't stand it anymore, so I piped up: "There are a multitude of women in this room and one man, and we again take our time focusing on men, what they do or don't do. Why are we giving them our time? This is an absolute avoidance of our work. If we get on with our work, the men who want to join in will show up. Let's put our focus where it does the most good." I got approving nods and a few hesitant claps, and a most exaggerated nod from the man. Then the room fell silent. We didn't know what to do. Look at ourselves? Find our spirits together? Go within? It was much easier to stay outer-directed. It's what women were trained to do.

If we're not ready to do our own inner work, then thank God for the men. We can be grateful to them for being the convenient distraction. But it's only a delaying tactic. Your personal work still awaits. What if he's already perfect? What if we chose him BECAUSE he is a rock? What if the last thing we'd ever want to see is how he really feels? What if the thing we dread most of all is his opening up that pain to us, or anyone else? Maybe we chose him because he keeps the lid on and avoids feelings. After all, if he stays closed down, we can be the ones to jump up. What if he's actually modeling some new behaviors that we want to learn? What if we're trying to learn how to contain our emotions, how to mitigate our excess feelings? There must be something for us to learn here. If not, why bother to get involved in the first place? Consider this question carefully.

ASK YOURSELF:

- How many relationships have you stayed in when you really wanted to leave?
- How many partners have you tried to fix?
- How many did you fix?

You Knew You Were a Snake

We choose who we are. We choose what and who we are ready for. When we were walled off and disengaged, that's the kind of man we picked. We might have told ourselves many things about what we were doing there; but essentially we were there to find a mirror. It gave us a chance to judge and criticize someone worse off, to feel "better than." You must accept that if you chose him, you're a bit like him. You must say this to yourself emphatically, because you have been so programmed into sweetness and light. Girls are made of sugar and spice and everything nice, and that's why they get fat so easily. It would be better if you owned a bit more of your sour side. Make sure you know what you're getting and from whom. Your Inner Self always knows—ask her. Ask her to help you get honest with yourself. Jim Croce sang a song about a guy helping a wounded snake, putting it in his pocket, carrying it home. Later the snake bites him. When he complains, the snake replies, "You knew I was a snake when you picked me up." It's time to know a snake when you see one—including your own.

Forgiving Your Snake

Eating-disordered women carry a heavy burden. They see the pain of Mom and all women in relationships, and then swear to themselves, "It won't happen to me." This is true whether Mom's love life appears idyllic or horrific. Either way, the daughter senses her mother's visible and hidden pains, and swears not to end up the same way. Oddly enough, she seems almost hypnotically to re-create the same patterns.

Please don't let this scare you. Just consciously being aware of the pattern will help you avoid it somewhat. For now, you have to deeply and profoundly forgive yourself for what has happened. It's only in that self-forgiveness that you have a chance to break the generational pattern.

■

EXERCISE 1

LOVE'S LABOR LOST

Write a history of the four most serious intimate relationships you've had in your life. It might help to unearth
your picture albums from years past, or to get out those
dusty old yearbooks and scrapbooks. Before you begin, re-
flect on the family and generational perspective by thinking
about couples in your family. You'll want to look at the biggest picture that you can.

1. Plot each relationship in time and space. How old were
    you? Where were you living? Where were you going to
    school or working? What was your frame of mind?
2. Were these relationships successful or unsuccessful?
    (Just because they ended doesn't mean they weren't
    successful for a time.)
3. How were each of these relationships similar? How
    were they different? What were the most memorable
    highs and lows?
4. Do these relationships bear any similarity to your rela-
    tionship with your mother?
5. Are you in a relationship now? How do you feel about
    it?
6. What were your patterns with food during each of
    these relationships?

■

EXERCISE 2

GOOD-BYE TO BAD LOVE—FORGIVING YOURSELF

Now you've taken a look at what occurred in your family, and in your relationships with men. You did this not to
judge or criticize what they did, but to see how generational patterns are affecting you today. You've also looked
at your own intimate history. It may not be a pretty picture,
but don't beat yourself up. Just acknowledge what really
happened.

It's time to forgive yourself. Release the pain and the
power of the past. Take out your journal now and write a

letter of forgiveness to yourself. Be gentle as you ask yourself:

1. What unconscious patterns did I bring to my choice of intimate partners?
2. What lies did I tell myself about my partner? What lies did I tell myself about my true needs?
3. What role did food play in the love picture?
4. What do I need to forgive myself for?
5. Knowing what I know now about myself, how can I honor and care for my Self in intimate relationships from now on?

Elizabeth came from a long line of strong women who worked hard. Although they often financially supported their men, all the while they pretended to be weak and helpless when the men were around. Her own mother couldn't play the strong role so she spent much of her life addicted, sickly, and in bed. Elizabeth donned the corporate cloak and achieved financial and societal success. No matter what, she vowed she'd never be sick like her mother. Her sickness showed up with 100 pounds of excess weight and abusive love relationships.

Here's what she wrote to forgive herself:

Dear Little Lizzy,

I can't believe how hard I worked to protect you. But here I've led you down the same suffering path as your mom. I became a career woman, swearing I'd never be dependent like she was. I swore I wouldn't blame my children for keeping me locked into a bad situation. Instead, I did it myself.

Despite different external trappings, every relationship I've had has been a repetition of what I watched my parents do. Mom played weak, but ruled the roost. I did the same. I so wanted to make these guys into my super heroes. I would pick men who couldn't match me. The match would be off somehow, either emotionally, intellectually, financially, or in terms of personal confidence. I'd pick someone I could judge, and then I'd feel "better than." I was terrified I'd feel as bad about myself as my mom seemed to.

Despite that early "superior" feeling that seemed to ensure I wouldn't be demeaned, I'd quickly lapse into subduing myself, my intelligence, my strong assertive style, my wit and insight. I'd tell myself the guys couldn't take my strength. I wanted caring, but I thought that meant I had to be weaker. Even though the work world appreciated my strengths, in my personal life I destroyed myself. I was split—between Mom and me and who I wanted to be.

I put up with very bad behavior in relationships. I excused men a lot. I chose men who were thoughtless and very self-involved, and then I whined and pleaded for the attention I "needed," but they just couldn't understand. I didn't choose guys who could understand. I didn't want to be a shrew like my mother, so I resorted to reading all kinds of books to learn how to talk to my man.

All the reading and practicing has left me frustrated. I want to cry now. Oh, Lizzy, I'm so sorry for how much I didn't take care of you. I put all the work on your shoulders, expected you to make things work, and never saw how much you needed to be cared for and understood. I don't have an answer, sweetheart, but I do think I'll start being more careful about where I take you. I don't think you deserve or can tolerate much more abuse, especially if you're not overeating.

For now, handling this eating thing will be a way I can provide caring and also get some caring from a sponsor. Maybe that experience will later show me how to pick a caring man. For today, I just want to go on record apologizing to you. I want to be more careful and more sensitive as far as you're concerned. I'm sure by keeping the food plan aligned you will feel things directly and you'll let me know if I take us into abusive waters. Say ouch and I'll stop. Again, I'm sorry.

This apology for self-abuse is a threshold you need to cross to be truly underway on the journey of listening for your true SELF to emerge. Rather than playing roles, you'll hungrily seek out your true, authentic self. You'll need to accept yourself as a needy, greedy, go-for-it gal. Otherwise, you'll only get what's in your plate. You must continuously ask that most selfish question of all—the one Mom never taught: "What's in it for me?" It's important to think of yourself as a high-ticket and high-maintenance item. If you plan to invest your heart, your soul, or both, make the price worth it. Make sure you don't sell yourself short—don't give yourself away.

We Must Be Bothered—Our Lives Depend on It!

As troublesome as they are, relationships are where we can grow. The struggle provides grist for the mill of our own evolution. Many of us judge ourselves harshly for choosing difficult relationships; but some deeper understanding within us knows that we needed this challenge. Sometimes even the pain is healing. Maybe this new relationship gives us an opportunity to cry unshed tears from our past. Maybe we need the catalyst.

Some women opt for finding the perfect, nice-guy-gentleman who won't cause them any trouble. Well, sometimes nice guys' wives finish last. Daughters of highly explosive, enraged mothers will often seek a mate who is quiet, withdrawn, and slow to anger. They've used up their fight on Mom, and as adults they seek a safe harbor for rest. Usually their mothers don't like this choice of mate. Such moms berate and criticize the quiet spouse, demeaning his manhood and strength. Unconsciously, what they're really afraid of is that their daughter is really calling off the entire fighting scenario. She chooses peace over war. Mom wants war.

Daughters who've been abused decide that what passes for love is actually the absence of violence, abuse, and criticism. They think that being left alone and not attacked means they are loved. Mothers see this as a threat. It's as though their daughter has gone over to the enemy. She's hanging out with the "normies," opting for a quieter, gentler road. Mom may complain, "He's such a wimp, it's hard to get a good fight out of him."

Actually these mothers may not be far off the mark. It seems that opting for this nice guy might not be too healthy a choice. Peace, love, and good vibes aren't necessarily the healthiest way to go. Statistically, wives usually outlast their husbands, but not so if they choose nonfighting mates. Just the opposite happens. Wives die first.

Recent research found that women married to mild-mannered guys died younger. Men who will not fight it out with their wives usually develop less interest in the wife sexually, ultimately rejecting her in bed. She ends up the loser. These wives die of benign neglect. They were grateful not to have married abusers. But, on some level, they got just as bad a deal. They blind themselves from seeing this subtle rejection by eating, instead. In the opening of May Sarton's book *A Reckoning*, the elderly heroine says, "A good marriage shuts out a very great deal." Even when it's good, it can still be avoidance.

RELATIONSHIP MYTHS. With all of the big questions looming for women today, it's no wonder we'd rather withdraw into food and drink. These comforts never fail us. We can control them. It's a game we know instinctively without having to develop new tools.

Perhaps the relationships we say we want are really fantasies of what was supposed to work for Mom, developed from her myths, based on what she was taught. Many of the old relationship myths were based on women disowning their power, acting weaker or dumber than we were. Living honestly may render us less likely to attract an "ordinary" man. Staying out of the food plate, with or without a mate, requires rethinking the meaning or value of relationships for your current functioning. Many mothers and daughters stay closely allied in the perennial complaint of how "no good" men are. Perhaps it's because the whole myth of "happy ever after" never did work, but we blame it on the men.

Ménage à Trois

You must carefully tease out whether your quest for relationships is about an actual man in your life, or whether it's more about healing some agenda with Mom. Is he someone you love, or is he a trophy on your mantel to show Mom? It's very important to sort out whether you're using your man to enhance your ego. Ask yourself: Do you depend on his advances as proof of your worth? Do the two of you get into power struggles around this issue?

Most addicted women have this problem. It's often an attempt to make up for what was missing with Mom or to prove something to Mom. Are you having a *ménage à trois*? Psychologically, is Mom in bed with you? Are you proving something to her? Are you teaching her something? Is there another side of you that shows up in bed? Is it a side not integrated into your regular life? Is this side of you something that Mom disowned about herself?

The Critical Choice: Relationship or Solitude?

Many of us who have spent our lives trying to please the crowds begin to feel a strange reality creeping in during recovery. We keep asking ourselves if, perhaps, we'd rather be alone.

You may find that you do, indeed, prefer to be alone, to be out of the race, away from the fray. Food helps us stay out there. We haven't yet found a way to accept how much we truly enjoy apartness and being by ourselves. If this is your choice, you need to find a way to welcome yourself, by yourself, without needing food as a substitute.

It's not about being liked. Many say they want to lose weight to "find a man," "be part of the gang," "gain acceptance and security." But what if that's not what we really do want? What if getting accepted, being chosen, hangin' out with the guys, isn't all it's cracked up to be? Maybe that's the disappointment we don't want to face. Maybe we don't want acceptance as much as we think we do.

Quite often it's very hard to take the acceptance and involvement we say we want. Sometimes we eat as a response to that acceptance. We have to keep asking, is this what we really want for ourselves. Do you remember Greta Garbo's line—"I want to be alone"? Perhaps Greta Garbo knew a thing or two.

WE WANT TO BE ALONE. Most of us have never explored the possibility that perhaps we want to be alone, that often we can't stand the company of others. This issue was easier to deal with when THEY were rejecting us. We could deny that we were the ones doing the rejecting. But we can't deny it when we're alone with the food, groveling at the plate. *Sometimes running to the food at social events is a way to keep away from people.*

Dr. Stanley Schachter did some interesting research at Columbia University in the late 1970s. He saw that food "worked" differently for different people. Obese subjects ate the least in a neutral situation where they were neither rejected nor accepted. Neutrality, being left alone, produced more normalcy in eating behavior.

Even when mated, we may not be sated.

Craving the Danger

Just as many of us have difficulty accepting success, we may also have difficulty being accepted in love relationships. Perhaps getting accepted and being mated is not such a safe place for us? Maybe it feels deadly? Maybe alone feels best. Maybe we actually crave insecurity and rejection. It is, after all, a safe harbor, a home base, predictable and survivable. Acceptance isn't so secure. Maybe addicts have a little more of that wanderlust; they crave excitement and danger.

Those of us who came from alcoholic homes are surely comfortable with excitement and chaos. We need the tension to feel at home. If it's not there, we'll create it. One sponsor told me that when she finds a newcomer who really wants to talk intimately, she takes her out to a bowling alley where they can relax to the sound of crashing pins. She says the familiar chaos makes it safer to COME OUT. Actually, if the mating we've chosen is fraught with ambivalence and insecurity, that may be just about as much "relationship" as we want. It keeps the action going. It may not fit the traditional model of coupling for safety.

Many who choose such excitement call themselves love addicts, codependents, or relationship runaways. Just as it's been said that compulsive gamblers play to lose, these people may enter relationships with their exit visas already stamped. If this feels familiar, it still may be very difficult for you to honestly stand up and admit that there's something appealing about all this insecurity and excitement. Perhaps it's helping you avoid the Inner Voice—that may be a bit too honest right now. But what if you actually went ahead and admitted it to yourself? What would it mean to acknowledge that you actually choose and savor getting out?

In fact, what if we seek relationships as an escape from the Inner Self? Mom taught us to run from it, no matter what. Most of us found that we'd ended up marrying our mothers. We marry the same power struggle, battling to be heard. If that battle gets removed, if we start choosing relationships for totally different reasons, how many of us will still want to get involved? Will it matter who we really marry? What if we chose our relationship not to get fixed, but to give service? That doesn't mean becoming servile—but rather serving your own highest instinct. That will bring out an entirely different agenda. If there are strange voices to hear, changes in store, we need to savor our alone time. What if we're not yet ready to hear the call, to travel to the alone, meditative, "sure-of-oneself" place?

The most preoccupying, involving business to take on is "having a relationship." Sometimes when I was developing a new relationship, my friends didn't see me for a while. They'd approach after a long absence with "Where've you been?" I'd answer as if it made sense, "Oh, I've been in a relationship." It was as though I'd gone to a foreign country.

My relationships helped remove me from my life. It was how I avoided myself. Finding a way to be in or out of a relationship, but always IN my life, is what my recovery has been about. It meant giving up the overriding fears that the culture instills in me about "being alone." Supposedly, the worst thing ever would be to end up alone. Why fear it so?

ASK YOURSELF:

◻ *Are you uncomfortable when you're not in a relationship?*

◻ *Are you afraid of being alone?*

◻ *Do your relationships help you avoid yourself?*

PURPOSEFUL RELATING

An important concept throughout your recovery will be to make all your endeavors count. What you do in relationships is all about helping you contact and embrace your Higher Self. Make sure your relationships do that for you. Maybe your relationship is making you look at how much you like to control things. Maybe it helps you see how insecure you are, and how much you need validation. Maybe it lets you see how much you flower with a bit of encouragement. Maybe it lets you see that you can make big mistakes, but people will still love you. Make sure you're using this experience to learn about yourself, to grow. Otherwise, you'll stagnate into business-as-usual. It is so easy to do.

Often recovery programs are criticized for breaking up marriages. What really happens is that someone who got married or involved—as a way to stay insulated and avoid the ebb and flow of growth—begins to see that this choice requires substance abuse to survive. But once they become motivated to go with the flow, they develop the energy and drive to get themselves out of stagnant accommodations. So, depending on your point of view, you might say recovery messed up the marriage; or you might say marriage messed up the growth.

However, it isn't always true that relationships break up in recovery. Some sponsors strongly recommend that you make no major life changes within your first year of recovery. This is partly because relationship struggles indicate areas where you need to do work on yourself. The other reason is that once you do this inner work, the relationship may evolve as well.

As Lenore's recovery from compulsive overeating moved into its third year, she was beginning to feel more comfortable with the new body, now minus 150 lost pounds. She loved the whistles, the compliments, the CLOTHES! My God! Trying on, and buying, all those clothes was more heavenly than any orgasm. But she'd also had a few thousand of those over the last two years. Her great fear about weight loss—that she'd go raping and pillaging—did come to pass. Despite an insatiable sexual appetite and ready access to numerous beaus, she came to me depressed about the prospects for her romantic future.

"I just can't seem to find a man for me. There are none out there. Every man interested in me turns out to be married, or some other type of 'nogoodnik.' I'm really scared that I'm going to end up like my mother, all alone."

I suggested gently to Lenore that some say, "We are what we do, not what we say. Perhaps there's a large part of you that actually wants to be alone. After all, your fat had served to keep men away. Just because you've lost the weight, why assume that you immediately want a man in your life?"

"Are you kidding?" she said. "I've been working like a dog to find a man to marry. I schlep to 'nice-Jewish-boy' dances, put up with 'the hand squeezer,' 'the foot stomper,' all the while trying to show everyone that I'm available, friendly, and interested. I've invested a lot of effort in finding someone. There's just no one appropriate out there."

I could tell we were treading on dangerous ground and Lenore could quite possibly reject therapy completely if I pursued this truth too quickly. All she wanted to see was that her efforts read as tragedy. But it was her way to stay busy with the project, and avoid the reality that she really wanted to be alone. She didn't see how she found men in order to leave them.

In each instance she knew exactly why she'd be leaving. She'd scope out his defects in the first five minutes but figured he'd be "okay"—with minor adjustments. These "adjustments," of course, were such things as "curing his alcoholism," "getting him to leave his wife," "teaching him how to dress and talk correctly," "getting him to stop smoking," or "helping him get a better job." There was always something.

If you asked Lenore, she'd protest that she did want a relationship. Just not with anyone she'd met yet. At one point, she'd even made up a list of men inappropriate for dating. These undesirables were: anyone at work; anyone in AA; anyone in the neighborhood. Basically, they were anyone she'd ever see again. Since some part of her knew in advance that things were not going to work out, she wanted to make sure she'd never have to encounter that person again after the breakup. Does this sound like someone who wants to be involved?

Shadow Boxing or Relationship?

It was difficult for Lenore to give up the shadow boxing of working on having a relationship. Almost as a last gasp of a "relationship" junkie, she suddenly found great stashes of accessible men wherever she went. Without even trying, she seemed to draw men toward her. One night she went to a club, was asked to dance every dance, and found three different men who wanted her to stay and talk. She just wanted to flit and flirt and kept herself circulating. For a girl who'd been fat all her life, who'd sat out every high school dance along the gym wall, this belle of the ball *role* was flabbergasting. She left early, giving no one her number, self-satisfied but alone.

Lenore reported to me the next day that when she put her key into the car's ignition, she'd had one moment asking herself, "Should I have stayed to encourage those men some more?" Her Inner Self's answer came instantly, and it was different from anything she'd ever learned in life: "No! I really want to be alone. Just because they want me doesn't mean I want them. There's no great shakes in being chosen."

This simple statement represented a great turning point in Lenore's recovery. And this realization seems to be the largest stumbling block for most of the women I work with. Trained since childhood to dress up and trot out the doll so someone will pick it up and take it home, we never even allow ourselves to look at whether we might not want it at all.

I suggested to Lenore again, "Maybe you really don't want a relationship." She argued louder and more frantically than before. "How can anyone NOT want a relationship? Isn't that what we're here for, after all?" Then she attacked, "Aren't you a family therapist? Isn't it your agenda to help people have meaningful relationships?"

I said I wasn't really sure I had an agenda, that my work was more responsive to helping her find what worked for her. I wouldn't lay a relationship on her, nor would I suggest she stay alone. I just wanted to help her find her own truth. Then, disclosing a little more about my own process, I shared with her what I'd found out about myself and my choice of career.

"Sometimes I think I really prefer the kinds of intimate relationships I'm able to establish in my therapy practice. They're time-limited, and I'm pretty much in control. People know I care about them intensely and deeply for the time we're together—they pay a fee for my time, so nothing is owed, there are no strings attached. It's clean. Real life is a lot more messy and bothersome. People don't play by the rules. They make them up as they go along. Relationships require a lot of flexibility and adjustment. That takes a hell of a commitment of energy and hard work. I'm not sure I'm up to it."

Lenore stared, dumbfounded. She looked at me as though I'd just attacked motherhood, the American flag, and apple pie. I could see she was questioning the whole nature of existence. She also seemed touched that I would be that honest with her. She told me she'd begin to consider the possibility that maybe she might want more apartness than she'd been able to admit.

"Okay," I countered, "why don't you do some homework for me before our next session. I'd like you to write a paragraph, or a page, allowing yourself the possibility that perhaps you really don't want a relationship. Just sit down and start writing and see what flows. I call this 'giving it the barest.' Just write as if there's the barest ounce of truth that maybe you'd rather be alone and not involved. It's a very safe way to just try it on for size."

Lenore laughed a bit ironically. "I certainly know about trying on for size," she said. "I squeezed my fat fanny into enough tight pants! Okay, I'll go ahead and tug this zipper and see what happens." She was still maintaining that self-abusive buffoonery, making fun of herself, still acting fat. She chuckled her way out as our session ended.

What She Learned

The next session she appeared ashen and entranced. As soon as I closed the door, she broke into sobs. After a few moments, when she was able to formulate words, all she could say, with smiles brimming through her tears, was "I do want to be alone. I would never have believed it. I certainly wouldn't cop to it if asked directly. But now I'm really sure I don't want a relationship."

"What's happened since the last visit? What did you write?" I had a million questions, but sat attentively and waited.

"First of all, I didn't write immediately. I left here angry and confused, and thought of calling another therapist. I think you're sort of weird, being a family therapist but encouraging me to value aloneness.

"But that night I had a crazy, upsetting dream. I was a woman warrior on a battlefield. There were many overturned cannons and carts and thousands of strewn bodies. It was smoky and foggy, but you could tell there'd been major mayhem. I roamed around sort of unbalanced, trying to maintain my footing. After a while I worked up some courage to take a closer look at the mess, to actually see the strewn bodies. They were all decapitated bodies. They were all ME!"

She couldn't stop the onslaught of tears, and I had no desire to change her focus. She cried for a full half hour and then her sobbing ebbed. I made no effort to touch her or console her. I waited.

She looked up, dry-eyed, and smiled at me—not joking or self-effacing, but sincere and knowing. "Those were all the games I've played for love."

"How do you know that's the message from your dream?" I was concerned that she might have been unduly influenced by me and was making up what she thought I'd want to hear. *Eating-disordered patients are skilled people-pleasers.* They can be difficult to treat because they are often so compliant that they perform in therapy the way they've performed all their lives.

Lenore, however, had found her own clarity. "It all made sense when I started writing the next day. I did what you said. I began with 'I'll give it the barest ounce of truth that maybe I don't want a relationship.' Then I just sat there and felt blank.

"Suddenly, I heard plop, plop sounds. There was nothing and no one around me that could make such a noise. I quieted myself to listen. I realized it wasn't plop, plop. It was sock, sock. It was fists hitting flesh. It was the sounds of someone being beaten. I started crying, but I didn't know why.

"Then I seemed to hear a children's nursery rhyme at the back of my ear. I couldn't make out the tune or words, but a little girl was humming. There was a crashing sound like glass breaking, and the humming got louder. I stopped and closed my eyes.

"In an instant I had a flash that illuminated all the blank space at the back of my lids. I saw, heard, and felt every bit of the scene. It was all so vivid, so clear. It was my parents. They were having a fight. I was five. They were running after each other through the house. I never saw the punches, but I heard them through the wall. I didn't see the cups either, but knew they'd been smashed over someone's head. I began to hum and rock. It would end soon. Just a few punches more I was sure. It didn't stop.

"I wandered into the hall. The place was a mess. What could I do? I got a dustpan and started sweeping. All I could do was hum. At least I'd help with the mess."

Lenore rocked herself slowly and in a few minutes opened her eyes. "That's what I know about relationships. Despite whatever I learned from Hallmark cards, and whatever lies my mother fed me to cover up the horror she'd lived, my wise little five-year-old knows exactly what it's all about. No thank you, sir. I'll do it myself."

There was nothing left for either of us to say. Lenore's journey into truth began that day. She'd explore deeper meanings for her fat, her loves, her personal integrity, and her boundaries. It began as it does for us all, by first accepting exactly and unequivocally just how it is. The truth sets us on the path, and our soul's quest for wholeness sets us free.

We've been so busy looking for union, we don't acknowledge our need for separateness and apartness. We don't know how to be alone. Mostly, we run in terror. We need to be alone to hear those inner voices. Togetherness too soon might be deadly, engulfing and overwhelming. Some relationships are like returning to the womb, home to Mom, to the deadly merger. Relating will feel like death.

ASK YOURSELF:

- *Do I really want a relationship in my life? If yes, why? If no, why?*
- *Can I be in a relationship without losing my Self?*

EXERCISE 3

GIVE IT THE BAREST POSSIBILITY

I now invite you to do the same writing assignment as Lenore. Write about some aspect of your life that you struggle and protest against. This may be your relationship struggles, your job struggles, your social life struggles, your family struggles—whatever is uppermost in your mind.

It may be a struggle because you just can't accept that this is how you want things to be. Just give it the barest possibility of truth. Try on the thought for size—that just maybe you want things exactly the way they are. That maybe your Inner Sensor knows exactly what she's doing and why.

Even if this all seems like a crock right now, even if you feel you'll write only lies, write it anyway. Just see what comes out.

For example, Helen was focused on relationships. She wrote: "I, Helen, do not want to be in a relationship." Just writing the words on paper left Helen in a cold sweat! But it opened her up to the barest possibility that her actions were speaking louder than her words.

Now it's your turn. Just sit down with your journal, take out your pen, and see what comes out. Complete the following thought:

1. My mind says I want _____
    My actions say I want _____
    Now I'm willing to entertain the barest possibility that what I really want is _____
    _____

Why Bother with Relationships?

All this discussion about relationships has been necessary so that we can take a realistic look at what we're after. We also need to acknowledge this to ourselves, and to accept the truth of our previous programming. Women may have very good reasons for avoiding men and relationships. Daughters who witnessed their mothers being beaten or berated by husbands—despite Mom's declarations to the contrary—developed their own opinions that coupling was not such a good idea. Even those who grew up insisting their lives would not turn out like Mom's unwittingly harbored some of Mom's judgments and fears. They weren't necessarily all that grateful about being chosen by such a lout.

Notice the prejudices in this culture. What daughters sense that mothers can't face is that women are still the ones who are blamed for a failed marriage. Relationships are women's work. If the woman has some type of addiction, it is triply her problem if things don't work out. If a woman stays with an abusive man, we mock and gibe with "Why doesn't she leave that S.O.B.!" Usually she stays because she has no resources with which to leave. However, if a man stays with an abusive, addicted, or fat woman, we exclaim, "What a prince of a guy he is!" No wonder daughters might not want to hook up so quickly. They see it as a way to get more abuse and criticism. Daughters listened closely to Mom's discontent.

IN RECOVERY—SEEKING THE COMFORT OF WOMEN. Only other women can understand and comfort your connections to Mom's pain—as well as your endless work on relationships. You must turn for comforting and consultation to other women who are trusting their Inner Wisdom. That will be very hard to do. You will have to overcome your fear of trusting your Inner Voice, the messenger of the Spirit. And you'll have to get past your internalized critic's assessments of other women. "Other women can't be trusted because they're getting the same messages I'm hearing," says the critic. She knows those messages are rumblings too dangerous for the social order, too threatening to the status quo. So she quickly tries to get you to disown them, to blind yourself again.

The Life or Death Battle of Trust

The reasons the messages from within are so threatening is that they move you away from Mom's teachings. They make you think about how you really view the world—and your life within it. More specifically, they make you think about the possibility that you can be content and happy though "alone." This idea is worth exploring whether you're mated or not. After all, even when we're in relationships, we often have to weather loneliness.

This isn't some coffee klatsch discussion of simplistic matters, such as which wallpaper to buy, or who does which dishes when. A conversation with your Inner Self is more about the meaning of life—your life. Just below the surface bubbles a tremendous sense of entitlement, a powerful "go for it" energy just waiting to be released. Moms tried to shield us from this voice for fear it would awaken their own. It was easier to teach us that we lived in a hostile, menacing universe—that way we shouldn't expect too much. "Trust us," they said. "We've been there, we know."

Mothers and daughters do great battle over trust. That particular battle involves the most important question for all humans on the planet. Should we live in fear or faith? Do we live in a benevolent universe? Is good meant for us?

No lesser a mind than Albert Einstein's posed this question. After he'd developed his relativity theory, explaining how the universe works, a reporter asked, "Now that we see how the universe works, what is the next great question for mankind?" He answered quite simply, "The most important question facing us now is: 'Is the universe friendly?'" Even if we understood its workings, we'd still need to take a giant leap of faith to believe that good was intended for us. This very issue is at the heart of the mother–daughter addiction struggle.

The addict's mother believes in a hostile universe. She's scared, and constantly giving warnings to her daughter. She figures the boys can take care of themselves. She panics when she sees how trusting her daughter is. Mom tries to shield the daughter from her own mistakes. She has a great ability to absorb the negative and a complete inability to believe in or trust the positive. Some modern moms have read enough self-help books to convince themselves and their daughters of the value of "positive affirmations." They propose faith, love, and good vibes. Their daughters sense the lie. They fight their knowing with food or booze, or they puke secretly, hoping to flush it away.

Dying to Believe the Lies

We also ignore our instincts so that we can continue to believe certain lies that we know would take too much to confront. Think about all the countless lies that women in this culture swallow hook, line, and sinker. For example, we're beginning to uncover numerous reports of male therapists having sex with their female patients, some even charging fees for the session! When such a therapist suggests that his penetration will help clear up troubles in her marriage, do you really believe she doesn't have some inkling that this may not be quite the best method? Does she think this is marriage counseling? She talks herself into it. Actually, what she's really doing is talking herself OUT of what she knows. She shuts out her inner voice by eating, drinking, and then, of course, screwing.

A scandal was recently uncovered in a farm community in the heart of America. It seems the local well-respected physician had been violating three generations of women and had never been confronted. All it took was one woman deciding to break the silence. She spoke of making an appointment for treatment of a head cold; but then she was placed in stirrups as the doctor probed. And this was not the first time!

Soon the whole town was a-buzz with stories. What made each of these women decide to turn off their instincts, to stop listening to their heart of hearts? When our bodies are violated, we can't pretend. The body doesn't lie. How could mothers take their daughters to the same physician, telling themselves it wasn't really happening? How could they take their granddaughters?

Blaming the poor, misguided, wretched doctor doesn't get them out of their own stupor. They have to wake up and face their own betrayal of Self—their own soul's crying to be heard, to be honored. But this is so hard. That's why most of us continue with addiction and choose not to know. We take a look only if we're forced to—only if our lives are at stake. With addiction, they are!

It will be helpful in your quest for your true Self if you look closely at the deals you were making with yourself when you believed the lies. You must have decided somewhere along the way that shutting up your Inner Voice was worth the price of the goodies you sought.

In most cases, the sellout was for power. We somehow thought that if we went along with the lies we'd eventually get some power over the situation. We'd be able to turn the tables and win. Most of us thought we could "manage" the situation. Just a few white lies, and patience, and it would all work out. Well, we also thought we could manage drugs, food, and sex.

Blaming the Victim?

We often tend to look at our lives from the victim–perpetrator point of view. We, of course, are the victims, succumbing to overwhelming power. We blame everything wrong in our lives on the perpetrator and fail to look at our part in the whole drama.

Now, it's hard to get this perspective. And I'm not saying this to put the blame on the victim. My intention here is to empower you as an adult, to help you step out of your victim shoes. To help you see some of the powers you had all along. Until you can acknowledge your own part in creating your life nothing can change.

We're the ones who betrayed our own trust when we decided not to know what we knew. We learned from watching our mothers how to be swept away and irresponsible. When your own time came to confront, rebel, and say no, you didn't. Perhaps you weren't willing to pay the price of rebellion. You hoped you could beat the odds and win. This is actually a subtle form of compulsive gambling. You thought you could get away with lying to yourself. You lost the bet. You survived on the outside, but your Inner Self went hungry.

Part of the problem has been your understanding, compassionate heart. You may have been too understanding. Part of women's work has been to understand. But while we're working so hard at understanding others, we completely lose ourselves. And even when others hurt us, we somehow end up feeling sorry for them. When I was a small child I was taunted for my obesity. Groups of mean-spirited children sang,

> *Fatty, fatty, two by four,*
> *can't get through the bathroom door,*
> *so she did it on the floor,*
> *licked it up and did some more.*

I looked at my abusers with a compassionate heart, feeling sorry for them that they didn't know how much they hurt me. When I wasn't focused on feeling embarrassment and shame for them, I took myself even farther out of the situation by considering my parents back home. I thought about how badly they would feel if they saw these people taunting me.

I was always able to feel and understand the feelings of others rather than my own. It's no accident I became an excellent therapist. In recovery, I had to learn to feel my own pain, and care lovingly for that wounded being. I'd learned that caring for others doesn't get YOU the caring you need.

Be careful now not to blame yourself. Just because you acknowledge your part does not mean that's all there is. Many of us avoided looking at our side in things because we're afraid that means we're totally responsible. But it's never one-sided. Guilt would be quite wasteful here. You must take an honest, clear, compassionate look, and then mourn for yourself and your previous inability to access your power. If there is any guilt, it may be toward your Inner Voice that you cut off and tried to shut up with substance abuse. You might give her a big hug at this point and apologize for copping out on her. There is no blame here. You have been hurt by your inattention more than anyone else. Think of it as benign neglect.

Time Out for Self-Love

Taking time out from intimate relationships gives us a chance to really listen to our Inner Voices. The old saw about a woman being nothing without a man is a lie! Healthy relationships can be delicious and exciting experiences. But relationships that make our companions the center of the universe are life-threatening. What we truly need to learn is never to sacrifice our Inner Self to an outer other.

Our relationship with our Inner Essence can be the most rewarding affair of our lives. It can enable us to find new joys and new satisfactions as we live a life no longer controlled by food.

ASK YOURSELF:

- *How have you blocked your Inner Wisdom in your intimate relationships?*

- *Are you willing to take a "time-out" from relationships to feel inner emptiness?*

- *Tuning in with your Inner Wisdom, how would you "do" your relationships differently?*

COMING HOME TO OUR LIVES. You are now invited to come home to your Self. This isn't a prescription for deprivation. It's really a loving invitation. You've already been more deprived than you can imagine. You've been deprived of your own counsel. I invite you now to turn on to your own life. Go for it! Remember who loves ya, baby! YOU DO!

Were you taught not to expect too much? That's another of those lies we swallowed. Your excessive eating is a signal that you are hungry for more out of life. I now invite you to the feast of life, but using a whole new approach. Instead of bingeing and starving, you'll model yourself after people who have been where you are, but who allowed themselves to become more "deserving." People like myself, who became willing to accept the good life with gusto. People who grew up and found home . . .

9

WELCOME HOME

"I found God in myself and I loved her fiercely."
—NTOZAKE SHANGE

WE ARE SPIRITUAL BEINGS TRYING TO HAVE A HUMAN EXPERIENCE.
Some say we were sent here from the spirit world to be tested
and to grow. Hindus even say we float around heaven looking
for an opportunity to complete our incomplete development.
We find the parents we need in order to get that work done and
then get ourselves born to them. We come to the earth to rub
and chafe and smooth our stone. When all our rough edges get
smoothed out, we're ready to return to the life of spirit. This last
chapter is about reclaiming your lost soul, your spirit, your essence, your reason for being here.

This reason for being, what the French call *raison d'être,* is
what you lost when you turned to food. You gave up on your
spirit. As a survival rather than growth maneuver, you chose to
stay imprisoned by your animal nature. Now as a recovering person, you will learn to integrate your animal and spiritual na-
tures. This is the challenge, the pain and the joy of your life.

LEARNING TO LISTEN

Each of us is part animal and part spirit; part body and part
soul. This is our blessing and our curse. Learning to integrate all
of our parts together into one whole functional being is our destiny. We have to grow, change, and stay ever flexible and open.

Ours is not a rigid existence. We have to remain what seems unbearably vulnerable. Angels have it much better. So do cows. Angels are born angels, float around heaven all day, and stay angels forever. Cows know only their animal consciousness. They chew their cud, have sex, produce calves, and die. They live a simple, earthbound existence. Humans are put in the ever-changing landscape between heaven and earth; the horizon between spirit and matter. On our journey we learn to balance these two states within ourselves, finding our own personal path on a daily, sometimes hourly basis. It can be a wonderfully exhilarating adventure, or it can be a terrible pain in the ass.

Which it is depends on our attitude, our abstinence, and our willingness to risk going with the flow. It also depends on staying in contact with our mentor, initially at least daily. She'll help you orient yourself and will alert you when you start running away from yourself. Without feedback from a significant other, you'll be the last to know this. I'd often have elaborate treatises for my mentor to explain some self-destructive plan which seemed like "a good idea at the time." She'd respond with "It seems okay on the surface, but something about your idea just doesn't smell right. I can't put my finger on it exactly, but something's wrong." She was trusting her instincts, flying by the seat of her pants, but honest enough to let me know it smelled a little rotten.

You'll have the same experiences and, if you're open to it, you'll meet the same kind, honest feedback. Your major questions will be about the use of power, when and how, timing, and style. Your mentor will help you see which part of the work is yours to do, and what work needs to be passed on to others. For example, early on I was instructed to put a yellow Post-it note on my phone with the question: "Is this your business?" I found that there were few situations that actually needed ME. I learned to delegate and get out of the way.

Regarding timing, the mentor will know when to drop the rock. She'll help you question and feel your body's signal about when you should make that phone call to find out how you did on the job interview. Regarding effort, the mentor will help you see when you've done enough. You may want to wait up for your alcoholic husband yet another hour, but she might advise a good night's sleep will better help you weather whatever is in store. Regarding style, the mentor will help you make it through like a lady. She might advise what OA calls "restraint of tongue and pen," a way to be less expressive, but more effective. We need help with these most difficult questions.

As difficult as life often appears, we have to become willing to ride our horse in the direction she gallops. Otherwise, we can't complain of a saddle horn up the rump! Excessive eating has been an attempt to insist that the horse turn around without our doing the necessary spiritual footwork.

WE ARE OUR BODIES. Lest we get too spiritual too quickly, we have to remember that we ARE our bodies. We were blessed with these sensitive bodies. We must keep our vessels slightly open and resonant so that we can listen correctly.

Our work in recovery is to re-own our bodies so that we can then let them go. When you first set out on this path, you may be totally disowning your body, talking about it as a foreign entity. "No matter what I eat or don't eat, this THING keeps gaining weight." "I really think it's out to get me." "It just won't get me up to exercise." Anorexics are even more divorced from their bodies than the overeaters: "My body just wants to waste away. I'd love to eat, but my body rejects food."

However, whether we like it, accept it, or rail against it, we ARE our bodies. The quality and quantity of your life will be determined by your relationship with that body. Whether you experience it as a demon or a vehicle, it is your home. You must make friends with it. The friendship isn't based on looks: it's not about evaluating and then finding your body "acceptable" by your standards. The friendship has to be based on function. Does your body serve you well? Do you give it the food and caring it needs? Does it give you back the signals you need to hear?

When you journey inward to listen to your own voice, then your body's function is to resonate like a tuning fork, picking up signals and sending them out. To read these signals properly you want to keep the cavity partly empty so the vibrations can sound clearly in their proper tone. If you're a compulsive overeater and your cavity is filled to the brim, oozing syrups, gurgling sauces, then you'll pick up only a dull thud. If you're anorexic, keeping that cavity hollow and empty, then you'll vibrate screeches and static. You need to find just the right level of fullness for your own best tones.

Tuning Your Carburetor

To achieve the proper resonance, most of us function best at the same level as a car's half-full gas tank. Recent research with rats showed that most lived longest and healthiest when they remained slightly underweight, eating a bit less than previously prescribed. In this book, we have focused very little on food as fuel. There are plenty of other books for that, and millions of food plans you and your mentor can choose from. Our work has aimed at cleaning out your psychic pipes so that you can feel confident that the signals you pick up are pure and true for you.

Since I love and drive old cars, I only recently became aware that newer cars don't have carburetors. Adjustments are now done automatically, with computers. Well, I find both my cars and myself often had carburetor trouble. The carburetor regulates the proper mixture of fuel to oxygen so that your engine performs well. You have to keep it clean, finely tuned, so it can do its job. All through this book we've been helping you adjust your spirit's carburetor so that your psychic engine will purr smoothly. You've cleaned out hidden areas of fear—no more cat dance in the sand box. You've taken a clear, honest look at the pains of others in your life. You've learned to separate your journey from theirs. Now you're ready for your own inward journey. When your psychic carburetor is clear and tuned and you're putting in high-grade fuel, that's when the engine begins to purr.

Listening to Your Engine

"Just sit." These are the instructions I get when on retreat at a Buddhist monastery. We're given work assignments, just like the ones I give in treatment. But large blocks of the day are spent staring at a bare white wall. This is where the experienced "macho meditators," as I call them, sit cross-legged for hours. They never blink, even when flies go up the nose. They talk softly all the time.

For me the instruction is "Just sit." But there's so much more than sitting in "just sitting."

Try it on for yourself right now. Find a straight-backed chair and sit in it comfortably upright, feet flat on the floor, with your weight distributed evenly. Keep your head erect, look straight ahead, hands down, resting on your knees.

Now JUST SIT.

Relax into the meditative state by focusing on your breathing. Watch how your body breathes in and breathes out. Just follow your breathing. Notice how natural it is. Notice how not-controlled it is. Your organism breathes in and out approximately twelve times each minute whether you think about it or not. So, now think about it. Put your attention on your breath. When other thoughts come in, try to blow them out on your out breath. Just sit. Just breathe.

Time passes. At first you may not be able to tolerate too much of this alone time. Do what you can. Some feel better taking time for reading as meditation. Just remember that if you choose reading, you are choosing FILLING. Meditation is about emptying, turning to the hollow, vacant place within. Feel the spaciousness. However, at the beginning, perhaps reading meditation books will help you focus more on the emptiness. For the simplest instructions I recommend Herbert Benson's *Relaxation Response*. But there are countless meditation guides out there for you.

Just remember, ACTION! It's not so much about knowing what to do, as about DOING IT. Action! Do what you can. Teachers of meditation usually recommend trying it twenty minutes, twice a day. Our patients do approximately one half-hour in the morning. Most can't stand that long at first. I recommend you put the clock away, just sit until you drool. As your mouth relaxes and you stay immobile, you might find a small spittle of saliva traversing down your chin. That's your drool time. Keep sitting still, but just notice it. It can be a funky, animal, "in the body" kind of feeling. That's the point. That's the goal. In that state, your body will speak to you.

Is That All There Is?

You may now be hungering for more entertainment. It sounds so boring and empty to think of sitting alone with yourself. And then, yech! DROOLING? You probably want me to tell you what to think, tell you what should emerge from within you, give you YOUR answers. If I wanted to look smart and impress you, I would. Probably many have already done that for you. It's much harder not giving you what you want. Unfortunately, at this point, getting directions is deadly. You will try to perform instead of letting go. Even if no one else is around, you will perform for your own little ego. That will still leave the Self unheard. Please trust me on this and sit and wait. Your Inner Self is ready. So are you.

WHAT'S IN THE SILENCE?

■

EXERCISE 1

In treatment we often put our patients on a "silence assignment" where they can't talk, can't speak on the phone, can't listen to radio or watch TV. They can only write. This assignment usually lasts for a day or less. At first some patients become agitated and irritated. But after experiencing a brief time in their own silence, many thank us profusely. They realize that they've never had such an opportunity before—to listen to and receive from Spirit.

A tremendous gift you could give yourself would be a full day of total silence once a month. In some religious traditions, this is called "going on retreat." But you can do it at home if you like. Or you can find some beautiful place in nature that you find inspiring. After such a day you'll find that your heart rate slows down, your breathing evens out, and new ideas come to mind quietly. You'll walk around with a smile on your face.

MY DAY OF PEACE AND QUIET

1. Decide on the day. Warn your family and friends that you won't be available. Run your errands and do your marketing the day before—just enough food to get through the day.
2. When you wake up on your Day of Silence, turn the ringer on your phone off—put your answering machine on. Hide the remotes for the TV and VCR. Turn off the radio, the CD, the hi-fi—all the clamor of modern life.

3. No reading matter is allowed—no newspapers, no magazines, no books.

4. Your only companion will be your journal.

5. Just be alone and quiet. Do kind and gentle things for yourself—perhaps beginning with a long walk.

6. In the silence, try to be quiet in yourself. Listen to your body. When this gets difficult, just sit quietly and focus on your breathing—in and out, in and out. Follow your breath. When you're quieter, write in your journal about how you're feeling.

7. Use your journal to keep track of your impressions hour by hour.

8. As you find yourself becoming more serene, listen for the still, quiet voice of your Inner Self. Use your journal to dialogue with her. Let her write and then answer back.

9. Try to listen to your body's need for food. Eat only when it tells you it's really hungry. Try to stop when it tells you it's almost full. Keep track of this in your journal.

10. Just before you go to bed, take a bubble bath, and then write a brief summary of your Day of Peace. You turned off your head and opened up to your spirit. How do you feel about this? How do you feel about yourself now?

11. Ask your Inner Self to send you a message in a dream that night. And when you wake up the next morning, lie still for a few moments recalling the dream you've just had, and write it down in your journal.

12. If you don't recall a dream, don't worry.

13. Sometime in the next few days, when you're feeling crowded by work, and people, and things to do, and the media is blaring in your life again—take a little time out. Remember back to this day of peace.

14. Go sit in a quiet space, pull out your journal, and reread what you wrote on this day. See if the memory alone doesn't bring back the feeling of quiet you had at the end of that special day. You can give yourself the gift of quiet whenever you need it. Simply take a few minutes out of your day, sit quietly, and think about how you felt in the silence. Let it wrap itself around you like a loving hug, until you have the feeling back again.

15. When next month rolls around, remember to give yourself the gift again. In time, you'll come to crave it much more than you ever did chocolate.

Holly came to us as a hospital administrator who was very secure in her analytic, organizing abilities, and wanted to be assigned the job of office manager. She weighed 300 pounds and she was actually dying in her competence. We had to give her a task where she felt incompetent and unsure. She was assigned window washing. She wasn't delighted with the idea, but projected a cooperative spirit and set to work. She revved up enthusiasm, and asked to play bouncing music to accompany her task. We explained how work assignments were to be undertaken in a more meditative mode. She was to focus on her actions, staying aware of internal senses while working. No music. She didn't like this at all. She was so accustomed to keeping her head busy, she wanted more external stimulation. She pouted, but set to work.

Later, a counselor discovered her listening to a talk radio interview with a secreted Walkman headset. Caught, she offered up the earphones and agreed to try again, quietly listening to her Inner Self. She was to go on "silence," so she wouldn't get distracted into chatter with other residents. By that afternoon she was sobbing uncontrollably. She came to group hysterical. The up and down motion of washing the windows, coupled with the silence, reverted her back to scenes at age ten, working with her mother, a maid. Her mom took her along on jobs, and Holly always wanted to talk a little. But

Mom was always too busy, and too depressed, to talk with her little girl.

At that tender age, Holly decided to occupy her own head and keep her own self company. She resolved never to need or crave that attention. She'd fashioned a financially successful life so she'd never suffer as her mother had. But she'd never realized how fast she was running. Only when the running stopped did she face the pain—hers and her mother's. Washing windows in silence brought it all up.

As a result of the work done in subsequent groups, Holly contacted a part of herself she'd never owned. She loved painting, an art form totally distant from her intellectual life. She set up an easel in her office and randomly during the day let herself use broad strokes to express an inner, untapped voice. When she craved a cookie, she'd grab a brush. It satisfied a deeper appetite.

SILENCE IS GOLDEN. The playwright Harold Pinter once said that he was more interested in what happens BETWEEN the words in his plays. What is happening when no words are spoken at all? Meaning is not in the lines, but in between the lines. It's very hard for us to choose that in-between place. We don't know how to stand quietly and wait. We feel we're doing something negative and unproductive.

However, today many women are becoming more secure and demanding what Virginia Woolf prescribed: "a room of one's own." Pinter said, "Speech is a constant stratagem to cover nakedness. When true silence falls we are still left with the echo but are nearer nakedness." It is this visible, penetrable nakedness that the recovering woman seeks. There was no way to know this while still bingeing or talking. Who wants a relationship where you can't get naked. Why bother? If you can't be real with others, it's better to be alone.

> *"The only cure for loneliness is solitude. . . ."*
> —*Marianne Moore*

When you have spent some time contacting your innermost Self, sitting with her quietly and appreciating her message, then you will fully understand the sweetness of solitude. For now, your work is just to learn how to listen. Paradoxically, you must listen to learn how much you already know. Confidence in your own intuition won't come right away. You'll have to keep testing it out in the real world. But once you develop and trust it, you'll wonder how you managed so long without it. At present it may be so far from your consciousness that you just have to let it continue to roam for a while. If you call your dog, but he's out of earshot, he just can't pick up your signal. It won't matter how much you holler. But as you develop your receiver, you'll vibrate a clear, true tone. Just as I finally learned to read as a child, you will eventually hear your inner voice.

You already know more than you think you do and more than you probably want to know, more than you'd like to admit. To recover from addictions, you must stay true to that knowing. You must also learn to respect the inner voice, whether it speaks with elaborate embellishments, or screeches. It will probably do both from time to time. Be careful not to belittle the voice if it's a bit unintelligible. Trust enough to keep listening.

Body Sense

This knowing sense—this knowing without knowing how— lets you receive direction and guidance from all the life around you. Some psychologists tell us that the unconscious is a highly sensitized awareness that picks up everything going on in the environment. It reads things we don't necessarily integrate on a conscious level.

Early studies showed that overeaters have a much greater sensitivity than most to external cues. We pick up and absorb more than most. For example, in one study, participants were sent into a room to observe what was there and report back. The "normal" eaters control-group subjects reported seeing "a chair, a desk, a lamp." The overeaters described such details as "a blue tweed chair, a Victorian lamp, and a picture on the wall of an autumnal scene with a tiny blue jay in a tree."

Those with eating disorders seem to be more sensitized not only to externals but also to their own internal energy fields. If not sedated with excess food, we are wiser and more perceptive than most. In fact, much of our eating has been an attempt to turn down the volume on all the information we were picking up. Just look at the language. When we listen to this side of ourselves, when we follow our hunches without concrete objective evidence, we call it a "gut feeling." Stuffing or starving is an attempt to quiet our gut.

The AA *Big Book* tells us: "We will grow in intuition." One of the "promises" of working the Twelve Steps is: "Situations that used to baffle us, we will INSTINCTIVELY know how to handle."

This is the goal of your Fat and Furious journey. You're going to reclaim the self you've always been. You're coming back into your own body, cleared and cleansed of others' baggage—and your own. Your psyche is lighter, your body will be soon, and you are available to surrender to your intuition. Remember that old phrase: "women's intuition." Have you noticed how seldom you hear it today? We've become so scientific that only hocus-pocus types talk about it anymore. Well, there are real benefits to plugging in to that "hocus-pocus."

Stephanie was walking home in the early dusk from her work at a Wall Street brokerage firm. That area clears out fast on weekdays. She was clean and serene. A man fell in step beside her to ask about directions to a local restaurant. He was well dressed and quite presentable, even handsome. For an instant she hoped he was flirting. But she didn't pick that up in her body. Although he seemed friendly enough, her body jumped. She described it as a rustling, like when a flock of birds whooshes out of the underbrush. Her whole body went "whoosh."

She turned, startled, and stared directly at this man, whose eyes bulged as he seemed to sense she knew something. Quickly, he pushed her and grabbed her purse. Prepared in advance, she pulled away and took off running. She quickly reached a populated corner and relaxed with the crowd. When she looked back, he was gone.

Later, reporting the incident, she marveled at what a responsive, aware, and self-serving organism her body was. She was amazed at how she knew on a body level that she was in danger long before her intellect had clicked in. Having safely survived the experience, she loved that it happened. She loved and respected her body and its instinctive wisdom.

Lorraine had a similar experience at work. Jean, her assistant, was extremely dedicated, came in early and left late. She was amicable and overly and effusively complimentary. She adored Lorraine and was very impressed at how far she'd come within the corporation. Jean went to great pains to tell Lorraine all the specifics of things she watched that impressed her. She was like an adoring teenage fan.

Lorraine was very uncomfortable with Jean's effusive style. Her skin crawled when she heard much of this. At first she judged herself to be "uncomfortable with compliments." Then she ascribed it to geographics—Jean was from a rural town in Texas where perhaps this was the style. Her head tried to talk her out of the discomfort, but her body balked as this woman flitted around her.

Remember Marlene, who suspected her older woman friend of flirting with her boyfriend? It's the same intuitive response that we try to talk ourselves out of. When your body is clean and serene, the signals come in loud and clear—they won't be silenced by your headtrips. Marlene waited years before her head was finally convinced of what her body had been sensing all along.

Lorraine's discomfort was soon cleared up. She discovered that her adoring assistant had been gossiping all over the office that she was having an affair with a senior official—intimating that's how Lorraine had succeeded so fast and so well. While offering excellent administrative support, Jean had been secretly stabbing her in the back. Her body felt the wound. When she confronted Jean, the sweet Texas girl just smiled. Lorraine felt sick to her stomach.

When your body is half empty and resonant, you will sense—and know—much more than the average person. You will walk in truth, although it may sometimes cost you a sick tummy. That isn't necessarily bad—it may just be your body's signaling device. Laurie Nadel, author of *Sixth Sense*, tells us that intuitive men get their flashes as a warmth in the chest, while women feel them as a tightening of the stomach or diaphragm. You will have to decide daily if it is worth it to you to know, feel, and sense so much. Most of us worked so hard to get here, we wouldn't have it any other way. We may sometimes get sick to our stomachs, but we won't leave home again!

TO EAT OR SENSE. The more you have experiences like these, meeting your intuitive inner self, you won't so easily and unconsciously want to leave her behind. Your decisions about whether and what to eat will have nothing to do with being "good" or

"bad." And they won't have much to do with weight and body issues. You know this ONE EXTRA HELPING isn't gonna make or
keep you fat. The real question is one of consciousness. "Do I
want to stay or leave? Do I want to feel more or less? Do I want
to be true to myself, find out what I really believe, or would I
rather go back to being a robot on an automatic running-scared
program?" No one will blame you for choosing to stay in the
dark. The problem is, it's usually just a stopgap measure, a delaying action. Your life wants you to move into the light.

Too Much to See

Acknowledging change, seeing it coming down the pike,
isn't a question of how smart you are, but rather how willing you
are to be aware of your inner voice and act on it. The question
may be whether you want to live a high volume or low volume
life. Do we have any choice in the matter? Well, all this time I've
been exalting your superb, exquisite sensitivity. However, being
too aware, too sensitized, could get you hearing all kinds of
strange voices. Sometimes too acute a sense of hearing can get
you hospitalized as a schizophrenic. With too much stimulation
you might want to get out of yourself. But what if your soul is
screaming to get out of the life you are living?

Clinicians are often concerned about bulimic women who
enter treatment and transfer obsessions. Some, when they're not
vomiting, cut their arms, pick their scabs, watch themselves
bleed. The spirit is screaming out a heartfelt cry, "I exist! This
is MY blood! This is MY body. MY life. Don't you try to work your
stuff on me. I am separate, an individual. I have to cut myself so
you and I can see!" These behaviors are sad and scary, but on
one level, very understandable.

We've all read of many suicides by people on Prozac, including 1960s yippie leader Abbie Hoffman. Prozac was prescribed
to quiet that pain-filled inner voice. The Prozac soothes the sav-
age rumblings just enough to get patients functional. They report that they're quite content and happy with their new ability
to concentrate and avoid depression. Then, suddenly and without warning, they commit suicide. Why? Perhaps these tragic suicides were a response to a desperate spiritual self rising in
rebellion, screaming, "Get me out of this Prozac shell!" The

spirit doesn't know any other way to free itself but to destroy the casing, and thus in effect destroy the body, and thus the being.

I am not at all proposing self-mutilation or suicide as an option here. I'm suggesting that all these events need to be explored to discover the message that the distressed spiritual being is trying to communicate. Reincarnationists regard suicide as a fruitless endeavor anyway, because the karma set in motion would repeat the same unfinished business in the next go 'round. My perspective is that some souls had such a strong life force that they rebelled against being overpowered by others or deadened by drugs.

Recovery offers a much better way if we are willing to face the fear, feel the pain, and wait. We know always "this too shall pass," and we are given some direction on how to proceed.

Allison wrote me from Texas. "After I left treatment, I changed my thinking from 'food is my enemy' to 'Judi Hollis is my enemy.' Jude, I hated you and everything you had to say. I watched in group as you relentlessly forced people to see their lies to themselves. I wanted to punch you the night you pressed Martha to finally admit she was jealous of her daughter. I screamed inside, 'Who the hell do you think you are?' I never said it though, 'cause I was leaving in a week, and I didn't care enough about you anyway.

"I was so demure, pretending, acting shy and a little dumb. I'd go back to the unit later and talk up a storm, making fun of you and others, dissecting, analyzing, psychologizing. I just couldn't speak out straight. I didn't want anyone coming back at me. I wanted to win and control. I wanted to sneak my power, and play safe by acting weak. I couldn't believe it one night in group when you mentioned to another patient that gossip was the last resort of the powerless. I thought you had my room bugged!

"I now see how we have to get honest when we want to cut down on food. I hated you so because you were showing me how to be a strong, confident, honest woman who trusted her instincts and her power. You just said what you had to say. It wasn't that you were at all mean or hostile. You were just direct. You called a spade a shovel.

"Now that I am back home, minus 72 pounds, I'm beginning to see some of the wisdoms I rejected before. It has been a very difficult time for me. I see myself so clearly that it's ex-

hausting. I got a sponsor here right away and started complaining to her about all the people at our home meeting. She told
me to write about them. Then she had me come to her house
and read her what I'd written. Each time we came to a word like
'dishonest, manipulative, coy, hostile, argumentative' that I'd
written, she'd ask me to circle that word. Then we went back
over the lists. She asked, 'Are you ever like these women you are
judging?' I answered indignantly, 'Well, I'm more subtle.' She
told me, 'Well, honey, if you spot it, you got it. All we can sweep
is our own side of the street.' Man, I see the danger of judging
others. Everyone is me and I am everyone. We're so much the
same. It's kind of fun to see my own little games and laugh at
myself. Only my sponsor and women at my meetings could understand. They know why I have to keep seeing myself.

"Since I've been home, I see I can't get away with sneaky behavior. Each time I try to be coy, I just can't pull it off. My soul
cries out, 'Come off it!' When I try to ignore her and play
dumber, I become ravenously hungry; I've even binged. Each
time, I later see, it's all about listening to the call to power.

"You were telling me that every day in treatment and even
modeling how to do it. Well, much as I resented your example
then, I'm here to shout hallelujah, 'It's the only game in town.'

"I feel so alive now. I want to be all I can be. My husband
loves my boldness in bed, but he'd still like me to act a little
shyer. Oh well. If I could, I would. Those days are long gone. So
are the size 20s. It's a fair trade."

At this point a few women will jokingly complain, "I wish I
didn't know so much." But I've never really seen anyone who
managed to come through this process of birthing and owning
herself, of tuning herself up to a vibrant life, who didn't thank
me. More importantly, most of these women thank their inner
selves for being so patient and waiting so long.

Birthing Takes Crying

You have to cry before you can soar. Your inner self will begin to cry as soon as you really settle in to listen. It will cry tears
of joy at finally making contact. She thought you'd never come.
When your body is abstinent and clean, you vibrate with wise
spiritual messages. You'll need training and practice in experiencing this voice, but once you learn how smart she is, you can't

pretend to be deaf to your inner self any longer. The more you listen, the less fearful and more welcoming you will be about what she has to say. Ultimately, you'll never want to lose conscious contact with her again.

You may cry more. You'll operate as a tuning fork, resonating, trembling, vibrating, alive. A slight tap will speak to you from the cosmos. That kind of connection is worth one, two, or even twenty-seven cupcakes. But to be a tuning fork, you have to put down the food fork. Put down your fork to BE one.

Have you ever encountered a foreigner who speaks little English? Notice how, in order to be better understood, you start speaking louder and slower. You may even resort to some baby talk in order to communicate. Does that help, or does it make you look a little silly?

Currently, the psychotherapy community seems directed toward those regressive practices. Rather than acknowledging what isn't working, they believe that relapsing into the "inner child" will help us become more authentic. While this approach might bring brief relief, your inner spirit knows it's been patronized. This infantilizing of spirit sends a confused message to our consciousness.

AVOIDING POWER AND WISDOM. Why can't we understand our own strange behavior? Why would we want to avoid power and wisdom? Why weren't we schooled in managing it?

When my residential center was in Hollywood, we had a number of plumbing and electrical problems. As things went wrong in the house, we used the experiences clinically as grist for the mill of patient recovery. Instead of a sanitized, all-needs-met hospital environment, our patients had to face real life problems without excess food. In the process, they learned a number of useful skills. How do you handle food decisions while calling the plumber? How do you cope with a car failure on the way to a meeting? As a joke, I suggested we name the place Tara for Scarlett O'Hara's girlhood home. The acronym that we devised for *Tara* was: *To Accept Recovery Anyway.* Years later I discovered that there is a Tibetan Buddhist goddess whose name is Tara. She represents "the wisdom that transcends understanding." "Wow," I thought, "divinely inspired." Many women disown Tara's wisdom. Our mothers weren't able to teach us to recognize and own such wisdom because no one had taught them to do it. Such wisdom is not honored in our society. And yet, it is exactly this wisdom that recovering women must tap.

Many of us have been taught to walk away from owning that wisdom, that power. We fear that it would render us too powerful and thus not mateable. We're afraid we won't be understood, that our precious gifts will be rejected or derided by partners who don't function on the same wavelength that we do. There may be some reality to this, as it takes a special man to be with a fulfilled woman.

However, there are some things we simply need to share with other women. Leave men out of it. But accepting this truth challenges myths about partnership—that when the right man comes along we'll be able to share everything with him. Well, there may or may not be such a man there for you, but your priority is to make sure that YOU are there. When YOU want what you have, others will too.

When you start to acknowledge and celebrate your intuitive, instinctual self, you will fall in love with yourself. You will curtail food abuse because you love yourself too much not to. You will listen to your own vibrations to find your next intended action. And you must take action. You must invest in your own life. What you were taught is that you must seek the source of power and knowledge, and if you're successful, you can capture that power and make it your own. You were sent on an outward journey. You were taught to search the universe instead of your soul. It got you lost because what you're really seeking is your own SEEKER. You must find the path here, now, within you.

This is not crazy or dumb. We're after something very real and very elusive—a personal love object that always seems to be waiting just around the corner. It's a dance-away lover, a teasing, bouncing carrot that snaps into thin air just as you think you've grabbed it.

After twenty years of exploring addiction, I've come to see that, at heart, we're all trying to operate with the same unmet basic needs. At bottom all addicts and codependents are questing for the same dance-away lover: THEMSELVES. Since the going gets difficult, and the SELF doesn't trust us yet, we tend to give up and get off track.

We use some very effective diversions. From my own personal and professional experience, I can tell you that psychotherapy and examining one's personal history is a major diversion. Seeing our internal rumblings as sick and needing adjustment is deadly; it's the basic thing that's wrong with us. We may take the call from an inner messenger, but instead of listening to and loving the call, we label and medicate it. The acting-out illness is a *signal*, not a curse. Carl Jung said, "We do not cure our neurosis, but if we are lucky, it will cure us." Eventually, when you've exhausted every escape hatch, you come to see that there is nothing you can eat, drink, buy, or kiss that makes any difference. You can't ignore the call from within.

ASK YOURSELF:

☐ *Are you blessed/cursed with exceptional sensitivity?*

☐ *Think of an example from your childhood when your senses gave you a message that contradicted other people's view of reality.*

☐ *Think of a recent experience in which your senses gave you a message unconfirmed by logic. How did this contradiction make you feel? What did you do?*

Spiritual Growth Is Organic

Every organism seeks its own growth. Spiritual growth is just as organic a part of us as physical growth. When that growth is thwarted, we develop illness. Our project as women is to make sure that the energies we're putting out are leading us to our own natural growth. Often our attention and energies get diverted into outer heroic battles, in order to ignore our personal inner battle.

Fritz Perls, the father of Gestalt therapy, said anxiety is measured by our exact distance from the NOW. In recovery, we will be less anxious, as we learn to live life as a succession of "Nows." Carl Jung said that when we experience anxiety, that is our soul or spirit knocking on the door of our ego-centered self, which is trying to win the race.

Our Higher Self is trying to get our attention to warn us that we're racing in the wrong arena. Our inner spirit keeps knocking until it finally gives up and walks away. That walking away results in depression. And it is our Inner Self that produces the primary symptom of this depression: disordered eating. Our Higher Self is launching its form of rebellion against foreign rule. It resents being ruled by the outer-directed ego. It keeps telling us that we must live our own intended life. The Hindus say, "Honor your incarnation." Twelve-Steppers say, "Bloom where you're planted."

Birthing Ourselves Again

There is a call from within us to honor that incarnation, to celebrate this life. When you give up an abusive lifestyle, the Self wants to come out to play. As you've worked through this book, you've stopped denying and running away. You've got your midwife ready. You've said good-bye to women who suffer. You've given up resentment about what you didn't get yet. You're ready to make it happen.

At this point, many of us develop SYMPTOMS instead of taking our next step toward growth. You can take doctor-prescribed drugs at this point to relieve that symptom. Or you can give up all forms of external coping, so you can fall apart and allow your soul to emerge. This feels like death. And it is a death, of sorts. It is really the death of the little self, the death of the ego. And this little death precedes our being reborn into our bigger Self.

When we learn to listen to that soulful cry, we find a depth of wisdom we can't explain. Call it intuition, or ESP, or a Higher Power—it is a power and resonance that can only be felt in an abstinent, drug-free body. A clarity, a sureness that requires no explanation other than "I know my own truth." It's the voice of our own personal God, speaking like Yahweh in the Old Testament: "I am that I am." Maintaining that contact becomes the recovering woman's reason to continue on the path. Fear subsides as we begin to trust our instinctive wisdom.

Seeking extremes and excesses has been our way to avoid the emptiness in the center of our beings. Carl Jung referred to addiction as the "spiritual thirst of our being for wholeness." Others have described this quest for spiritual filling as a longing to reclaim the unlived life. So many of the substances or activities we've used have been so transitory. They've let us down again and again. But our instincts are here forever. And until we can accept and be comfortable with emptiness, we will continue foraging and continue getting lost. Our Self awaits in that empty place. We must learn to trust, to be comfortable telling ourselves—and others—"It just FEELS right. I just know this."

EXERCISE 2—PART I

YOU'RE INVITED: A COMING-OUT PARTY

It's time to have a celebration, and the guest of honor is your Inner Self! So grab your journal, it's time to send a letter of invitation to your lifelong party.

Begin with "Dear Inner Self," or perhaps give her a name. The name can change. Mine has been named Claudia, Samantha, and Dr. Jude.

1. Let her know you're ready to give her some time and attention.
2. Tell her how eager you are to listen to what she has to say.
3. Let her see how interesting it will be for the two of you to work together.
4. Sell her on how willing you are to be cooperative.

This is what emerged when Sarah sat down with her journal to invite her Inner Self, whom she calls Olivia, into her life.

Dear Olivia,

I'd like to invite you to join me in this life I've been granted. I'm finally at home and ready to receive you in the manner that you deserve.

I've stopped eating compulsively. And I've been working with my tough but tender sponsor who keeps me honest. I've now spent enough time on empty to know a rumble of Spirit from a grumble of stomach.

I welcome you, exquisite part of my self that I nearly lost. I've missed you and know that our reunion is long overdue. I'm ready to sit still long enough to hear your wise counsel.

EXERCISE 2—PART II

DEAR OUTER SELF . . .

Now you're going to write a reply from your Inner Self.

1. Allow yourself to be empty, to be still. And wait. When words or thoughts come to mind, just write them down.
2. Ask questions if you like. Wait quietly. And write down whatever reply floats up from your Inner Self.
3. Keep going as long as you like, as long as answers keep coming.
4. In your journal write: Dear —————— [add your own name]. You have just begun a lifelong dialogue with your most intimate and loving friend.

Here's what "Olivia" wrote back to Sarah:

Dear Sarah,
I always knew you'd find me. You're too wonderful a woman, too strong and brave, to have lived your life without connecting with the "me" that is "you."
Sometimes you've been so scared that your petals would never open that you've stopped your own growth in mid-bloom. I've been determined to be awake and alive and free in this lifetime—no matter what the price.
Always remember, we're in this together, sister! If you tell me the truth, I promise to tell you the truth. There's nothing in you I can't handle. Nothing in you I can't love and accept. I want what's best for you, and I'm willing to stay up all night when you need an ear to hear, or a shoulder to cry on.
We are one. Our separateness is an illusion. As long as you remember that you work the outside, and I work the inside, we'll be fine. All you have to do to call is close your eyes and breathe.

LETTING GO

When you're willing to listen again to your inner self, you give birth to your own freedom. People who trust their own inner wisdom are unpredictable and uncontrollable. And they don't always seem to be able to explain "why" they do things. They might decide to go home by a new route on the freeway. Not for any good reason, just because it feels right. They'll also gravitate toward some people and shun others, all for reasons they can't explain exactly. They simply trust their instincts. You too will grow to trust your own instincts. When you trust yourself more, you will be able to "let go."

You've probably heard this message to "let go" many times in your life, but didn't know how. Sometimes you were letting go and didn't even know it. And sometimes you might have thought you were "letting go," but instead you were pushing, striving, and winning. You might have thought that "letting go" meant giving up your power to others, taking their advice above your own counsel, becoming a nonthinking follower instead of a unique arbiter of your own fate.

I'm not suggesting that type of letting go or surrender. This true letting go experience is even more difficult. You will have to stay involved, connected, and invested. You will have to participate fully. Then at the same time, you'll have to let go of the outcomes of your actions. Most of us want to totally manage and control the situation, or give up the farm and turn it over to someone else. Both those positions are cop-outs. Once you've done your footwork, you must take a leap of faith and leave the results to the universe. It's like those pledge breaks for public television. A donor will match your gift. So you put up your footwork and see how it gets matched. Trust the process. For example, when you're on a weight-loss food plan, let results happen in their own good time. In other words, don't jump on the scale every half hour.

My Resistance

I couldn't accept any of this at first. I had a food plan in order, and had lost sixty pounds. But I was still very resistant to this idea of listening for inner wisdom. I was willing to grant that the "airy fairy" stuff might work in Twelve-Step meetings. Still, I didn't see how it could possibly filter into real life—certainly not MY real life.

My first "spiritual experience" happened more than a year later, and it was related to my work. This was perfect, of course, because work was my whole life. I had already opened the first hospital eating-disorders unit. And I'd been teaching many people all I'd learned about addictions and food obsessions.

I was then scheduled to speak to the medical staff of another hospital, where I would convince them of the viability of such a unit and encourage their support. I was petrified. I hadn't yet earned my Ph.D.; in medicine no one is much without "Doctor" in front of their name. At that time, no one else in the country was treating patients by using this model.

The problem I was facing is that time-honored medical practice founded on the CYA principle—"cover your ass." If you can convince doctors that someone else has already taken the risk and researched results, then they will follow.

So, I set about researching what I could find about what others had done. I borrowed from every discipline I knew—the behavior modification people, hypnotherapists, sound nutritional counseling, exercise physiologists—so I could show them that I wasn't really asking them to try anything too new and daring. I was totally well rehearsed with graphs, flip charts, and even a pointer. I knew I could knock their socks off.

A half-hour before that luncheon meeting, I took one last look at my notes. I couldn't make out one word of what I'd written! I panicked and called my mentor, hysterically screaming that I'd have to cancel the talk. She tried to soothe my anxiety by suggesting that I quietly meditate and then pray.

"WHAT!" I screamed. "That's fine for 'those meetings,' but this is MEDICINE!"

She answered with what a fellow-traveling, wounded healer always says that stops you cold; "Well, that's what I would do." Action, action, action. Do what I do.

So, I did. I meditated. And I got calm. Then I slowly walked to the podium and gave what I felt was the singularly most boring talk I'd ever delivered. I lost all my New York pizzazz—and I felt like a California surfer with no smarts and no energy.

But the docs loved it! And the gift from the universe was the proliferation of eating-disorder units across the country. My Inner Self, the one I'd meditated quietly to contact, knew exactly what those conservative doctors needed to hear.

Like Jack Webb, they wanted "Just the facts, ma'am." They didn't want to hear my glitter and jazz. They wanted it dull. It made them feel more comfortable and confident, rather than "sold." Because I let go, my inner sensor picked up what THEY needed. My ego wasn't that impressed or happy—but it was really none of MY business. My job was to do my preparation, the necessary footwork, and then suit up, show up, and let go. The results speak for themselves. I had stopped focusing on outcomes so that my soul could orchestrate the process.

This was a major turning point for me. I didn't give up my intellect. I didn't stop trusting all I'd learned. But I began to allow in the idea that perhaps it wasn't ALL about me, or how I thought things should be. Perhaps there was more going on than my brain could fathom at any one time. That meant that I needed to trust other, deeper sources of my inner awareness. I may still have to go within for guidance. I may have to trust energy, "vibes" that my abstinent, resonant body picks up. I may have to trust a "wisdom that transcends understanding." It wasn't an abandonment of myself. Rather it was a broader reading of SELF.

Once you learn to listen and to trust this instinctual part of yourself, nothing will ever be the same. She will let you know when you are tired, when you've had enough to eat, how your running regimen is going each day, who is your friend, and who is out to get you.

SWEEP YOUR OWN SIDEWALK. Until we learn to focus on self and away from others, we will continue to hunger in perpetual longing. Most of us have an overdeveloped sense of responsibility. We chose drugs to avoid the questions entirely. Whether the physical addiction is to alcohol, sugar, or mind-altering chemicals, the personality conflict is about CONTROL. That wish for control is coupled with an unrealistic sense of our own ego boundaries: We don't know where we end and the other person begins. Moms taught us to work at control, instead of letting go.

You didn't learn about the conscious strength of vulnerability. That you must melt and allow in before you begin to be affected by life. You only knew the extremes of managing and holding tight, or dropping it all and giving up. Wanting to be liked more than respected, needing approval from others more than personal integrity, you developed an "as if" personality—acting as if you really were the person that others wanted you to be.

Many of us turn to our addictions to ease the pain of this inner dilemma. But when the drugs are removed, the same basic issue lies in wait for us. We suffer from a mistaken sense of responsibility. And we first recognized this loss of control over our own identities, our own lives, by watching our mothers' pain, and being unable to heal it.

You've beaten yourself up fighting other people's battles all your life. In recovery, you'll learn to separate areas of responsibility. You'll discover how to look for clues that tell you when to do more, and when to let go. Ultimately, you'll find that there are no secure outcomes. In order to stay open and flexible enough to deal with these day-to-day insecurities, you need to consider your own needs and abilities. You must separate and live your own life. This is not selfish. This is HEALTHY!

Sibling Rival with Your Inner Child?

It's not about returning to childhood. Rather, the task of recovery is to assume the spiritual responsibilities of adulthood. Don't infantilize or patronize your Self in the process—it's very easy to do.

I'd been scheduled to speak at a national convention for Adult Children of Alcoholics. They'd appreciated my descriptions of codependency, illustrated in my first book, *Fat Is a Family Affair*, and had heard of the specialized family week at my treatment center. Since my treatment programs focus on today and tomorrow, I was concerned about a conflict between my message and their focus on childhood trauma. I didn't want to alienate anyone.

A few years earlier I had presented a lecture to this same group, and had met with resounding silence and blank stares. I had been emphasizing the importance of getting the food in order before examining "family of origin" issues. I'd explained there was a definite disservice in stirring up childhood trauma, if the person still ate compulsively.

The message was a bit premature for that group. Many had been instructed by therapists to relive their childhoods and let themselves be kids. In fact, a common sight at the convention was adults clutching teddy bears—ostentatiously declaring it was time to "let their kid out." Many felt they'd grown up too quickly and needed a chance to let it all hang out in the playground.

But despite all the furry stuffed appendages wrapped around so many "playful" waists, the tear-stained faces belied the effectiveness of this approach. These folks attended many such conferences, but seemed to find little fun in them. A prevalent message was about "reparenting the inner child." There were books for sale and workshops galore, teaching methods for contacting the inner child to give it long-needed nurturance.

I was confused about discussions of the inner child's neediness and instructions to heal its wounds. Something didn't quite work for me, but I didn't know what it was at the time. But somewhere during those first three days, halfway down the winding, confusing halls of the Opryland Hotel, I discovered what was wrong with this picture. I was reminded of my own initial contact with my own "inner child," and how that contact had helped me into recovery.

It was Thanksgiving morning of 1974, and I woke up crying and shaking in sugar withdrawal. I knew I couldn't make it through Aunt Myra's Thanksgiving dinner, especially since I'd baked all the desserts. Panicked and in stark terror, tears streaming down my face, with sponsor's instructions I managed to get myself quiet by focusing on my breathing.

Presently, I saw a vision of myself as a little five-year-old walking home along a cracked sidewalk. The crying stopped as my vision took me under a large chestnut tree. I felt comforted as I heard an overriding message: "Everything is going to be all right. It's all taken care of."

My sense was that this little five-year-old had some kind of connection to the universe, that her umbilical cord stretched into yet another place and time, where she had contacted a wisdom greater and more profound than my worries about pumpkin pie. I stopped crying. I sensed at a deep level that there was much more going on than my adult head dreamed of, and that whatever I'd find to worry about was already in the hands of a consciousness wiser and stronger than I. I felt very relaxed. I followed my vision of this little girl. She looked back and smiled. "Don't worry. Your job is to walk the path. It's all taken care of. Just focus on the cracks in the sidewalk or the chestnut shells on the ground. Stay focused on what's put in front of you. Be here now."

Little did I know how meaningful and timeless this message would be. My five-year-old Self knew much more than my adult self. She became a source of wisdom and strength. I recognized her as my Higher Power, the spiritual voice I would listen to with such gratitude in years to come. I later found that many of my adult concerns were issues I'd learned to obsess about in the psychobabble jungles of twentieth-century living. Some things were simply not as important as my colleagues and I had decided.

My inner child was saying, "Just keep on truckin'. Stay on the path." I'd learn my own truths by walking through what was put in front of me, not what was littered behind me. She wasn't calling out for me to help her. She was guiding me back onto my own spiritual path that I'd strayed from. She wasn't the needy child—I was the misguided needy adult.

It suddenly clicked for me what hadn't fit in with the teddy toters. I'd recovered by EXALTING my inner child, while these participants were NURTURING theirs. I had learned that the child within was stronger, wiser, more perceptive, capable, and resourceful than my adult self. In actuality, she needed absolutely nothing from me except attention. It was ridiculous to even think that this adult could nurture that child. The child had the situation very well in hand, thank you! That is what nagged at me when I saw the teddy bears. I saw people trying to infantilize a power much greater and wiser than they. They'd forgotten the biblical injunction: "And a little child shall lead them."

Penetration

For me, those people who were trying to "nurture their inner child" were missing out on the opportunity to listen and learn. They'd been misguided and psychologized into trying to become the care-givers for an inner source of strength that was much greater than themselves. The lesson wasn't about giving—it was about receiving. And for us, receiving is always the harder thing to do.

These teddy bear huggers needed to learn more about letting go in order to be truly filled. It was something they'd never been taught by their mothers. In recovery they'd have to work overtime to learn to open themselves up to receive. The first step was to stop acting, and start listening.

My little five-year-old had given me a model for faith. She

knew that all was taken care of—and her faith reassured me. Faith precedes understanding. It's all about trusting the emptiness, accepting the unknown, learning how "not to do."

But there was more. The whole codependency movement had arisen because of people's needing to learn about giving up control, letting go, letting God in. But instead of just trusting and letting go, they were working at "understanding," at trying to gain more control over their neuroses. When I turned my life over to the care and guidance of that five-year-old, I had to take a leap of faith. I had to trust the wisdom of her guidance without any objective evidence to back up her advice. I had to trust the calming, soothing sensation I felt in the pit of my stomach when I listened to her. This meant that I also had to trust the wisdom of my physical body.

For years, AA oldtimers had been telling me, "Either God is, or He ain't!" Trusting that this little girl was God helped me calm the raging beast within. Whether she was or wasn't didn't really matter. It simply felt better to believe. It felt even better to believe without knowing for sure. In some strange way, it felt calming to trust a five-year-old.

The last thing I needed to hear at that falling-apart moment was that there was work for me to do in "healing my inner child." I'd been giving to others long enough. I just wanted to let it all go, and this five-year-old's instructions let me do just that. She said she had the situation well in hand. Fine. Let her handle it. My letting go of control was such a gift. It allowed me to relax and feel more secure.

Years later I would learn about hooking up that youngster's sensibilities with the wisdom acquired through a woman's life experience. It wouldn't be a question of the woman having more to offer than the child, but rather a mutual relationship where each had a necessary and distinct function. My inner child was that still, small voice within. I would learn to follow the sailors' instruction: "Pray toward heaven, but row toward shore." Life required effort from me, and results from the universe. Could I stand to be in a cooperative relationship, neither managing and steering everything NOR giving up the farm? It was a matter of whether to pity or respect that child, whether to trust or doubt, whether to hold on or let go. The child whose praises I'm singing is one to be approached gently, with utmost admiration. She needs nothing. She's already survived more than you can imagine. She knows it's too late to have a happy childhood. That child survived and has a life now. The happy childhood is a long-gone myth. Have you been trying to re-create it for your mom? Why bother? You can't go home again.

Channeling the Light

Now that you've forgiven your mother and yourself, now that you've accepted new birthing with a parental surrogate of your choice, you simply cannot go back to the dark side. That is both the blessing and the curse of this kind of recovery. You just can't eat the same old way. In my own life, the person, the being, that I am today, cannot live in the obese body I once had, and my former fat self can't live in this size 8. We have separated, individuated—we cannot merge again.

The project of truly, responsibly creating our own lives seems so vast. In AA literature we read about newcomers moaning, "What an order, I can't go through with it." But the literature then asks the newcomer to quiet down and not be discouraged: "We are not saints. We seek to grow along spiritual lines. We claim progress, not perfection." Facing life on life's terms, seeing clearly, we can follow the Buddhists' advice: "Begin AT ONCE and do YOUR BEST."

LIFE IMITATES ART. You will make your life a work of art. It's quite natural to feel fearful. Everything you've known is about to change. It's okay to be afraid. The whole point is to feel your fear and do it anyway. What you're really afraid of is facing how you've been living from day to day. Up to now this has all been going on in your unconscious. But listening to the messages from your Inner Self means it's beginning to be conscious. And this is right and proper. After all, before you can create a life, you first have to see what's already there—this is true whether you're redecorating a house or a life.

This is a courageous and creative act. You're consciously, confidently, and maturely setting out to re-create your own life. Your traveling companion is the SELF who has been part of you forever. She is the painter of your canvas, the choreographer of your dance, developer of your print, writer of your book, shredder of your cabbage. It's only through abstinence, through sitting quietly, that you will discover your own true art form—yourself!

Martha Graham, the choreographer, said it well writing to her young protégé, Agnes de Mille. Agnes was disillusioned and complaining about her artistic development. She didn't like herself or her dancing. Martha wrote her the following:

> There is a vitality, a life force, an energy, a quickening
> that is translated through you into action,
> and because there is only one of you in all of time,
> this expression is unique.
>
> And if you block it, it will never exist through
> any other medium and it will be lost. The world will
> not have it. It is not your business to determine
> how good it is
> nor how valuable
> nor how it compares with other expressions.
> It is your business to keep it yours clearly and
> directly, to keep the channel open.
>
> You do not even have to believe in yourself
> or your work. You have to keep yourself open and
> aware to the urges that motivate you . . .
>
> Keep the channel open. . . .
> No artist is pleased. . . .
>
> There is no satisfaction whatever at any time . . .
> There is only a queer, divine dissatisfaction,
> a blessed unrest that keeps us marching and
> makes us more alive than the rest.

Agnes de Mille later went on to have a career as brilliant as her mentor's, but uniquely different.

Coming Home to the Body

It's no accident that I've quoted a dancer here—a person very much in touch with the body and its signals. You probably began reading this book because you wanted to see your body change. But the more you got into it, the more you began to see that it was YOU that had to change.

As these changes begin to happen, the body you are meant to have will develop for you. It may not be the body popular magazines tell you to want. It may not be the dress size you're pushing for. But, then again, it may. Your body may become more "attractive" than you ever imagined. Nevertheless, it isn't about looks; it's about function.

In keeping your food in order, your primary purpose is not to attain a given body image, but rather to keep yourself available to hear your Inner Voice. Now you can trust your body and its signals. Your fear can subside, as you realize that the body doesn't lie. The head can talk us into all kinds of things, but the body knows the truth. It will always serve us and respond appropriately.

You may think you have the option of not knowing what you know, not seeing what you see, not feeling what you feel. Well, you do if you eat. Unfortunately, though, we've already seen that food doesn't work anymore. Your body is living your life, whether you dull the pain or not. Your body responds beautifully and organically to all the stimuli brought in from life.

If two men sit in a dark room, moving small pieces of wood shaped like kings, queens, and bishops across a black-and-red-checkered board, their individual bodies respond with the same "fight or flight" responses as a cave man facing Tyrannosaurus rex. They may appear quite calm and composed. But their foreheads bead with sweat, they get a tremendous urge to urinate, and their jaws clench tightly. The body lives it all. Which part is real life?

Seeking a Real Life Means Seeking a Real Body

The proper body proportion will evolve as a by-product of your work. And you'll find that by the time it does, it won't really matter.

For example, Lil wanted to lose 50 pounds. She said it over and over again like a mantra, from her first day in treatment, all through her first six months of abstinence. "I gotta lose 50 pounds!" But then we stopped hearing so much about her goal. It wasn't as though she'd lost sight of that agenda, and was just eating and giving up. She was steadily losing weight. What actually happened was that her way of talking about herself and her projects changed.

Lil had more things to say about what she was DOING in her life that made her feel good about herself. She started meditating. And she began to hear a voice that was somewhat shrill at first, but then deepened and resonated more softly. As people complimented her on her weight loss, she smiled sweetly, looked excited and appreciative, but didn't have a comment or explanation.

When she first came to treatment, Lil talked about herself as an object: "Look at these fat thighs. I've just gotta lose some weight. I'm such a pig." She had objectified herself, seeing herself as a thing, an animal. As her recovery progressed, Lil's self-respect deepened. Although she was concerned about her body, she began to realize that she was much MORE than her body.

Daphne wasn't pleased by the culture's standards for her body, but learned to trust her Inner Wisdom. "I'm swimming every day now and my legs are hard as rocks. But they're big. My stomach is tight, but it's still rounded. I'm in great shape, but I still wear size 14. All I know is that I feel very serene, extremely attractive, sashay like I'm sexy, and trust my instincts. I may not be a *Vogue* model, but I'm sure that it's ME!"

ASK YOURSELF:

- *Are you capable of living with—and loving—the body you have today?*
- *Are you willing to consider that you are MORE than your body? What will that mean?*

I'M BORN AGAIN. As we progress, we feel as though we're dying to get reborn. We keep changing our position, our viewpoint, our standards, all our old ideas of how things should be. We're letting go. We keep having to trust a new way of living, a new way of seeing, a new possibility, though giving up old myths is often too hard to bear. It's not just about dying, but about giving up CONSCIOUSLY in order to get. In other words, it's about being present, and paying attention. It means not focusing on what "they" do, but focusing on what "is." In other words, "What am I doing here? How does this struggle serve to lead me home?" Rather than seeing the struggle as negative, diseased, sick, we begin to understand the underlying healing that's going on in our lives! We know to ask ourselves: What are we after? Why take on this battle here and now?

So, our life's question is: "How can we have a good time in the midst of a hard life?" Or "Where does our own personal responsibility begin and end?" Ultimately, this becomes our own individual quest. Avoiding this question is what food, sex, and rock and roll are all about. Finding other sources of comfort and joy are what this journey is about. How can we allow a loving, witnessing, no-bullshit, consequence-carrying adult to flower within us, while also listening to an inner childlike wisdom that knows what is ultimately true and best for us?

Many say that once we have formulated the question, we already know the answer—that the questions are vastly more important than the answers. As I've participated in Buddhist ceremonies, watching monks query their masters, I've seen what careful thought and effort must go into such questions. I now invite you to sit quietly, and wait until your next question bubbles up.

ASK YOURSELF:

▢ *Fill in this blank with your best question for today*

Spiritualizing Your Relationship with Mom

Now it's time to get a little perspective on the exquisite beauty of your new, emerging life. We've analyzed your relationship with your mother. Now it's time to spiritualize this relationship and to understand it, not from an ego-based perspective, but from the Soul's perspective. It is time to put Spirit first in every aspect of our lives—including our relationship with our mothers.

At the beginning of this chapter we talked about acting "as if" it was our Soul's greater wisdom to choose the parents we had. Now we're going to look at how our battles with food and our stand-offs with Mom have tilled the soil for seeding the growth of our Soul.

■

WHY DID YOU CHOOSE THIS MOM?

Just for now try on the idea that, on a spiritual level, we choose our own parents.

Bring out your journal and sit quietly with your Inner Self. Ask yourself these questions:

1. Why did I choose this particular mother and this particular struggle?
2. How have I, as a spiritual being, used this experience with this mother, and with this illness, to hone myself into the sensitive instrument that I am?
3. How have I used this experience to develop the core of my Inner Self?
4. What strengths did it develop? What has remained underdeveloped?
5. How has this struggle with Mom determined my views on dependence and independence? How? Why?
6. What have I discovered by "swearing off" certain behaviors: "I'll never _____ like Mom!"
7. What has this taught me about vulnerability?
8. What has this taught me about control?
9. What better opportunities have I had that Mom didn't? What opportunities did she have that I haven't?
10. Has our relationship helped Mom grow?
11. Is there any struggle I would have traded this one for? Why?
12. How has this relationship served my Soul?
13. I'd like to take this opportunity to thank Mom for

_____

_____

THE HUNDREDTH MONKEY

Is it time for us all to change? Are all our struggles actually the birthing pains of a spiritual revolution? Perhaps the answer lies in the tale of the hundredth monkey. From anthropological research comes the story of an island in northwestern Japan where a young female monkey was digging in the island's sandy soil for a wild sweet potato to eat, just as her species had done for eons. When she found one she made a breakthrough decision: *She decided to wash the sand off the yam before she ate it.* This had never been done before in her culture.

Then she taught all the members of her family to wash their yams too. They taught others—although a few grumpy oldtimers stubbornly kept eating their sandy yams, and wearing down their teeth. As time passed, more and more monkeys began to follow her lead. The story goes that, at the moment when the hundredth monkey washed the sand off its yam, every monkey on the island began to do the same thing! Instantly, it became an established ritual—part of their way of life. Soon, no one could remember a time when it hadn't been done. It had endured the test of time and practice, and had been incorporated into everyday life.

It was later found that, strangely, after the hundredth monkey had washed her yams, ALL the monkeys on the neighboring islands—who'd had no contact with the first one—began adopting the same practice. Was it time for them to hear and receive that message from the universe?

Is it time for us to hear our own inner messages from the universe? Can you take it? Are you perhaps the hundredth monkey? Am I?

Once, during all the changes I was making in my life, I got panicked and depressed. I knew I needed help, so I called the sweat lodge lady, Grandmother Little Moon. I told her of my fears, and she answered: "You are a medicine woman. A leader. Great medicine is coming down to the world. We will all have to be strong. Medicine women are given the testing first so that we can help the others."

I wailed back: "I don't want to help the others. I want to be at the end of the line."

"You can't run from your medicine," she replied.

Are you a leader, a woman strong enough to listen to the messages you channel, and act on them? Your food problem says you MUST listen or else you'll have to eat. Can you swallow your own medicine? As more of us stand together, we'll reach a time when we no longer remember when we used to avoid the truth. We're the first monkeys and the medicine women. We were given this supersensitivity as an opportunity and responsibility. Instead of lamenting your past or present, feel blessed to have this supersensitivity and awareness, so that you can wash yams for yourself and your mother. The truth will set us free.

AN IDEA WHOSE TIME HAS COME. Your mother birthed you the first time. Now, with the help of spiritual mentors, it's time for you to quietly, slowly, and contemplatively rebirth yourself into a whole new way of being—within this very lifetime. This new life will be one in which you take responsibility for all your choices, from here on out.

Once daughters are able to take full responsibility for creating their own lives, they can see life's ups and downs as opportunities for growth; they rarely blame, choosing instead to own their power. They have compassion for men, and work together to accept mating as a high spiritual experience. They are not attached or threatened, but flow freely, meeting life on life's terms. For some, this may mean leaving Mother behind.

Our newly birthed selves are open and vulnerable. This is a whole new world and lifestyle—one in which healing and recovery can occur. We have learned to follow the guidance of our spiritual mentors so we can later trust our own. We've been learning to walk all over again—but this time we'll be more sure-footed, and supported by a healthy attitude, loving friends, and our own internal messenger.

Standing quietly together, women such as we create a roar heard round the world, but more importantly, deep within.

"We shall meet some of you in the fellowship of the Spirit as we trudge the road of happy destiny. May God bless you and keep you until then."

—AA *Big Book*

AFTERWORD

*"Integrity is not a given in everyone's life. It is the result
of self-discipline, inner trust, and a decision to be relentlessly
honest in our response to all situations in our lives."*
—HAZELDEN RECOVERY CALENDAR

Think about your life as if lived in four acts.

ACT I   I walk down a street.
I see a hole.
I fall in.
I am lost and helpless, but it is not my fault.
I have great difficulty getting out.

ACT II   I walk down a street.
I see a hole.
I fall in.
I see it's an old habit, and I take responsibility.
I get out faster and with less difficulty.

ACT III   I walk down a street.
I see a hole.
I walk around the hole.

ACT IV   I walk down a different street.

Recovery is about becoming more conscious of our life patterns and choices. Over time, our growth experiences teach us to stay conscious. We learn to walk between Act III and Act IV. We wish we'd walk down that different street more often, but there seem to be many old patterns we still have to work through and change.

Therapy and insight can bring us to Act III. But then we need a lot of courage and encouragement to help us make the conscious choice to take that different street. The blessing and curse of recovery and abstinence is that we become fully aware of what we're doing. We outgrow denial. We stop lying to ourselves. We learn to pray for the help and discipline we need to walk down our own intended street.

Bit by bit, our days begin to flow more easily. We make plans, we're more responsible and effective. But we're no longer driven. At first, we may think that operating in a lower gear means we're not working hard enough. But before long we discover that we're actually producing more and delivering a better quality of life to ourselves and to those around us.

We learn to trust and be guided by an intuitive, organic part of ourselves that we can't really control. And it's that very lack of control that's so exciting and scary—like an orgasm. As we welcome ourselves into the world of intuition, we join a sisterhood of like-minded women who respect themselves, while continuing to own and embrace all the pain and joy of their lives.

For people like us, the outcome of all this effort and confrontation proves to be worth the price. We begin to gain the right things, the right way—a body we've come to love and appreciate; our own personal integrity; and a deep sense of inner knowing, trust, and peace. The further we travel, the more we become who we always were. We find ourselves facing life with a childlike wonder, coupled with a woman's wisdom. The fear and rage were all cover-ups. As psychiatrist Harry Stack Sullivan said, "Mental health is close to childlikeness."

We find, to our surprise, that we look and feel much younger and healthier than we did when we started this journey. And other people are noticing it and telling us so. So what has changed? We haven't had a face lift. It's been a lift all right, a spirit lift—a lightening of fear and the emergence of courage. We're lighter, but now grounded in the good and steady company of our Inner Self. As King David said in the Twenty-third Psalm, "I shall fear no evil, for Thou art with me."

This connection with the Inner Self unites us with more power, wisdom, and confidence than we ever thought possible. We find ourselves standing solidly on the Earth as whole beings.

We have an organic integrity and a healthy sense of self. With this feeling of wholeness comes a sense that anything is possible.

We find ourselves doing more in a week than we used to do in a month, and with energy to spare. That energy comes from more than just eating appropriately. It comes from tapping into a whole new source of energy—the wellspring of life. And we're learning to trust this energy because it's made us survivors. No matter what life throws at us, we bounce right back.

We continue to do the footwork we need to change and to keep living our new lives. And, just as importantly, we meditate, create peaceful alone time for ourselves, and practice loving self-care. We listen to and honor our Inner Self. Then, when it's time to get out there and participate in life, we do so with renewed energy and courage, following our intuitions.

We don't have to work as hard as we used to to get things done. We send out our intent in a burst of energy, and then sit back and wait for what comes next. We create an atmosphere of cooperative interaction with everyone and everything in our lives. Together, we create a third reality—not my reality, or your reality, but OUR reality. We're all in it together. It's like making love with the whole world!

And speaking of sex—all this work with body and spirit has transformed our outlook on sex. The more we access and appreciate our spiritual nature, the more we honor the temple of our bodies, the core of our beings. We trust an inner sense of peace and balance. We discover that allowing anyone to enter the boundaries of our body requires a spiritual negotiation. We can no longer take our body where our soul cannot follow. This leads some of us to deeper, more conscious relationships with our partners, and others of us to a very comfortable celibacy.

We discover that we love our alone time, that we are content with our lives. We keep ourselves focused on, and engaged in, things we find stimulating. We bring people in as we feel the need, and we also keep to ourselves when necessary. We now hunger for the filling we get from accessing that resonant empty place within. We're shedding our fears of not being liked or accepted. Instead of wondering if we're liked, we continue TO BE SOMEONE WE LIKE. We want to surround ourselves with people who like this person, too, people who can share and benefit from the journey we've all been on. We've given up old, stuck patterns of relationships, as well as a number of old friends and lovers who haven't been able to grow and change with us. We now seek relationships that encourage us to open up. We can no longer spend time with experiences or in relationships that force us to shut down.

We've come to trust and follow the wisdom of our organism. Because of this our food consumption is moderate and healthy on most days, and we know how to listen to our body, as it keeps us conscious of how we're living.

In learning to trust ourselves, our bodies, and our Inner Selves, we have developed the courage to speak our own truth. And that is the most profound teaching of this entire book: *To thine own self be true.*

The more we learn to trust ourselves, the more we learn to trust that a Higher Energy than ourselves is operating in our lives. We take full responsibility for the life we're fashioning, but we also remain open and available to "a little help from our friends." This rebirth of the Self allows us to consume less, and to open up and let go more. Our journey into consciousness has taken hard work and a great deal of love and help, but it's been worth every step. I wish you solid footing as you head into Act IV of your new life.

Index

and craving emptiness, 42–43
difficulties in, 18–20
evolutionary, 15–21
and focusing on present, 66–68
and forgiving yourself, 43
fruits of, 16–18
and handling competition, 69–71
and importance of intentions,
41–42
as invitation vs. deprivation, 21
keys in, 38–44
and learning to be nurtured, 40–44
and meaning of recovery, 30–31
necessity for, 22–31
overeating therapies for, 24–25
and playing the game, 65–69
power and, 65–76
and surrendering ego, 43–44
and weak and helpless types, 71–76
competition, 69–71, 76, 83, 86, 114
compulsive eating disorder, 35–36

death wishes, 8–12, 145, 185
denial, xv, 128, 222
depression, 28–29, 67, 161
and forgiving your mother,
199–201, 204–5, 210, 213, 218,
222–23
power and, 67, 69–70, 84–85
spirituality and, 261, 266, 272

eating:
changing relationships with, 5
defiant, 217–18
as reciprocal, intimate experience,
8
as sedative, xxv–xxviii, 2
eating disorders, xiv–xvi, xxiii–xxv
as blessings vs. curses, 31–34
categories of, see specific eating
disorders
current epidemic of, xiv
as diseases of childhood, 56
similarities between alcoholism
and, 12–13, 24, 28, 31, 34, 37
stigmas associated with, 19
emptiness, 222
cherishing of, xxvii–xxviii

craving for, 42–43
life calls and, 5–6, 21
spirituality and, 272–73

family and families, 212
and mother–daughter
relationships, 26–28, 99–127
treated by Hollis Institute, 26–29
food plans, 66, 126, 221, 275
abstinent, see abstinence
sponsors and, 156–57, 160, 170,
181
forgiving your mother, 190–227
and absence of help from your
mother, 213–15
and alliances, confidantes, and
images of self, 203–4
and ambivalence, 202–11
and befriending women, 211–12
and defiant eating, 217–18
and doing your best, 215–16
exercises in, 194–96, 206–10
and facing disappointment, 213
and feed me or starve me attitude,
219–23
and hitting bottom, 200–203
and jealous mothers, 191–215
and letting go of your mother's
pain, 224–25
and life, 191, 200–202, 206, 210–11,
221, 223–25
and love, 191–96, 201–3, 206, 210,
215–16, 222
and making amends, 208
and passing the torch, 223
and paths we choose, 222–23
and Pollyannas, 225–27
and postpartum depression, 204–5
and rotten–daughter syndrome,
198–200
and seeking out punishment, 218
and telling your mother what she
missed, 208–9
and thanking your mother for the
good things, 209–10
and wake–up calls, 226–27
and wanting a larger piece of the
pie, 221–22

abstinence and, 50

and getting in touch with your inner child, 278–82

Hollis's resistance to, 275–77

penetration and, 280–82

and sweeping your own side of the sidewalk, 277–78

life and life styles, 1–21, 38–44

and body images, 14–15

and death wishes, 8–12

evolutionary change of, 15–21

as fearful, 39

and forgiving your mother, 191, 200–202, 206, 210–11, 221, 223–25

and forgiving yourself, 229–30, 237–38, 241, 244, 249–50, 253

good, 58–59

as if lived in four acts, 290–91

in imitating art, 282–83

and moderation, 13–14

and power, 65–69, 87

risks in, 178

and spirituality, 3–6, 272, 281–86, 288–89

and sponsors, 173, 178

therapy as substitute for, 67–69

listening, xxxii–xxxiii

death wishes and, 8–9

learning about, 254–74, 277, 280, 282, 288–89

and love of self, 149

separation and, 138

sponsors and, 165–67, 171, 176, 186

of witnesses, 142

to your engine, 257–58

love, xxxi

and forgiving your mother, 191–96, 201–3, 206, 210, 215–16, 222

and forgiving yourself, 228–41, 245, 252–53

of self, xix, 148–49, 253

sponsors and, 187–89

meditation, 258, 276, 284–85, 292

menstruating, 144–48

mother–daughter relationships, xiv–xv, xxi–xxiv, 37, 83–155

absence of blame in, xxiii–xxv, 122

adolescence and, 144–48

announcing self–interests in, 142

beneficiaries of, 99–100

chooser vs. choosen in, 78

control in, 180

crotch watch and, 83–86

and daughters saving marriages, 110–13

and daughters who want to help, 89–92

death wishes and, 10–11

and dos and don'ts for mothers, 125–26

families and, 26–28, 99–127

and finding self–love, 148–49

and forgiving your mother, see forgiving your mother

and forgiving yourself, 228–29, 231, 233–38, 240, 246, 248–51

and healing present, 151–54

incest events and, 122–25

and nurturing Self, 135

power and, 55–56, 61–63, 65, 72, 76–89, 98–99

primal shrugs in, 126–27

rivalries in, 76–89

and secrets that make you sick, 113–20

separation in, see separation and separating

spirituality and, 261, 277–78, 280, 286–89

and spitting up your mother's pain, 94–102

sponsors and, 157–58, 161–63, 169, 173–74, 176, 178–80, 185–89

survival decisions and, 109–10

and telling your mother's story, 94–98

timing in, 153

triangulation and, see triangulation

and trying to salve wounds of your mother's disappointments, 93–127

Other Materials by Dr. Judi Hollis

Judi Hollis has devoted the last twenty-five years to educating recovering individuals and their families. Thousands have benefited from her residential and inpatient treatment programs and nationwide seminars. The following resource list is provided to assist you in your further exploration of the ideas presented in this book.

Also by Dr. Judi Hollis:

BOOKS
  Fat Is a Family Affair (Harper/Hazelden)
  It's Not a Dress Rehearsal (HOLSEM Productions)
  Let Them Eat Cake (HOLSEM Productions)

PAMPHLETS
  "Accepting Powerlessness" (Hazelden)
  "Relapse for Eating Disorder Sufferers" (Hazelden)
  "Resisting Recovery" (Hazelden)
  "When AA's Go to OA" (Hazelden)
  "Humility vs. Humiliation" (Hazelden)
  "Transferring Obsessions" (Hazelden)
  "I'm Not Ready Yet" (Hazelden)

VIDEOS
  "Family Matters" (Hazelden Foundation)
    Dick Young Productions, New York City
  "Dark Secrets, Bright Victory" (Hazelden Foundation)
    Dick Young Productions, New York City
  "Dignity Dine" (HOLSEM Productions)
  "Live to Eat—Eat to Live" (HOLSEM Productions)
  "Starving for Perfection" (HOLSEM Productions)

CASSETTES
  "Hope for Compulsive Overeaters," Vols. 1 & 2 (Hazelden)
  "Fat is a Family Affair" (Hazelden)
  "Codependent Compulsions" (HOLSEM Productions)
  "Y2 OA?" (HOLSEM Productions)
  "Let's Talk Radio"(HOLSEM Productions)
  "Going Deep" (HOLSEM Productions)
  "Fat and Furious" (HOLSEM Productions)

For ordering or more information about videos, audiotapes, books, and seminars please call: 1-800-8-ENOUGH